THE LAPPS

THE
LAPPS

BY

Björn Collinder

GREENWOOD PRESS, PUBLISHERS
NEW YORK

PREFACE

THERE are about twenty thousand Lapps in Norway, less than nine thousand in Sweden, twenty-five hundred in Finland, and eighteen hundred in Russia. Because of their picturesque costumes, their old-fashioned way of life, and the sense of beauty which they display in the ornamentation of their household goods and implements, they have attracted the attention of innumerable travelers and men of science from the beginning of the Christian era up to these days. They have been described in hundreds of books and thousands of articles. And yet little is known about them in the great countries of the Western World. Apart from the remarkable *Muittalus samid birra*, written by the Lapp wolf-hunter Johan Turi and translated into Danish, Swedish, English, and German, no broad survey of this subject has appeared in the English language since 1674, when Johannes Schefferus's learned compilation *Lapponia* was published in English translation under the title *The History of Lappland*. It is the aim of the following pages to fill this gap.

A linguist and philologist by profession, I do not pretend to cover the whole field of Lapp studies. My firsthand knowledge of the Lapps is incomplete, although I have made thirty trips to them and spent about three years of my life in their entertaining company. I cannot mention here the names of all those friends, Lapps and non-Lapps, who have given me valuable information; but I should like to acknowledge my indebtedness to Dr. Israel Ruong, who is a Lapp by birth and is second to none in matters of Lapp ethnology. Most of the photographs presented in this book are his.

Uppsala
March, 1949

Björn Collinder
Professor of Finno-Ugric Languages
in the University of Uppsala

CONTENTS

CONTENTS

THE LAPPS

Wisely they
Despise the insensate barbarous trade of war;
They ask no more than simple Nature gives;
They love their mountains and enjoy their storms.
No false desires, no pride-created wants
Disturb the peaceful current of their time,
And, through the restless ever-tortured maze
Of pleasure, or ambition, bid it rage.
Their reindeer form their riches. These their tents,
Their robes, their beds, and all their homely wealth
Supply, their wholesome fare, and cheerful cups.
Obsequious at their call, the docile tribe
Yield to the sled their necks, and whirl them swift
O'er hill and dale, heap'd into one expanse
Of marbled snow, as far as eye can sweep
With a blue crust of ice unbounded glazed.
By dancing meteors then, that ceaseless shake
A waving blaze refracted o'er the heavens,
And vivid moons, and stars that keener play
With doubled lustre from the radiant waste,
Even in the depth of polar night, they find
A wondrous day—enough to light the chase,
Or guide their daring steps to Finland-fairs.
.   .   .   .

Thrice happy race! By poverty secured
From legal plunder and rapacious power:
In whom fell interest never yet has sown
The seeds of vice; whose spotless swains ne'er knew
Injurious deed; nor, blasted by the breath
Of faithless love, their blooming daughters woe.

JAMES THOMSON, *The Seasons.*

CHAPTER I

THE LAND OF THE LAPPS

THE land of the Lapps is part of Fennoscandia, which consists of the Scandinavian peninsula, Finland, Karelia, and the Kola peninsula. The territory where the Lappish language is spoken has about the same configuration as a Greek Γ. The stem of the letter covers more or less the mountain ridge that divides Sweden from Norway, whereas the horizontal bar runs east across the extreme North of Finland and along the middle of the Kola peninsula. The extreme points of the territory are Storvätteshågna, the highest mountain of the province of Dalarne (Dalecarlia) in central Sweden, and Cape Ponoi on the eastern coast of the Kola peninsula. The southernmost point of the territory is situated on 62° N, at the same latitude as the southern bend of the Yukon river. The northernmost point is on 71°, at the same latitude as the northernmost point of Alaska. To the east of the Tornio river, which divides Sweden from Finland, the Lapp territory does not extend further south than to 67° N.

The westernmost point of the Lapp territory is situated on 11° E (Greenwich), on the meridian of Firenze; the easternmost point is on 41° E, on the same longitude as the eastern boundary of Kenya.

From north to south, this territory covers one-eleventh of the total extent of the Old World (from Cape Chelyuskin to the Cape of Good Hope). From west to east, it occupies about one-fifth of the northern coast of the eastern hemisphere, and (what is really important) the only part of the arctic sea coast which is free from ice during

3

the winter. Thanks to the vicinity of the Gulf Stream and the absence of cold arctic currents, this territory, and especially the stem of the Γ, is the only part of the arctic coast line which does not have an arctic climate. Here are a few figures to illustrate this fact.

Let us first take the July isotherm for +10°C (50°F). It runs to the south of the arctic coast almost everywhere, but from the Kanin peninsula east of the White Sea it makes a slight bend to the north, touching Lappland at 71° N. Point Hope on the coast of Alaska, two degrees to the south of Hammerfest, is on the northern side of the isotherm for +5°C (41°F).

The January isotherms show quite remarkable differences between western Lappland and the rest of the Arctic coast. The isotherm for −10°C (14°F) goes to the north and east of the whole Norwegian coast; off the Atlantic coast of North America it touches the northernmost point of Newfoundland, and from there it goes to Montreal; it reaches the Pacific coast at 62° N.

The year isotherm for 0°C (32°F) goes north and east of the whole Norwegian coast. It crosses the Atlantic coast of North America north of Newfoundland and reaches the Pacific coast at 60° N.

Russian Lappland, Finnish Lappland, and that part of Swedish Lappland which is situated above the Arctic circle enjoy about the same temperatures as the southern half of the Labrador peninsula.

Nowhere on the earth can rye, barley, or potatoes be grown above the Arctic circle, except in Fennoscandia (not including the Kola peninsula). In America the northern boundary of the cultivated soil goes from the Gulf of St. Lawrence to the Alexander Archipelago; its northern peak, west of the Great Slave Lake, is at the same latitude as Hälsingland in Sweden, where even wheat and tobacco may be grown profitably.

Geographical conditions have made it possible for a cattle-breeding population to settle down at the eastern sea coast of Fennoscandia as far north as the Arctic circle, and along the Atlantic coast even up to 70° N. It is to be

4

understood that up to the nineteenth century, agriculture played only an accessory role compared with cattle breeding in the northern parts of Fennoscandia, beyond about 63° N. Today the farmers in these regions have to buy a considerable part of their food. Their ancestors were often if not usually short of bread, and lived chiefly by fishing and hunting. In the Middle Ages and still earlier, there was a big export of wild skins from this area. Fishing also played an important role. Thus, for instance, in the fifteenth century the Birgittine nuns of Vadstena in southern Sweden owned the salmon fishery in the Edefors rapids of the Lule river, not far from the Arctic circle, where there was hardly any settled population before the thirteenth century. Along the Norwegian coast, fishing, including whale and seal hunting, was of primary importance, as it still is.

The wheat boundary goes from the northern tip of the Ladoga northwest and reaches the Bothnian gulf at 64° N. In Sweden it follows the same latitude westwards to the mountain region. In the last mentioned region it descends to 61° N. Along the Atlantic coast of Norway it rises to 65° N.

In the Fennoscandian wheat region the Scandinavian population can be traced back to the Stone Age, and there is no evidence of an early occurrence of Lapps in this area. The coastal region between 68° and 70° N was a contact area, where Scandinavians and Lapps had a long-lasting commercial and social intercourse from the middle of the first millennium of our era or still earlier.

In Norway the Lapps live chiefly in the two northernmost provinces even if there are Lapps as far south as Røros (62° 30' N). Finnmark (literally "the Lappish border region") comprises the whole north coast of Norway, from Varanger in the east and including the Lyngen fjord in the west. The province of Troms (Tromsö) occupies the northernmost part of the west coast down to a point a little north of Narvik.

The numerous fjords are a dominating feature in the northern Norwegian landscape. They have been a decisive

5

Political boundaries in Lappland.

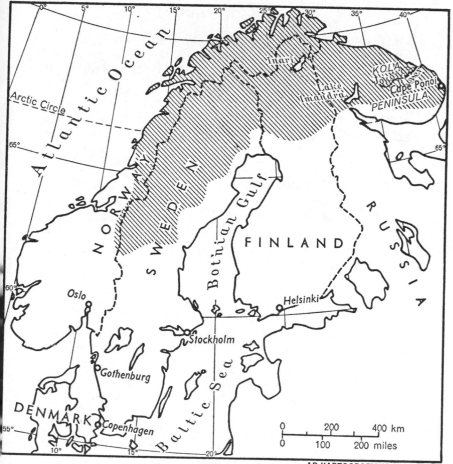

Distribution of the Lapps in Fennoscandia.

factor in the settling of the country, perhaps to some extent
even in the formation of the national character of the Norwegian people. In many places the snowy mountains extend to the sea coast. Even in the valleys, the arable area
is small, and the bulk of the comparatively low country
between the fjords is chiefly covered with spruce, birch,
moss, and lichen. It is an excellent land for fishing. Lofo-
ten, at the mouth of Ofoten fjord off Narvik is world-
famous in this respect. In the valleys there are good grazing-grounds for cattle, but the conditions of agriculture
are precarious, especially in Finnmark. The breadth of

7

the country, from the sea shore to the Swedish and the Finnish frontier, is small, if we disregard the parish of Kautokeino and adjacent parts of Finnmark, flanked in by the western arm and the "head" of Finland. The mountainous tracts (apart from the grassy slopes of the glens) are mostly fit only for reindeer breeding, but the nomads must be careful to avoid trespassing on the tilled soil.

To the east of the Norwegian-Russian frontier the Arctic sea shore has the character of a tundra, without high mountains. South of the tundra there are vast birch forests, marshes, and numerous lakes, the biggest being Lake Imandra; and still farther south, facing the White Sea, are dense timber forests. The Russian part of Lappland is the largest and the least populated, at least in so far as the Lapps are concerned.

The fishing industry along the Arctic coast is very important on both sides of the frontier. It has even caused political friction between Russia and Norway, and this has had its repercussions on reindeer breeding not only in Norway but also in Sweden, as we shall see below.

Finnish Lappland chiefly consists of the western arm (Enontekiö) and the "head" (Utsjoki and Inari). Until 1809, when Russia conquered Finland and the adjacent parts of northern Sweden, Enontekiö belonged to the so-called Tornio Lappmark, and the rest of what is now Finnish Lappland formed the Kemi Lappmark. The western parts of this territory have about the same character as the inner parts of Finnmark, whereas the eastern part of the parish of Inari (Enare), rich in big and small lakes, supports a relatively numerous population of fishermen.

Lappland (Finnish: *Lappi*) nowadays forms one of the administrative provinces of Finland; Rovaniemi is the seat of the provincial government.

When the Swedes speak of Lappland they mean only a part of Norrbotten and Västerbotten, the two northernmost administrative provinces of the country, situated to the west and north of the "Lappmark frontier." This

8

demarcation line was drawn in the middle of the eighteenth century in order to protect the agricultural population of the coast districts from excessive migration on the part of the nomad Lapps. This line mostly runs at a distance of about sixty miles from the coast. Actually the nomads in the winter often go far beyond this line with their herds, and sometimes extend their migrations even to the sea shore. But there are Lapps also in the mountainous western parts of the administrative province of Jämtland, ceded by Norway-Denmark to Sweden in 1645, and including the historical provinces Jämtland and Härjedalen. Earlier there have been Lapps in the southern parts of the province Dalarne, and even in Värmland. Late in the nineteenth century a nomad Lapp family was admitted to the parish of Idre in Dalarne.

"Lappmark" is a term which apparently dates from the Middle Ages. The old lappmarks were named after the principal commercial centers along the northernmost part of the Botnian Gulf—Kemi, Tornio, Luleå, and Piteå. Thus the Lappland part of the province of Norrbotten consists of the lappmarks of Tornio, Lule, and Pite respectively. Subsequently the term was applied also to southern Lappland, which was divided into Lycksele Lappmark and Åsele Lappmark. Even outside Lappland proper the term has been used; thus Ångermanna Lappmark formerly meant those parts of the historical province Ångermanland where Forest Lapps dwelt up to the latter half of the nineteenth century.

There is another geographic division which chiefly concerns the Swedish and Finnish parts of Lappland. In northern Lappland the nomads from time immemorial were organized in communities, each of which occupied a territory of its own. In so far as the members of the horde were the owners of the territory, they owned it in common. When the Lapps lost their political independence, this arrangement was confirmed by the new authorities (Norwegians, Karelians, Finns, and Swedes) and is still maintained, especially in Sweden. Rather recently it has been extended to regions where earlier the principle of individual ownership, or at least individual right of using the land, prevailed. In southern Lappland, according to the indigenous customary right acknowledged by the Swedish authorities, each nomad disposed of a territory of his own, which nobody else was allowed to use. Even if the Swedish Crown did not accept the theory that the nomad *owned* the territory, his exclusive right of using it was seldom contested; he paid taxes for it, and it was called his "tax land." But towards the end of the eighteenth century, if not earlier, colonists were admitted even to such tax lands, and later the district community principle was extended to all those parts of northern Sweden where Lapps are allowed to move with their reindeer herds. The whole Lapp territory in Sweden is divided into fifty nomad districts. Thus, for instance, the Tornio Lappmark consists of two parishes, Karesuando and Jukkasjärvi, and the main part of Karesuando is divided into two nomad districts, Könkämä and Lainiovuoma.

In Lappland, and especially in Swedish Lappland, the great rivers are the arteries of communication. Up to the present the compass-rose was determined in each region by the main direction of the river, not by the needle or the sun. This is true of the Finns and the Scandinavians as well as of the Lapps. In the last three centuries the Scandinavian settlers have been moving slowly upstream from the coast region. The annual migrations of the nomads mostly follow the rivers, or the tracts between the rivers, up and down, with few or no variations.

In Lappland the height above sea-level makes much more for climatic differences than latitude. Each of the lappmarks is a pageant of botanical geography. There are three principal regions from southeast to northwest—the conifer zone, the zone of the big lakes, and the alpine zone. The prevalent evergreen in Swedish Lappland is the spruce (*Picea abies*); the Scottish fir (*Pinus silvestris*) is less abundant. The fir is concentrated in the river basins while the spruce is characteristic of the ridges between the rivers. Both grow slowly in these northern regions, but the timber is excellent in those parts where the soil is dry. Much of

10

the conifer zone consists of marshlands. The natural conditions of cattle breeding are good along the rivers, except in the extreme north (Karesuando), but mediocre or unfavorable on the morain grounds between the rivers. In the watery parts there are vast natural (unsown) meadows. On dry soil the reindeer lichen (*Cladonia rangiferina*) is plentiful, not only to the west of the Lappland frontier, but right down to the sea coast. Earlier these forests were very good hunting-grounds, and everywhere there were plenty of fish in the lakes and streams. Nowadays the valuable game (wild reindeer, beaver, black fox, elk, etc.) is extinct or scarce, and in most places fishing plays only an accessory role, if any. The most important source of livelihood in these regions is forestry, but the bulk of the forests belongs to the Crown or to joint-stock companies.

In Swedish Lappland all the big rivers and some of their tributaries come from long and comparatively narrow lakes, or more or less continuous chains of lakes, which are with one or two exceptions about 1,100 to 1,300 feet above sea-level. Most of these lake chains extend from the alpine region almost half way to the coast. Spruce and fir grow in the lower parts of this region; the typical tree of the higher parts is the birch. If we disregard southern Lappland, the conditions of cattle breeding are fairly good along the lakes in the eastern part of this zone, and unfavorable or bad or even nonexistent elsewhere. The fishing opportunities are good; the chief kinds of fish are whitefish (*Coregonus lavaretus*), redbelly (*Salmo alpinus*), and trout (*Salmo trutta*). Even here the reindeer lichen is abundant, but in these days it is more or less cropped by the reindeer in the northern parts of this zone.

Northwest of Lake Torneträsk the birch region extends to the Atlantic. In all the other parts of Swedish Lappland the tree-limit goes west of the great lakes.

In the lowest parts of the alpine region there are bushes such as juniper, dwarf birch, and certain willows. The most conspicuous herb is the *Angelica archangelica*.

11

Higher up the willows are only knee-high, and the dwarf birch creeps. Still higher up there is not much food for the reindeer, and one can hardly find anything else to make fire with except the scrub of the *Andromeda*. There are spots where the snow never melts in the summer. A few herbs, as the eatable sorrel *Oxyria digyna*, grow still higher, close to the never-melting snow. Such grass and herbs as the reindeer eat in the summer are abundant in many places in all the zones, especially in the lower strata of the alpine zone.

From the first half of the seventeenth century mining has played a role in Swedish Lappland. The silver deposits of Nasafjäll, in the parish of Arjeplog close to the Norwegian frontier, raised sanguine hopes during the Thirty Years' War, but the enterprise turned out to be a failure. The copper mines of Svappavare, in the parish of Jukkasjärvi, of which the exploitation began at the same time, are not operated now. But the iron ore of Kiruna in the same parish and Gällivare is a factor in the world market. The Russians have considerable mineral deposits on the Kola peninsula, and the nickel factory in Petsamo is of no small importance.

Briefly, such is the geography of the land of the Lapps, and an understanding of the geography is necessary to an understanding of the history, condition, and future of the Lapp people.

CHAPTER II

THE HISTORY OF THE LAPPS

IT MAY be asked whether the Lapps really have a history. We have but little information about them from the time when they were politically independent. For all we know, the Lapp people may always have been split up in small tribes without any political or military organizations. According to their own popular traditions, confirmed by historical documents, the Lapp tribes or hordes earlier had judges of their own, but we are not told to what extent such a judge had the authority of a ruler. The Norwegians at the end of the viking epoch thought that there were or had been Lapp chieftains. In the short prose introduction to the Edda song on Völund (the Daedalus of the ancient Norsemen) it is said that Völund and his brothers were the sons of a Lapp chieftain (*Finnakonungr*) and that they were ski-runners and hunters.

The Icelandic saga of Egill Skallagrimsson was probably written in the thirteenth century; it has been suggested that it may be a work of Snorri Sturluson. The first chapters deal with events that are assumed to have taken place in the second half of the ninth century, during the reign of King Harald Fairhair. According to the saga, an opulent Norwegian land owner named Thorolf Kveldulfsson went in two subsequent winters to what is now Swedish Lappland (and Norwegian Finnmark) to raise taxes from the Lapps in the name of the king of Norway. In order to emphasize the just and righteous claim of the Crown, Thorolf had an armed retinue of about one hundred men. There were also other tax-cravers and merchants moving around in those regions—Karelians, Kolbyags (descendants of Swedish colonists in Russia?), and Quens. The last-mentioned may or may not have been identical with the Finnish-speaking *Kainulaiset* of northern Ostrobotnia; some scholars think that they were Scandinavians. Thorolf allied himself to the king of the Quens, and together they fought the Karelians.

That the Lapps had to pay taxes to their Norwegian neighbors is confirmed by the relation of Ohthere, quoted by King Alfred the Great (see below, Chapter XVIII). From the *Egilssaga* we know that the northern Lapps were attacked from other directions too. It may be that the Lapp legends about the raids of the Chudes (or Karelians) are reflexes from the time when Karelia was independent, that is to say, before the beginning of the fourteenth century. In these legends there is little mention of battles or even skirmishes; almost always the enemies are outwitted by the Lapps, or by a single Lapp.

One of these legends tells us how the Lapps once killed a lot of Russians (or Karelians) by letting down a heap of logs on them when they were climbing a steep hill. This story has been localized to several different places. According to Per Högström's description it happened at Käppuvare in the parish of Gällivare. The Russian historian Dergachev[1] says that this legend reflects a battle fought by Lapps and Russians in 1318, but I do not know where he has got this sensational information. Here is a variant from Jockmock, taken down in 1943 (phonograph collection of Uppsala Landsmåls- och Folkminnesarkiv):

"Once I heard a tale about the old Russian war, there on the southern side of Peuraure. There was a cliff, a huge steep cliff. The Lapps knew that a horde of Russians were approaching their settlement. . . . First they made a path and this path they made slippery with ice; then at the top they made what the Lapps in the old days used to call a *satim* or *pärtom* [a trap for big beasts]. . . . Two children were out of doors the day the Russians were expected to

---

[1] Quoted by Kharuzin. The only sample of Dergachev's work which I have seen is defective and does not contain this passage.

THE HISTORY OF THE LAPPS

reach the camp. One of the children gave a sign and said, "Look, a dog is coming." The Lapps heard, but paid no attention—they were sitting and eating in the tents. Then the child gave another sign (gave alarm again) and said, "Look, another dog is coming." But the Lapps still gave no indication of being frightened. Then the child pointed to the third Russian and said, "Here comes still another dog." By this time three Russians had managed to climb up the path, all the way to the tents. The Lapps rushed out and shot the three Russians with their bows and arrows, and ran to their traps which they had prepared in order to kill more Russians.

"By now the Russians were on their way up the side of the cliff. The Lapps had made fast logs with rope and twine; that was their trap. Now they cut the ropes and the logs thundered down the path which the Lapps had covered with ice, and on which the Russians were approaching. And in this manner they killed many Russians. . . . And so peace was established in the tract where the Lapps had killed the horde of Russians by the cliff. And the cliff has since been called *Karjelpakte*."

Let it be said once and for all that the folklore of the Lapps can hardly be given credit as historical evidence. Most of these legends are probably items of migratory fiction, attached to certain places in an arbitrary fashion.

In the thirteenth century the whole north coast of Fennoscandia was a bone of contention between Norwegians and Karelians. After the Republic of Novgorod (shortsightedly founded by Swedish Vikings in the ninth century) had annexed Karelia, the conflict was settled by a peace treaty in 1326. The frontier between Norway and Russia has not changed much since then; the overlapping economic and fiscal claims survived to some extent and appeared again as late as the middle of the nineteenth century.

The first frontier between Russia and Sweden-Finland was drawn in 1323. According to the opinion of many modern historians, the boundary line crossed the Finnish peninsula from southeast to northwest, reaching the Bot-

15

nian gulf at 64° 40′ N. Swedish popular traditions make it plausible that the Karelians up to that time had laid claim to the western coast of the gulf north of that latitude. It must be kept in mind that northern Ostrobotnia was more or less uninhabited at the beginning of the fourteenth century, and the settlements on the opposite coast, in what is now called Norrbotten, were scarce and recent. The Karelians, on the other hand, had a firm foothold on the west coast of the White Sea even in the ninth century. We know from the *Egilssaga* that they made raids into the Scandinavian part of Lappland. They could reach western Lappland along different routes. It is highly probable that they went along the Ule river to the Botnian coast, crossed the gulf, and levied taxes on the western Lapps. But this means of livelihood became precarious as soon as the Swedish Crown succeeded in colonizing Norrbotten, in the thirteenth century. From this epoch dates a Swedish-Finnish expansion, which was not checked until the beginning of the seventeenth century.

Immediately after the peace of 1323, the Swedish Crown started a farsighted colonization in the Uleåborg (Oulu) region. This was only the beginning of a movement that almost two centuries later bore fruit in the peace treaty of 1595, which confirmed a boundary line which in its northern parts did not differ much from the Finnish-Russian frontier of today.

The peace of 1595 secured Kemi Lappmark to Sweden-Finland. Tornio Lappmark had been taken earlier, though not from the Russians or the Karelians. The Tornio valley was a Finnish sphere of interest as early as the thirteenth century, perhaps still earlier. It had been occupied by Finnish hunters and fur traders, known under the name of Bircarls (Swedish *birkarlar*, Finnish *pirkkalaiset*).

The first mention of the bircarls of which we have a record was made in a document from the year 1328, in which it was stipulated that nobody was allowed to hinder the Lapps (*homines silvestres et vagos vulgariter dictos Lappa*) in their hunting, or molest the bircarls who visited

16

the Lapps. In 1358 the king of Sweden confirmed the trading and tax-raising privilege of the bircarls.

Bircarls no doubt means the inhabitants of *Pirkkala* (*Birkala*). Pirkkala is nowadays a country parish close to the factory town Tampere (Tammerfors) in southwestern Finland. In the Middle Ages the territory of Pirkkala was very large, and it is one of the old centers of civilization in Finland.

According to the Finnish historian Jalmari Jaakkola, the landowners of ancient Pirkkala developed an important fur trade in the twelfth century and earlier. Every year they went on hunting expeditions northwards, chiefly along the rivers which run from their region to the coast of southern Ostrobotnia. Those far-flung enterprises called for a military cooperation, because a Swedish population dwelt in the coast region. In northern Ostrobotnia it was not safe to move under any circumstances, because this was a Karelian sphere of interest. Avoiding the estuaries of the rivers which came from the territories of the warlike Karelians, the Vikings of Pirkkala crossed the gulf northward and got a foothold in the Tornio valley, which at the beginning of this millennium may have been no man's land.[2] They subdued the Lapps and made them pay taxes, preferably in wild skins. Later they profited from the adversities of the Karelians and extended their sphere of influence. When Sweden incorporated Norrbotten, the Swedish authorities confirmed the existing arrangement as they found it, as far as the Finnish fur trader companies were concerned. Probably the same privilege was given also to fur traders of Swedish extraction; but all the privilege-holders were called by the established name of bircarls.

In the old lappmarks (Kemi, Tornio, Lule, and Pite) were the chief residences of the bircarls. The Lapps of these lappmarks seem to have been regarded as the serfs of their respective bircarls, whereas the Lapps of Väster-

---

[2] It should be noted that the Finnish dialect of the Tornio region points towards southwestern Finland, especially towards the Pirkkala territory.

botten (southern Lappland) were called "the King's Lapps."

The halcyon days of the bircarls lasted up to the reign of Gustaf I (1521–1560), even though there may have been some kind of royal jurisdiction in Lappland as early as the beginning of the fifteenth century. At the end of the sixteenth century their privilege was very much reduced, and their influence was soon brought to nil.

King Carl IX († 1611) tried to bring the whole land of the Lapps under the Swedish Crown. He laid an explicit claim on Finnmark and tried to erect a fortress at Vadsö, and one of his Finnish chieftains raided Petsamo, the residence of the famous Russian missionary Trifon. (The Russians later repaid the visit with interest.) But Carl IX was not successful. Denmark-Norway declared war in 1611, and in 1613 his successor, Gustavus Adolphus, had to renounce the title of "King of the Lapps."

In Russian Lappland the exploitation of the Lapps seems to have been organized in much the same way as in Finland and Sweden. In Russian documents from the fifteenth century, concerning the sale and letting of landed property in the Kola peninsula, mention is made of the "five families (or clans) of sons of Karelia" as the righteous owners of the land. Karelian landowners could transfer upon others the right to trade with the "wild Lapps" (Dikaia Lop') and exact *prazga* (land rent) from them. According to Geiman, Lapps are even mentioned as objects of sale in documents from that time. Besides Karelian landowners, boyars from Novgorod are also mentioned. Strife between Novgorodians and Karelians was sometimes settled by alternating use of the land, so that there were "boyar years" and "Karelian years."

The political contentions between Swedes, Danes, and Russians were detrimental to the Lapps. Apart from the devastations brought about by warfare, many Lapps had to pay taxes to two or even three governments, and sometimes they were fined by the officials of one state for having paid taxes to another. The iniquities of bureaucracy were multiplied.

In Norrbotten the mining industry caused much suffering to the Lapps about the middle of the seventeenth century and even later. There were no roads from the mines to the smelting factories, or even from the factories to the highway that runs along the sea coast, and the Lapps had to transport the ore and the metal with their reindeer. The only thing that kept the authorities from dealing violently with the Lapps was the consideration that the Lapps might emigrate to Norway if they were ill-treated in their own country. We must remember that this was the age of mercantilism; the rights of the individual did not matter much when commercial interests were at stake. But even this circumstance does not make it understandable why part of the cartage should be paid to the Lapps in the form of raw spirits, as we are told by Janrik Bromé.

It is natural that the Norwegians were the first to preach the Christian faith to the Lapps. The first endeavors in this direction were made in the thirteenth century. There were single Christians among the Swedish Lapps in the fourteenth century; a Lapp woman named Margaret made a journey to the southern parts of the realm in order to direct the attention of the reigning Scandinavian queen, her namesake, to the deplorable spiritual state of her pagan compatriots. The only known result of this journey was a Latin letter from Queen Margaret to her Lapp subjects.

The Russian Lapps were converted in the sixteenth century, but their Christianism remained rather superficial for at least two centuries.

Carl IX, "the King of the Lapps," had a few churches built in Lappland, and he made up his mind to provide priests who were able to preach to the Lapps in their own language. To that purpose he ordered one of his trusted men to collect Lapp boys who might be trained for the ecclesiastical career. The man went to Lappland and kidnapped sixteen boys. Six of them he turned over to the Lapp sheriff in Tornio to be taken to Uppsala by ship. Of the other ten, one fell sick and could not be taken, and the other nine were taken to Gnarp in Hälsingland, where two of them escaped. The seven boys who were left were delivered to the sheriff in Gävle. What became of them is not known.

In the middle of the seventeenth century the prayer book of the Swedish church was translated to Lappish; from that time on Lapps are found among the pastors of Lappland.

The decisive steps in the Christianization of the Norwegian Lapps were taken in the first quarter of the eighteenth century. To the devoted Norwegian evangelists, teachers, and priests of that epoch we also owe the main part of our knowledge of the old pagan religion of the Lapps. These missionaries gained the confidence of the Lapps, and they made a point of making themselves acquainted with the pagan beliefs and superstitions in order to combat and eradicate them. In the wake of the zeal to convert the Lapps went a positive scientific interest.

Influenced by the Norwegians, the Swedish authorities carried out their part of the Christianization of the Lapps chiefly in the second quarter of the eighteenth century. It was stipulated that nobody could be admitted as priest in Lappland without knowing the Lappish language, and a literary language was created, chiefly on the basis of the dialects spoken in the center of Swedish Lappland. The New Testament appeared in this language in 1755. The same standard language was codified in the *Lexicon Lapponicum* of Lindahl and Öhrling (1780).

In the lappmarks of Kemi and Tornio the work of Christianization proceeded as in the other parts of Swedish Lappland, with the only difference that in those parts of the country where the settled population was Finnish-speaking, Finnish was usually adopted as the medium of preaching, to the detriment of Lappish.

The Lapps readily accepted the Christian faith. Nowadays they are at least as good Christians as their Scandinavian, Finnish, and Russian neighbors.

In the middle of the nineteenth century the rector Lars Levi Laestadius in Karesuando started a lively religious

movement among the Lapps and Finns of northern Lappland. This was both a religious and a moral awakening.
Laestadius raged against drunkenness, which he regarded
as a basic evil.[3]

In his sermons he used drastic language, threatening
with fire and brimstone. He did not break with the established church, but he denounced its representatives, or at
least most of them, as hired shepherds. He created an
unorganized community, with preachers who were simply
approved by this community (it did not matter if they
were ordained priests, like himself, or lay preachers, like
most of his collaborators). The cult of the Swedish church
he left untouched; but the divine service, as he practiced
it, was marked by a strong element of religious ecstasy.
The movement soon spread to the Tornio valley and to
the adjacent parts of Finland and Norway. In our days
there are many Laestadians also in southern Finland, and
even in the United States, especially in Michigan. Calu-
met, Michigan, is one of the centers of the movement.

Laestadianism has been a good influence both for the
nomads and for the settled population in northern Lappland, improving the moral and economic conditions; but
sometimes it has been accompanied by spiritual pride,
self-sufficiency, and fanaticism. During Laestadius's life
the movement, when it reached Kautokeino in Finnmark,
took a violent turn and led to two murders. In his book
Muittalus samid birra (An Account of the Lapps) Johan
Turi has given a vivid account of these events.

I have already said that Lapps and Scandinavians lived
together in northern Norway before the viking epoch.
According to Wiklund there are a few Lappish place-
names in the southern part of Swedish Lappland, which
the Lapps must have borrowed from Primitive Scandinavian. But if there was a Scandinavian population in that

[3] To give a hint of how bad things were in this respect, I will cite the following from the preacher Bodell, who was active in southern Norrbotten at
the same time: "We cannot dam up the flood of intoxicating liquors which
pours over our country, wasting such an infinite amount of material and
spiritual values; but we can raise cries of distress on the banks and salvage
as much as possible."

21

region thirteen hundred years ago, it must have disappeared later, perhaps in the fourteenth century. In the sixteenth century Swedish Lappland was exclusively the land of the Lapps. The colonization of the "lappmarks" began in the first decennium of the seventeenth century, on the initiative of the Swedish government. The Crown wished to get new taxpayers and encouraged pioneers by promising them immunity from taxation for a certain number of years. It was expressly stated that the nomads should not be molested or ousted, and that there was space enough both for reindeer breeders and for colonists. It can hardly be maintained that the Crown intentionally favored the settlers to the detriment of the Lapps. When there arose conflicts about fisheries and hunting grounds, the Crown resolved that the farmer should not go into the woods farther than three miles from his farm. But often the relations between the two groups were regulated by the law of the wild rather than by royal edicts, and as a rule the settler had a stronger position than the nomad.

In most cases the relations of the nomads and the settlers were peaceful, or even friendly, not only because there was no inevitable source of conflict between their trades, but also because they could be useful to each other. From the account of Ohthere we know that as early as the ninth century Norwegian landowners had reindeer, which in all probability were tended by nomad Lapps. In Swedish Lappland this custom still exists. It stands to reason that such transactions both imply and develop friendly relations.

Wherever a piece of land can be tilled with profit, it feeds more people than if it is used as grazing land for reindeer. This is an economic iron law, which in the long run determines the issue of the conflicts that arise between nomadism and agriculture. Of course the attitude of the authorities may temporarily reverse the trend, but even legislators find it difficult to kick against the pricks. In Swedish Lappland, as in northern Finland and in Finnmark, agriculture (in this case cattle breeding, combined with the raising of forage and potatoes, or, earlier, turnips) has proceeded upwards along the rivers nearer and nearer to the snow-clad mountains. It is worth noticing that conflicts with the reindeer-breeding Lapps have arisen chiefly in regions where agriculture is not very profitable or has remained in a primitive stage. Much trouble has been caused by farmers who are the descendants of nomads. In many places Lapps who have lost their reindeer have settled down at a lake high up in the birch zone to live by fishing and hunting. The grandchildren of such colonists may have a horse and two cows for each family, and a potato patch, but no agricultural crops and no regular meadows; the fishing produces very little and the hunting grounds next to nothing. The fodder for the cattle is taken from more or less distant sedge swamps. After the hay has been mown in July, it is left there for months; there are no haybarns, and no fence around the ricks. Such natural meadows attract the reindeer in the autumn, and a reindeer may spoil a whole haystack to get a mouthful of horsetail-grass, whereas normal cow-fodder leaves it unaffected. According to Swedish law, the Lapps have to pay the damage only if they have caused it intentionally or by carelessness. Of course, much depends on how the law is applied; and even if the authorities should be with the Lapp, he will prefer to pay than expose himself to the animosity of the landowner.

It would be unjust to draw a parallel between the treatment of the Scandinavian Lapps and the treatment of the Indians in the United States,[4] at least as far as Sweden proper is concerned. Sweden still acknowledges the principle that the Lapps have a hereditary right to the land of their fathers. The right to keep reindeer on alien grounds (whether the land belongs to the Crown or is private property) is the exclusive privilege of the descendants (children or grandchildren) of nomad Lapps. And this grazing right is not limited to the region west and north of the Lappmark boundary; in the winter the nomads are allowed to go beneath the boundary as far as

---

[4] The Lapps of the Kola peninsula have proved unable to withstand the competition of another reindeer-breeding people, namely the Ziryenes, who began to establish themselves there in the eighties of the last century.

they are accustomed to go, some places even down to the sea coast. The last-mentioned right is probably less than two centuries old. In the latter half of the nineteenth century a so-called cultivation boundary was drawn through Lappland in order to check further colonization; to the west of this demarcation line only the nomads are allowed to fish and hunt. The Lapp privilege includes the right to use the fishing lakes and hunting grounds.

After Jämtland and Härjedalen had been ceded to Sweden in 1645, the authorities had some trouble with nomad Lapps who had recently established themselves in the southwestern part of this territory. First they were regarded as intruders both by the authorities and the landowners, but on second thought the Crown accepted them as regular taxpayers. The farmers persisted in their opinion, and after three centuries there is still something left of the old tension. The folklore of the Lapps of Härjedalen shows that their ancestors were afraid of the farmers. It is worth while to give a specimen of this folklore, but it must be stated that the following story is pure fiction.

"In that time the farmers planned to murder the Lapps. Then it happened that a married woman came to the priest, and the priest was just about to read a letter which the farmers had written to him. But then somebody drove up before the house, and the priest went out to meet him. The woman hastens to take the papers, and she tears other papers into pieces and throws them in the fire. Then she gives a paper to the priest's little child and tells the child to throw it in the fire. Then the priest comes back and asks what has happened to the papers. The woman says, 'Your little child has thrown them in the fire.' The woman returns home, and she takes a hand-sledge and puts her two children on the sledge. She puts on a fur coat and also dresses the children in fur coats, and then she starts for Stockholm, pulling the sledge and the children. She comes to Stockholm, and there she meets a gentleman, and he was the King. The King was astonished

that there are in his kingdom people who are covered
with hair. The King stopped and asked, 'Of what nation
are you?' She answers that she is a Lapp woman from the
mountains and she has come to meet the King. The King
himself shows her where she can get accommodation. Then
the gentleman says, 'At one o'clock you are going to see
the King. . . . But you shall come to the King in the same
costume.' Then on that day there came a dignified gentleman to take her to the King. Then the woman shows the
papers which the priest and the farmers had written. Then
the King reads this letter and sees that the farmers
planned to murder the Lapps. The King promises the
woman that he will help the Lapps. . . ."

This is a legend, but a popular tradition about a Lapp
family that was murdered near Ljungdalen at the boundary of Härjedalen and Jämtland has a historical background.

The legend expresses a real attitude. There has been
some animosity between Lapps and landowners in Härjedalen, which culminated in 1891 when hundreds of reindeer were highhandedly shot on the lands of the foundry
of Ljusnedal.

Another front of dissension was—and is—Arvidsjaur in
the center of Swedish Lappland. This is one of the biggest
and most desolate forest regions in western Europe. Arvidsjaur has been the El Dorado of the Forest Lapps. The first
outsiders arrived there in the second half of the eighteenth
century. According to Lapp tradition one or two of them
were killed immediately by the Lapps. It should be kept
in mind that they settled on the tax lands of the nomads
and consequently were, from the viewpoint of the Lapps,
unlawful intruders.

In the central part of the parish of Arvidsjaur is the
village Lomträsk, which is nowadays inhabited by both
Swedes and settled Lapps. The configuration of the place
is exceptional. Most of the families live on a narrow land
tongue, which has a length of two miles. At the point
where the land tongue is connected with the mainland, its

breadth is about 150 feet. The Lapp to whose tax land this place belonged nearly two centuries ago used to keep his reindeer herd on the land tongue, especially during the rutting season in the autumn. There came a colonist who without permission built a house at the very entrance to the land tongue. The Lapp set fire to the house. The settler built a new house exactly on the same spot. A little later the Lapp was walking in the forest with his wife and quite unexpectedly met the colonist. He threw his lasso and caught the colonist and tied him firmly to a tree. Then, aided by his squaw, he put four piles of wood around the tree, set the piles on fire and withdrew. Fortunately the wife of the settler heard the cries of her husband and came in time to rescue him.

I do not know whether this story is true or not. I heard it from a Lapp who lives in the same village, and I am glad to say that he most decidedly disapproved of the attempted murder. I asked the opinion of the Swedish farmer who is the offspring of the first settler, and he said that he found the behavior of the old nomad quite understandable.

A third theater of conflict has existed in northernmost Jämtland. In 1813 a family of settlers was extirpated by Lapps in the parish of Frostviken. According to a popular tradition, Lapps had earlier been murdered by settlers in the same region.

Such misdeeds were sporadic symptoms of a tension which in itself was of a local and transitory nature. In the present territory of Sweden this tension seems to have originated chiefly in the middle and the second half of the eighteenth century in regions where the Crown encouraged settlers to occupy parts of the tax lands of the Lapps. In Härjedalen the trouble may have started in the seventeenth century.

Today there is not much left of the old antagonism even in the regions I have spoken of. But as late as the end of the nineteenth century an overbearing attitude towards the Lapps prevailed in the areas of conflict. A century ago the surveyor A. F. Rennerfeldt wrote a description of

Frostviken, in which he says: "It cannot be denied that farmers and homesteaders . . . often treated the Lapps both insultingly and cruelly."

To this the ethnologist Levi Johansson, who spent most of his youth in Frostviken, replies that there is no evidence of such cruelties, but he adds: "However, what he has to say about the overbearing attitude, the sneering pride and the refusal to recognize the Lapp's equality as a human being is, unfortunately, all too true, and has in fact been a general and stubbornly persistent trait of the population in the more prosperous and thickly settled part of the parish. In the Lapp territory, the *lappmarken* (the thinly settled and mostly untilled part) relations have, on the other hand . . . been good between the Lapps and the settlers, and this because both very soon realized that they needed each other's help, and because they had more to thank each other for than mischief."

Finland, with Russian Karelia all the way east to Lake Onega, seems to have been the homeland of the Lapps at an early epoch, perhaps as early as about one thousand years B.C. (We must keep in mind, however, that archeological reasons are often far from cogent in determining the language or the nationality of the bearers of a prehistoric civilization.) It is problematic whether they expanded to the Scandinavian peninsula before the beginning of the Christian era. It seems that Tacitus was right when he placed them in the neighborhood of the peoples that lived to the south and southeast of the Finnish Gulf.

According to the opinion of most archeologists, the Finns came to Finland about two thousand years ago. At that time there may or may not have lived Scandinavians in some coast districts and in the archipelago (certainly in the Åland isles, at any rate); the rest of the country probably belonged to the Lapps. The Finns soon learned the profitable business of levying contributions on the Lapps, and as early as about A.D. 500 they seem to have extended their hunting and tax-collecting expeditions to northern Ostrobotnia.

27

There is ample evidence, place-names as well as written documents and popular traditions, to testify that Lapps have lived in central Finland and even in southern Finland in the Middle Ages and later. We should make an important distinction here. There is hardly any certain evidence of Lapps in the coastal regions (except around the outflows of the Tornio and Kemi rivers) or southwest of the diagonal which separates the territory of the western Finnish dialects from the rest of Finland (approximately a line drawn from Hamina [Fredrikshamn] to Gamla Karleby [Kokkola]). On the other hand, the province of Savo (Savolaks) was for a great part a "lappmark" as late as the time of the Reformation, and there were Lapps even in the southern part of the province in the second half of the seventeenth century. There is no doubt but that the Savoans have a strong admixture of Lapp blood. In the first half of the eighteenth century there were probably still Lapps in Suomussalmi, half-way between the southern and the northern end of Finland. About the middle of the same century the Lappish language died out in Kuusamo, just below the Arctic circle. North of the Arctic circle Lappish was spoken to some extent in the eastern regions during the nineteenth century. Today the Lapps are chiefly restricted to the left arm and the "head" of Finland, namely the parishes of Enontekiö, Utsjoki, and Inari, north of the sixty-eighth latitude. The Lapps of Sodankylä, south of 68° N, are the descendants of late immigrants from Inari and Enontekiö. Towards the end of World War II some four hundred Skolt Lapps were evacuated from the Petsamo area, and they have a reservation in southern Inari. Utsjoki is the only parish in Finland where the Lapps are in a majority; there the prospects of the Lappish language are favorable, because, as Doctor Toivo Itkonen remarks, "there are no longer any tracts left for settlers to cultivate or use as grazing land, and, besides, among the Utsjoki Lapps one finds a more conscious nationalism than among other Finnish Lapps."

28

We have already mentioned the efforts of King Carl IX to unite all the Lapp regions under the Swedish crown, and how they failed. Sweden had another setback in the middle of the eighteenth century. In 1751 the delegates of Sweden-Finland and Denmark-Norway met to settle the question of the frontier in northern Lappland, where there had been a kind of undefined joint ownership for centuries. The Swedes were persistent in claiming Kautokeino, which is the mainland of Finnmark and where Sweden had a firm foothold. They might have succeeded if the Danish delegates had not made a most unexpected move. Now we must go about a hundred years further back in the history.

In 1644, when there was a war between Sweden and Denmark, the rector of Älvdalen in Dalarne called out his parishioners and conquered the adjacent Norwegian parishes Särna and Idre. In the following year Denmark ceded Jämtland, Härjedalen, Gotland, and Ösel to Sweden, but out of sheer forgetfulness Särna and Idre were not mentioned in the peace treaty; they simply remained under Swedish domination. Then in 1751 the Danes handed over the bill; indignantly they asked to get the two parishes back without delay together with a fair indemnity for all the loss and damage which had been caused to the Danish Crown by this unlawful annexation. Sweden's international position was rather shaky at this time, and the Swedish Crown renounced the nomad districts of inner Finnmark.

In 1809 Sweden lost to Russia the Kemi Lappmark and the greatest part of Enontekiö in Tornio Lappmark. According to the peace treaty the status of the Enontekiö nomads remained unchanged.

The controversial border questions on the Arctic coast were settled by Norway and Russia in 1826; but a quarter of a century later the Russians revived the old question of the season fishing along the coast, claiming certain rights all the way down to Ofoten. When the Norwegians did not give in, the Russian emperor in his capacity as Grand Duke of Finland shut the Finnish frontier to the

Lapps of Finnmark in 1852. From time immemorial the nomads of Kautokeino had enjoyed free access to the grazing-grounds of Enontekiö, and they needed them. In the Danish-Swedish treaty of 1751 it had been stipulated that the nomads should be allowed to migrate as they had done earlier. The first effect of the Russian move was that many nomad families emigrated to Karesuando (Enontekiö) in Sweden. In the eighties the Russians made new difficulties, and the Finnish frontier was shut to Swedish Lapps too.

When the Swedes acknowledged the dissolution of the union between Sweden and Norway in 1905, they did this on certain conditions, one of which was that those nomads who were Swedish citizens should keep their right to take their reindeer to Norwegian grazing-grounds in the summer, in accordance with the principle that was laid down in 1751. The Norwegians agreed to this, but the application of the principle was so complicated and difficult that it took many years to get to a practical solution of the problem. Joint committees were appointed, with sub-committees in which the nomads were represented; even Finnish experts were invited to preside over such committees, in order to smooth out the controversies between the Swedish and the Norwegian members. Philologists like J. Qvigstad and K. B. Wiklund were engaged to go deep into the past in order to determine whether the annual migrations of the nomad Lapps across the mountain ridge is an ancient phenomenon or not. The zoölogist E. Lönnberg arrived at the conclusion that the reindeer are driven more or less by a biological necessity to migrate to and fro across the Scandinavian peninsula.

The chief trouble was with the nomads of the four northernmost districts, between Lake Torneträsk and the Finnish frontier. They cannot prosper without moving to the Norwegian sea coast in the summer. Before 1905 they were allowed to take their reindeer to the isles off the coast of the province of Tromsö. The Swedish Lapp Anta Pirak has given a clear account of the question:

"The Karesuando Lapps and some of the Jukkasjärvi

Lapps do not have, on Swedish territory, mountains where the reindeer herds can graze during the warm months of the summer, and they have to migrate to Norway during the warm months, some of them leaving even in the Spring. For there are snow-clad mountains on the islands and on the capes in the ocean, where the reindeer can graze during the summer. These Lapps were accustomed, generation after generation, to migrate to Norway during the summer, and some of them had let their herds swim across to the rocky islands in the ocean, and spent the warm season there. But when the Norwegian population increased, and inhabited the forest regions along the rivers and creeks, and homesteaded in every forest-clad valley, they gradually settled the forested regions surrounding most of these snow-capped mountains and moved in on the lands reaching to the very foot of the high mountains. Then the settlers and the Lapps began to dispute with each other. The reindeer destroyed the settlers' mountain pastures, their meadows and grass-covered slopes, which were the summer grazing lands for their cattle, sheep, and goats. . . . The settlers demanded compensation from the Lapps when the reindeer herds trampled the grass in their pastures, and then the Lapps would protest, saying: "My reindeer have not been there, or trampled anything; that is the other Lapps." Then the Norwegian government stepped in and section by section divided up the mountains where the Lapps kept their reindeer herds in summer, and which were situated so close to each other that they formed a common grazing area for certain Lapps during the warmest period. . . . The commission was to investigate how many reindeer could be kept in this or that district without damage to the settlers' crops. . . . These settlers had been awarded legal title to the areas surrounding their houses. The commission usually asked, 'How far does your land reach up towards the mountain?' The Norwegian would answer, 'To the highest mountain.' . . . Then the commission had to investigate to what extent grazing lands could be set aside for the reindeer in more distantly situated grass-covered slopes high in the inaccessible tree-line and around mountain peaks situated at great heights."

The Norwegians were very particular about stipulating a maximum number of reindeer to be admitted to the Norwegian grazing-grounds in summer. In order to fix this number, inquiries were made in the different nomad districts as to how many reindeer could be fed in each district. Apparently the Lapps did not know the purpose of the question. After an agreement had been arrived at in 1919, it turned out that the Lapps of the districts to the north of Torneträsk had a total of sixty thousand reindeer, whereas by the agreement, only thirty-nine thousand could be admitted to Norway. This impasse could not be settled solely by reducing the reindeer herds. It proved necessary to order a considerable part of the reindeer owners to migrate with their reindeer to southern Lapland, where there were still pastures which were not used to their full capacity. It seemed questionable whether the Lapps could be forced southward. Actually only those Lapps were asked to move south whose ancestors had come from Norway in the nineteenth century. Everything went smoothly in so far as these Lapps were concerned, but it is understandable that they were not welcome everywhere in those regions to which they moved. The chief source of discontent on the part of the southern Lapps was that the northern Lapps had other methods of tending their reindeer. In most places these intruders proved successful in their trade, to the detriment of the indigenous nomads.

This peculiar demografic movement has been advantageous in one respect; it has solved the difficult problem of a literary language common to almost all the Scandinavian Lapps. The northern Lapps are more numerous than the nomads of the southern regions, and by now most of the pupils of the nomad schools speak the Finnmark dialect. And as there are northern Lapps all the way down to Härjedalen, Finnmark Lappish has been adopted in most of the schools. In 1948 a common orthography was adopted in Sweden and Norway. In Finland the same literary form of Lappish is prevalent, though the spelling is slightly different.

Some people think that too much is done for the Lapps, and that the Lapps would be better off if the governments did not interfere with their trade and their mode of life. The committees that have dealt with the Lapp problems have been expensive, and it seems that this diplomatic and legislative work never comes to an end. The Lapp Administration costs a lot of money, and so do the nomad schools. Big appropriations have been made for the support and promotion of nomadism. It has been asked whether the five hundred nomad families in Sweden could not be cared for in a less cumbersome and less expensive way.

Those who ask such questions seem to forget about the moral and legal aspect of the problem. All the nations which have in the course of history taken the land of the Lapps by force have acknowledged the hereditary rights of the nomads, and Sweden has done so quite especially by granting them the privilege of reindeer breeding. It would be inconsistent if the treatment of the Lapps should be regulated by fiscal considerations.

CHAPTER III

THE LAPPISH LANGUAGE

THE language of a people is an important feature of anthropological character, both in itself and as the basic form of its literary self-expression. But there is also another reason why an account of the Lappish language should be added to the description of the Lapps and their life. The documentary evidence on the history of the Lapps is scarce up to the seventeenth century, and archeological finds cannot tell us much about their prehistory. Specialists in race biology cannot give us much information either, at least in the present stage of their investigations. So we have to turn to the history of the language.

First of all comes the question whether Lappish is an isolated language (like Basque, for instance) or is related to some other language. It is true that linguistic relationship is no evidence of racial relationship. The Negroes of Haiti speak French, and French derives from Latin, which five hundred years before the Christian Era was one of the many Indo-European dialects spoken in central Italy. On the other hand, no people ever adopts the language of another people without having lived in a long intercourse with that people; and the lower the level of civilization is, the more intimate the intercourse must be in order to bring about a complete language shift.

The Lappish language belongs to the western division of the Finno-Ugric branch of the Uralic family (which comprises also the Samoyed languages, spoken along the Arctic coast of European Russia and in western Siberia, and probably Yukaghir, spoken along the Kolyma river in the northeastern corner of Siberia). The other languages belonging to the same western group are Finnish (with Estonian, Livonian, Vote, Vepse), Mordvin, Cheremiss, and Permian (Votyak and Ziryene). Of these languages, Finnish is most like Lappish. It will appear from the following specimen that there can be no possibility of mutual understanding:

> Finnish: *Jos joku lyö sinua oikealle poskelle, niin käännä hänelle toinenkin.*
> Lule Lappish: *Jus kuhtik chormot tu oalkes nierrai, te yorkole sunyi nuppeu ai.*
> English: *If somebody hits thee on thy right cheek, then turn to him the other too.*

This sounds a little too bad indeed. Apart from the first word (which may be a Finnish loan-word), the Lappish sentence differs as much from the Finnish as does the English equivalent. Even if these sentences are not typical, they are quite illustrative. The words *chormot* "hits," *oalkes* "right," *nierra* "cheek," *yorkole* "turn," and *ai* "too" simply do not occur in Finnish. The pronouns *tu* "thee" and *sunyi* "to him" are no doubt of the same root as *sinua* and *hänelle* respectively. The basic stem *ku-* in *kuhtik* "somebody" may be identical with Finnish *-ku* in *joku; -k* in *kuhtik* is more or less identical with Finnish *-kin* "too"; and the basic stem *nu-* in *nuppeu* "other" is the same as Finnish *muu* "other, another," which is synonomous with *toinen* "other, the other." From this we may infer that Finnish and Lappish must have diverged considerably in their phonological development. As a matter of fact, Finnish is conservative in its vowels, whereas Lappish is conservative in its consonants.

Both languages use case endings where the English language has prepositions, for instance Lappish *tu* "thee," *su* "him," *tunyi* "to thee," *sunyi* "to him," Finnish *poski* (the) "cheek," *poskelle* "on the cheek." This feature occurs in many languages (take for instance Latin *Romae* "in Rome," *Romam* "to Rome,"*Româ* "from Rome"); even Old English has traces of a locative case.

In Lappish words, *c* should be pronounced (approximately) as *ts*, *č* like English *ch* in *chin*, *z* as *ds*, *š* like English *sh* in *wash*, *ž* as *d* + *sh*, *ð* like English *th* in *bathe*, *ai* like English *I*, and *aw* like English *ow* in *now*.

According to some scholars, Lappish is closely akin to Finnish, much more than to any other Finno-Ugric language. In view of the fact that the Lapps are of quite another race than the bulk of the Finns (Estonians, etc.), these scholars assume that the Lapps about two thousand years ago or a little earlier adopted the language of the ancestors of the Finns or a language that was very nearly related to the language from which Finnish, Estonian, etc., have developed. Karl Bernhard Wiklund went as far as to identify the speakers of this hypothetic language with the *Chudi* (a word used by the Russians to designate Finnish tribes, especially Votes, Vepses, and Karelians) and the mythical *Chudes*, who according to Lapp popular legends formerly used to invade Lappland, and to whom he attributed the so-called comb-ceramic Stone Age finds in northern Finland. In the opinion of Wiklund the Lapps must have adopted their Finno-Ugric vernacular in those same regions.

According to other scholars there is no reason to assume that Lappish is more closely akin to Finnish than to Mordvin or Cheremiss. In matter of flection Finnish and Lappish have several traits in common which do not occur in the other Finno-Ugric languages, but at least part of these traits are found also in Samoyed, which seems to prove that they are inherited from the common Uralic parent language. In its word formation (derivation) Lappish may have been influenced by Finnish. As to the vocabulary, it is often difficult to make out whether a word that is common to Lappish and Finnish is a Finnish loan-word in Lappish; and there are hundreds of Finno-Ugric words in Lappish which do not occur in Finnish.

It is obvious that this controversy is of basic importance to the prehistory of the Lapps. If Wiklund's theory is true, then neither the Samoyeds nor the Ob-Ugrians (i.e. the Voguls and the Ostyaks in northwestern Siberia, whose languages are Finno-Ugric and closely akin to Hungarian) can have spoken Uralic languages from the beginning, and we get three hypothetic language-shifts instead of one. This difficulty can be avoided if we assume that the common ancestors of the Finns and the central Uralic peoples (Mordvins, Cheremiss, Permians) at a remote epoch changed their vernacular (perhaps an Indo-European language) for the Finno-Ugric language of the ancestors of the Lapps, and that the Lapps together with the Ugrians (Voguls, Ostyaks, Hungarians) and the Samoyeds are the descendants of the people who spoke the common Uralic parent language. It is the business of the specialists in race biology to judge the plausibility of this hypothesis. It might be argued that the demographic figures are against it, as the number of the Lapps is to the total number of the Finns (Estonians, etc.) and the central Uralic peoples as 1 to 250. But this argument is not decisive. It is impossible to predict the increase and decrease of population for thousands of years. We know that Hungarian is closely akin to Vogul and Ostyak, and that the ancestors of the Magyars, after having parted from their Ugrian kinsmen, assimilated Turkish tribes; now the total number of the Voguls and the Ostyaks is to the number of the Hungarians as 1 to 400.

The Lapps have been the neighbors of the Finns for many centuries, perhaps for two thousand years (or still more). The Finnish influence has left many traces in the Lappish language. The dialects that are spoken in Finland and in the Tornio Lappmark abound in recent Finnish loan-words.

The Scandinavian loan-words in Lappish give a striking evidence of the lively intercourse between Lapps and Scandinavians (up to the seventeenth century perhaps chiefly Norwegians). There are about three thousand such loan-words, and at least two hundred (probably many more) of them date from the epoch of Primitive Scandinavian or still earlier times; that is to say, they are at least about thirteen hundred years old. They belong to the same language as the Scandinavian runic inscriptions from the time between A.D. 200 and A.D. 700. Of course the Lappish language has not remained unaltered during thirteen centuries, but many of these loan-words have changed very little or not at all, and in most cases it is easy to reconstruct the old Scandinavian form of the word.

Most of the old loan-words are culture words, terms which have been adopted together with the thing or notion which they designate. But some of them simply give evidence of intimate intercourse—for instance *fawro* "fair, beautiful" (of a woman; Prim. Scand. *fagru* feminine form).

Among the old Scandinavian culture words the terms of navigation play a conspicuous role. Almost all the parts of a sea-going boat have Scandinavian names in the Lappish language, and so have the whale and the cod and almost all the other sea animals except the different species of seal and the halibut.

Here is a list of Lappish words which immediately display their Scandinavian origin:

akšo "axe"; *bardne, barne-*, "son, boy, child" (cf. Scottish *bairn*, Old English *barn*); *barko* "bark (of a tree)"; *biello* "bell"; *borde* "board"; *buwre* "shandy, shed" (cf. *bower*, OE *būr* "chamber"); *dames* "tame"; *dawgas* "tough"; *dielde* "cover (for the feet and legs) in a Lapp sleigh" (OE *teld* "tent"); *diibmo, diimo-* "hour" (cf. *time*); *divtes, diktas-* "tight" (Middle English *tiht*); *diwras* "dear" (OE *dēore*); *diwre* "animal, beast" (OE *dēor;* English *deer*); *fales, vales* "whale"; *farro, faro-* "company, party, travelling companions" (OE *faru* "journey, expedition, companions"; English *fare*); *fatme* "embrace, the outstretched arms" (OE *fæðm;* English *fathom); fiidno, fiino-* "woodpile" (OE *wudu-fīn); fuolke* "folks, family"; *galbe* "calf"; *garde* "enclosure" (OE *geard,* English *yard); garno* (in the obsolete hunters' jargon) "the intestines of the bear" (OE *gearn,* English *yarn,* originally "intestine") *garves* "ready, prepared, yare" (OE *gearu,* genitive *gearwes); gielas* "keel"; *golle* "gold"; *gordne, gorne-* "corn, cereals, barley"; *habag* "hawk" (OE *heafoc); laðđe* "cloth" (OE *clāð); liidne, liine-* "linen" (a Latin loan-word in the Germanic languages); *libre* "liver"; *marke* "mark" (weight and coin);

38

mielke "milk"; *niekke* "the lower part of the back of the head, the upper part of the back of the neck (of persons),'' (OE *hnecca* "nape of the neck"); *nuoges* "sufficient, enough" (OE *genōh*); *rasse* "grass"; *riððo, riðo-* "storm, gale" (OE *hrīð*); *ri(e)vtes* "right" (OE *riht*); *ruottas* "root"; *salte* "salt"; *snarro* "a snare"; *soames* "some"; *suwle* "something which gives the food a flavor" (OE *sufl* "food," English dialects *sowl*); *šallja* "sallow, Salix caprea" (OE *sealh*); *ullo* "wool" (OE *wull*); *varro, varo-* "ware"; *vielpes* "whelp"; *viides* "wide"; *viises* "wise"; *visses* "certain" (OE *wiss*).

The origin of Kola Lappish *lambes* "lamb" is obvious; but in all the other dialects the consonant clusters *mb, nd,* and *ng* have changed into *bb, dd,* and *gg* respectively; thus "lamb" is *labbes* in Finnmark Lappish. The following words are likewise of Scandinavian origin: *badde* "rope, band"; *budde* "twenty pounds" (cf. *pound,* OE *pūnd;* this is a Latin loan-word in the Germanic languages); *digge* "district-court sessions" (OE *ðing* "council," English *thing*); *gonagas* "king" (OE *cyning*); *radde* "brand" (piece of burning wood); *ragges* "narrow" (cf. *throng,* OE *ðrang*); *rigge* "iron chain for hanging cooking pot or kettle over the fire in the tent" (cf. *ring*); *rosse* "horse" (OE *hross*); *uddo* "scar" (cf. *wound*).

The diphthong *ai* developed into *ā* in Old English and *au* into *ēa.* This accounts for the following identifications: *airo* "oar" (OE *ār*); *daige* "dough" (OE *dāg*); *gaica* "goat" (OE *gāt*); *laibe* "bread" (cf. *loaf;* OE *hlāf* "bread"); *(s)laive* "weak, light, insipid, flat (of coffee and other drinks, etc.)" (cf. *slow,* OE *slāw*); *maidne, maine-* "defect" (OE *mān* "damage, pain, crime"); *raido* "string of baggage reindeer tied together, caravan" (cf. *road, raid,* OE *rād* "a riding, a journey"); *raipe* "rope" (OE *rāð*); *awros* (in the obsolete hunters' jargon) "the ear of the bear" (OE *ēare* "ear"); *lawgo* "(hot) bath" (OE *lēah*); *lawkes, laffes* "flea" (OE *flēah*).

The following words would need a few commentaries if this were a scientific treatise: *arbe* "heritage" (cf. OE *yrfe*); *arvas* "generous, munificent" (OE *earu*); *awje* "hay";

awjo "edge"; *bodne* "bottom" (OE *botm*); (*b*)*ruwdas* "bride" (OE *brȳd*); *dadne, dane-* "tin"; *darfe* "turf, peat"; *darbo* "(the) need, (the) want" (OE *Þearf*); *farjo* "cloths," *varjo* "shroud" (cf. *wear*); *galdi-* "geld"; *gasse* "rennet" (cf. cheese, OE *cēse;* this is a Latin loan-word in Germanic); *laðas* "joint, articulation" (OE *lið*); *loppe, lobe-, love-* "permission" (cf. *leave*, OE *lēaf*); *males* "meal, repast"; *manno, mano-* "moon"; *muoldo* "mould, earth"; *nawle* "nail, peg" (OE *nægel*); *niibe* "knife" (the initial consonant has been dropped in Lappish as in English); *raves* "grey"; *saddi-* "send"; *sawdnje, sawnje-* "seam"; *spanas* "shaving," "chip of wood" (OE *spōn,* English *spoon*); *spierde,* Lule Lappish *svierde* "sword"; *spiidne, spiine-* Lule *sviine* "swine"; *stalle, stale-* "steel"; *stawdne, stawne-* "prow, stem" (OE *stefn);* *vaðas* "frieze-cloth" (cf. *weeds,* OE *wǣde* "garment"); *vievses,* Lule *viepses,* Kola *vīsves* "wasp."

These and many other words form an authentic vocabulary of Primitive Scandinavian. The way in which the Scandinavian words are reproduced and preserved in Lappish shows that in that distant epoch there must have been Lapps who thoroughly mastered the language of their Scandinavian neighbors. This is enough to refute the opinion that the Lapps are savages who have lived in isolation for many centuries. On the contrary, as long as thirteen centuries ago the Lapps, or at least part of them, had learned much from their more advanced neighbors. They seem to have been keen on procuring new sorts of tools and implements, just as they are today. The Scandinavian Lapps use Mauser guns for hunting and Zeiss field-glasses for looking after their reindeer, they cross the lakes in boats driven by the most up-to-date outboard motors, and the Lapp women sew their garments with Singer sewing-machines.

CHAPTER IV

RACE AND NATIONAL CHARACTER

LIKE all other European peoples, the Lapp people is a mixture of different races. All the neighbor nations have contributed to the racial pattern of the Lapps, especially in the last three centuries. This accounts for a good deal of the average differences between Lapps of different regions. In Tornio Lappmark, tall strongly built individuals with more or less pronounced Scandinavian (Nordic) or Finnish (East Baltic) characteristics are much more frequent than for instance in Jockmock. Such family names as Tornensis and Helander, fairly common in Kautokeino and adjacent districts, bear witness to the remarkable fact that descendants of Finnish clergymen and merchants have been assimilated with the Lapp population to a considerable extent. It should be noted in this context that the Finns (and the Karelians) have not been averse to matrimonial connections with the Lapps, as the Scandinavians have been.

According to Bryn and Czekanowski, the Lapps are racially akin to the Samoyeds. Czekanowski uses the term "lapponoid" in a wide and vage sense. In the opinion of other scholars, the Lapps form a race of their own.

Some authors have remarked that the Russian Lapps are unlike the Norwegian and Swedish Lapps in certain respects. According to Kharuzin we have to deal with two types of Lapps, of which the type represented by the Scandinavian Lapps is the more genuine. Lundman speaks of a Northern Lapp race, consisting of the Kola Lapps, the Skolt Lapps on both sides of the Finnish-Russian (-Norwegian) boundary, the Fisher Lapps of Inari and (earlier at least) the Sea Lapps along the Arctic coast, and secondly a Southern Lapp race, including all the other Lapps. Broadly speaking, the northern race coincides with the groups speaking Eastern Lapp dialects or, in other words, the fishing Lapps of the extreme North. The two races differ in two respects, both important from the point of view of somatic anthropology: the relative height of the skull, and the blood group characteristics. The southern Lapp race is "high-skulled" and shows four per cent of the so-called blood allele q, whereas the northern Lapp race is "low-skulled" and shows very high figures of q (fifteen to eighteen per cent). For the sake of precision I shall quote Lundman's definition: "By the HLI [the height-length index] is meant the distance from the foramen magnum at the base of the skull to the crown of the head expressed as a percentage of the length of the head (i.e. the distance from a point between the eyebrows to the remotest point on the nape of the neck; the ordinary so-called head index, the breadth-length index, on the other hand, is the greatest breadth of the skull expressed as a percentage of the length)."

Lundman has shown that in the extreme North of the Lapp territory the HLI is 69–70 (or a little more) and in the South [Swedish Lappland) it is 76 or more, "while the variation in the *whole* of Europe is not greater than about 68.5 to somewhat over 78."

Lundman further says: "Attention should be drawn not least to the fact that the typical South Lapp triangular face is probably almost entirely absent among the pure-blooded North Lapps. In these we find instead certain Mongoloid racial features, such as slanting eyes, much more frequently and more pronouncedly. Such types resemble most closely Samoyeds and, at a further remove, certain Kirghiz tribes, and far less the real Mongols living farther east, with their broad, flatter faces."

Without dwelling on the ethnological implications of Lundman's statement, I will try to describe the Lapp type chiefly as it occurs in Scandinavia.

The Lapps are remarkably short of stature. In such

regions where no considerable recent admixture of foreign blood is known, the average height of adult men is five feet or a little more; the women are about four inches shorter. In addition, it seems that the relative length of the legs is less than in Scandinavians, at least as far as the men are concerned. Otherwise their extremities are shapely and proportional except for a kind of hip-bone dislocation which is not uncommon in some regions. I do not know whether there are more bandy-legged individuals among the Lapps than among other peoples. The feet are fairly small and narrow, with high-arched instep, not deformed by tight and stiff shoes.

The Lapps are brachycephalic (short-headed). The average breadth-length index is probably about eighty-four. The Lapps think that a round head is a thing of beauty, and in some regions the mothers are reported to have kneaded and wound the heads of their babies in order to make them as round as possible.

The upper part of the face is broad, with protruding cheek bones. The chin is narrow and weakly developed; hence the face is pear-shaped.

The eye fissure is fairly narrow, usually not slanted. The color of the iris is brownish grey, brown, grey, or blue (listed according to the order of frequency).

The nose is straight, not very broad, and low at the root.

The hair is mostly brown, light brown, or black, and straight, sometimes even coarse. Lapps seldom turn grey before old age. Baldness is rare. The beard is scarce and grows slowly.[1]

The muscular strength of the Lapps is remarkable, especially if their small size is taken into account. Still more remarkable is their power of endurance. Many a Lapp is able to go on skis for two days and two nights at

[1] Karl Bernhard Wiklund writes as follows: "The type which with full reason may be called the pure Lapp type, is characterized by low stature (150 cm. [4' 11"] or a little more for the males), short legs in proportion to the trunk and arms, small hands and feet, very short skull in proportion to the breadth (average index about 82) , and broad and low face, prominent cheek bones, feebly developed lower jaw with pointed chin, . . . brown eyes, hair dark to black, lank, coarse, beard or moustache straggly or scanty."

an average speed of six miles an hour, with little or no sleep, not to speak of the achievements of distinguished wolf-hunters. The Lapps are expert path-finders (although there are exceptions, of course). They can find their way even in dense fog in a terrain where there are no roads or tracks, at least if it is not quite calm. Their eye-sight is very sharp, at least in their young years. They are less sensitive to sudden temperature changes than are Scandinavians.

The health of the Lapps has been investigated by Dr. Sven Ekvall. He has observed only the Lapps of Väster-botten, and he makes no broad generalizations. In his opinion, the health of the Lapps has deteriorated during the last decades because of "a change in national nourish-ment from a diet rich in albumin to one rich in carbo-hydrates." Among the Lapps, as among the Eskimos of Greenland, this change has brought about a substantial increase of tooth caries. Rachitis has been found in almost every second baby. Ekvall states however that the health of the Lapps is good on the whole. They have as a rule a good physical condition, good musculature and flesh, and their skin is fine. The infant mortality is relatively high. Tuberculosis is not particularly frequent, "but when it gets into a family its spread is general, and it often as-sumes severe and acute forms." Organic heart diseases, anemia, and diabetes seem to be rare, according to Dr. Ekvall's observations. Dyspeptic troubles are not infre-quent.

One would think that rheumatism must be common among the Lapps, considering that the nomads have to work hard in all kinds of weather and that their dwellings are very draughty and otherwise unsatisfactory. Dr. Ek-vall says:

" 'Rheumatism' in the shape of neuralgic-myalgia symp-toms was usual both in old and young. . . . I observed stiffened backs in the relatively young and signs of ar-thritis deformans in the elderly and even in younger per-sons, also flat foot. On the other hand, I have not found acute or chronic rheumatic polyarthritis in any nomad, which appears to me particularly worthy of note. Otherwise it might readily have been expected that this disease would be usual among them on account of their mode of life. That rheumatic polyarthritis must be rare among them will be evident from the fact that, during the ten years the department for rheumatic diseases at Umeå Hospital has been open, no nomad has yet been admitted for that disease (on the other hand some settled Lapps have been admitted for it)."

Mental diseases are not very common among the Lapps. Neuroses are not unusual.

A book about the Lapps would be very deficient if it did not give a description of their mental qualities. But this is a very difficult task. The opinions of previous authors are too disparate to admit a synthesis and mostly too subjective to be relied upon, and my own personal observations are chiefly restricted to the Swedish Lapps, even though I have met and spoken to Lapps from all regions except the Kola peninsula. It is easy to generalize one's impressions, but it is difficult to make just and adequate generalizations. There are so many differences among the Lapps in matter of region, education, and even profession. The autochthonous nomads of Jockmock and Arjeplog are very different from the adventitious Kautokeino Lapps. The Lapps of Jämtland and Härjedalen are mostly so highly "civilized" that it would seem that they cannot be genuine Lapps, and yet they are no doubt much more genuine from a biological point of view than the Lapps of Tornio Lappmark. A research worker who had lived for two weeks in the house of a Lapp reindeer-owner in Härjedalen was rather surprised when he asked what he owed the landlord for board and lodging, and got the following answer: "Doctor, I and my wife would feel flattered if you would permit us to regard you as our guest." This attitude, which I have met myself among Lapps in Jämtland, conforms to a standard which was kept a half century ago by opulent farmers in remote parts of Jämtland, but has now been done away with by modern tourism. In this context the mode of expression is more symptomatic than the degree of hospitality. All Lapps are hospitable, at least to the same extent as the settled population with which they are in regular contact. Tourists do not always realize this when they make themselves comfortable in a tent which is the only room of a well-to-do and proud nomad family. In Tornio Lappmark the rule seems to have been that nobody was charged anything for the first meal. A stranger who has dwelt longer in a Lapp family and asks the housefather what he has to pay, is told to ask the housewife, and she charges him approximately the cost of the food he has consumed.

Even if there are average mental qualities common to the nomad Lapps of different regions, it is not easy to find out to what extent these are racial qualities. They may also be due to the geographic surroundings and the types of work they do. The Lapps do not appreciate such adages as "East, West, home is best," or the Finnish "Listen to the spruce, at the root of which your dwelling is." They say instead: "It is better to move than to stay." Like Odysseus, the average Lapp has seen the towns, or at least the villages, of many people and learned to know their ways. His experience gives him a feeling of superiority. Once when I was on a long foot trip with a poor old Forest Lapp, we came late in the evening to a Finnish-speaking farmer, who was unwilling to give us accommodation for the night. Only by referring to the Right Reverend Chapter of Luleå and the Illustrious University of Uppsala did I succeed in getting shelter for both of us. When we were alone, my Lapp companion said indignantly, "You see, these people have not seen more of the world than what is between their cottage and their cowshed; how could they have any human education?"

The nomad looks at the farmer much as an old tar looks at a land-lubber. In so far as national consciousness exists among the Lapps, it is no doubt linked to reindeer-breeding. Once when I told a Lapp about the life of the Samoyeds, he said, "Then they are Lapps too!" On the other hand, the Mountain Lapps of Gällivare and Jukkasjärvi have a rather poor opinion of the settled Forest Lapps, who cannot even sit (squatting), and they call them "Half-Laddek." *Ladde* (plural *laddek*) or *laddelaš* means "stranger," i.e. "non-Lapp," and it has a more or less disparaging connotation. The Finnish geographer Rosberg was mistaken when he thought that *ladde* is the same word as Finnish *lanta* "manure"; it is not quite as bad as that. The word *ladde* is of Scandinavian origin; it may be identical with English *land* (in Swedish Lappland the coastal region to the east of the Lappmark frontier was earlier called the "land"), but it may just as well be Norse *landi* "fellow-countryman" (in Norway, the Icelanders were called *landar* because they addressed each other that way).

The Lapps call themselves *samek* or *sabmelažžak* (singular *sabme, sabmelaš*). As the bearer of the national consciousness of the Lapps, this name has been adopted in Scandinavian and Finnish usage [*same* (plural *samer*) and *saamelainen* (plural *saamelaiset*) respectively] to some extent.

In order to illustrate the role which the costume has played as a national characteristic, I should like to quote the following anecdote from Härjedalen:

"When the Plague was moving to the *Laddek*, it happened that a Lapp who was tending his reindeer, noticed that somebody came upon his back, in his knapsack. He asked, 'Who are you?' The other one said, 'I am the Plague.' The Lapp went uphill, carrying the other one in his knapsack, till he began to feel cold and wanted to come down from his back; but the Lapp would not let him come down before he had promised never more to come to the mountains to visit the Lapps. And in order that he should know that they are Lapps, they should wear their own attire."

Patriotism is by its nature conservative, because its roots go deep into the past. The Norwegian missionary Isaac Olsen, one of the fellow-workers of Thomas von Westen, has handed down to posterity a pathetic testimony, in which folkways and vernacular are united with the remnants of paganism in a national pattern. According to this account, the subterranean people, who live like the Lapps in every respect, tell the Lapps to keep the same kinds of dwellings, customs, and garments, as well as the language. It is in particular the duty of the *noaides* (sorcerers) to do so, as they have to educate the others. "They talk to them in Lappish and warn them not to cultivate any other language except Lappish, as this is the best of all languages, used by their gods and by their forefathers and created by their first *noaide* and their fairy-people and the other people of old—if they wish to live long and well and prosper in their trade and keep themselves and their reindeer in good health."

It is difficult and audacious to ascribe to any people a "national character," but if carefully done it can aid the outsider to understand the people, if he is willing to remember that there are tremendously wide variations of individual character within any nation, and that perhaps no individual would be accurately described by the "national character." My impressions of the Lapps have not changed greatly since 1932, when I dared to formulate the generalization given below:

"The Lapp usually possesses a clear head and an alert mind, as well as a lively imagination. His power of observation is by nature good, and well-trained; and he has a marked ability to classify and register the things that fill his thoughts. He easily comes to know the characteristics of his fellow human beings, above all their weak points. His sense of humor is decidedly on the sarcastic and satirical side, which often finds expression in taunts and name-calling. He thinks easily, and without effort he can put his thoughts into colorful words, expressing himself in picturesque language. Like the Russian, he often says more than he means or can prove, and promises more than he can later stand for; in the eyes of the taciturn, straight, and conservative northerner he therefore appears rather unreliable. In trade and other dealings he is greedy and sly; life has taught him to be so, and it would be childish to condemn him because he does not live up to

Sunday-school morals. The Lapp does not lack respect for right and fairness, and property rights he regards as sacred; but reindeer rustling is here and there considered less shameful than other kinds of thievery.

"The Lapp is far more sociable than his neighbors. He lacks the stiffness and shyness so inherent in both the Swede and the Finn. His unrestrained frankness shows itself in a usually well-mannered way, but occasionally it is apt to lead him to impertinence. Coarse rudeness is foreign to his nature."

An infinitesimal people, forming no national unity and scattered over regions that are all but uninhabitable, cannot be expected to take active part in the cultural development of mankind. Yet one will find among the Lapps an enlightened desire for knowledge. Rosberg tells a tale of a Lapp who had heard the rumor that there are still in Russia Lapps who are pagans. In order to find out whether that was true, he made up his mind to go to the Kola peninsula. He persuaded another Lapp to accompany him; that is to say, he organized a little scientific expedition. On returning, he was glad to tell his acquaintances that there are no longer any pagan Lapps. The rumor that the Russian Lapps worshipped idols was false; he had made sure himself that they are good Christians, and in their huts they have an image of the Saviour hanging opposite the entrance so that they shall always have him before their eyes.

On his expedition to Greenland in 1883, Adolf Erik Nordenskiöld asked two Swedish Lapps, Tuorda and Rassa, who belonged to his staff, to make an excursion on skis to the interior of the country, where nobody had been before. They started from the turning-point of the expedition, and when they returned they had covered 290 miles in fifty-seven hours. As there were people who afterwards doubted about the authenticity of this achievement, Nordenskiöld in the following year arranged a long-distance competition on ski in Jockmock. Tuorda took part in the race and covered the distance of 220 kilometers (137 miles) in twenty-one hours and twenty-two minutes.

The achievement of Tuorda and Rassa gave Fridtjof Nansen the idea of his famous ski expedition across Greenland. He too was accompanied by Lapps. Tuorda later on took part in the explorations in the difficult Sarektjokko mountains in Swedish Lappland.

Tuorda's and Rassa's skiing on the inland ice of Greenland seems to have revived the interest in skiing in Scandinavia and even in other European countries. Thus it is fair to think that the Lapps have indirectly influenced modern sport and warfare.

The Lapps have also had an influence on the American continent. In 1890 there was a dire famine in Alaska. In order to improve the livelihood of the Eskimos, Commissioner Sheldon Jackson suggested the idea of reindeer breeding. Reindeer were imported from Siberia the following year, and Chukchee instructors began to teach the Eskimos how to handle reindeer. But the Chukchees proved a failure, and then the American authorities sent for Lapp instructors. The first Lapps came from Norway in 1894, and achieved a brilliant success. In 1906 the reindeer stock in Alaska had increased from 1,280 to 6,500; in 1922 the number was estimated at 200,000, and probably there are now more reindeer in Alaska than in Norway, Sweden, and Finland.

A few Lapps have managed to get advanced modern education. At Uppsala four Lapps have taken degrees at the University; one is a Doctor of Philosophy and a lecturer in Lappish, and the others have made contributions to Lapp ethnology. A Lapp elementary school teacher has done excellent field work in ethnology and has written an important paper on Lapp cult places and traditions attached to them. In the future it is possible that the entire investigation of Lapp culture and Lapp language may be done by Lapp scholars.

There is also a young Lapp, Aslak Partapuoli, who, though he is without formal schooling, is working on radiotelephone systems to facilitate communications between nomad Lapps.

CHAPTER V

LAPP CLOTHING

AUGUST STRINDBERG in his great ethnographic work on the Swedish people showed that most of the traditional peasant costumes which were used in Sweden in the last century are of comparatively recent origin. They represent fashions which the rural population has adopted from the higher classes. Some of the "national garbs" of the men are old military uniforms, and not very old at that.

To some extent the same is true also of the garments of the Lapps. But even in this domain the Lapps are more conservative than their settled neighbors, and here the mixture of ancient and recent styles is interesting and puzzling.

In describing the Lapps and their life we must always take into account that everything that is peculiar and characteristic is fading away in these days. When we speak of the Lapps we think as a rule of the oldest generation and the object of our description is a state of things that is vanishing or has already vanished in the melting pot of our modern European-American civilization. This should be kept in mind especially when we deal with clothing. The traditional Lapp costumes have been best preserved by the Mountain Lapps of Finnmark and northern Norrbotten. The Russian Lapps[1] are the least conservative in this respect, and next to them come, among the nomads, the Lapps of Västerbotten. In the dropping of the old fashions there is to some extent a sequence common to

[1] "Russian Lapps" includes also those Skolt Lapps (of the Russian orthodox confession) who became Finnish citizens in 1920 and now live in southern Inari.

51

the different regions. In general the women are more conservative than the men, which is natural, as they are in less frequent contact with strangers. The first thing that the men are prone to change is the headgear. (In this respect the Russian Lapps form an exception.) It must be admitted that a felt hat or a flat cap of the so-called sixpence model is more practical than the old conical cap without a peak. On the other hand the woman's cap is the most resistant part of the old garment among the Russian Lapps. The winter clothes are more resistant than the summer clothes, and the winter fur coat is the last genuine article to disappear. Blue blouses and lumber jackets have been taken into use recently in southern Lappland. A complete Lapp garment is expensive, and so it is understandable that modern ready-made clothes nowadays find their way to the Lapps.

The Russian peasant wears his shirt outside his trousers, and this is a very old habit. The shirt as we use it is a comparatively recent style. The Lapps adopted it in the second half of the nineteenth century or still later. The frock which they use is historically a kind of a shirt; the same model was used by the Scandinavians about fifteen hundred years ago. The man's frock reaches to the knees or a little farther, the woman's frock is considerably longer, but both kinds are tucked up by means of the belt. In eastern Finnmark and in northernmost Norrbotten the frock is shorter but a little wider than in southern Norrbotten. On the man's frock there is a high, more or less stiff collar. The collar is a relatively recent feature which may be due to influence from military uniforms which were used at the beginning of the nineteenth century. The Russian Lapps still wore frocks in the eighteen-forties, but from that time they began to use a kind of Russian caftan. The southern Mountain Lapps in Sweden use a kind of cassock. In Västerbotten it looks much like a frock but it is open in the front and buttoned or hooked up. In Jämtland the cassock is shorter. The coat of the Forest Lapps in Pite Lappmark and the adjacent regions has regular buttons and turned-down collars.

The Lapp frock is usually dark blue, but it may also be grey or even green. In Finnmark white frocks also occur, and earlier authors occasionally mention red frocks. A woman's red frock is preserved in the Finnish National Museum.

The frock is decorated with cloth-ribbons of different colors sewn to the seams on the shoulders or the upper part of the back at the height of the shoulder-blades, or as linings on different places. The most splendid decoration is found in northernmost Sweden. In northern Norrbotten red and yellow ribbons are used. In some parts of Finnmark the red color prevails, whereas in some districts one sees ribbons of many different colors hanging loose. In Jockmock narrow red, yellow, and green linings are used. On the other hand the dicky, the piece of material which covers the neck-front and is kept in its place by a ribbon tied around the neck, is here and in the southern regions decorated with tin embroideries, whereas in the northern regions it is usually made of cotton and of a simple quality. Also in the southern lappmarks the decoration of the coat is sober; in Västerbotten the prevailing colors are red and green.

A Finnish adage says that bronze is the gold of the poor, tin is the silver of the miserable. The Lapps have used their own poverty to advantage by developing the craft of tin embroidery. The tin thread is fabricated in the following way. A birch or alder twig is split in two halves, the marrow is removed and the two halves are put together again and bound together with strings. By pouring a melted mixture of tin and lead into the cavity one gets tin bars of adequate thickness. The thread is made by means of an oblong slab of reindeer horn with a series of circular holes of different size in it. First one presses and pulls the tin bar through the biggest hole, which is a little too narrow for the bar, so that the bar is made slenderer by the procedure. Then one pulls the bar through the hole next in size, and so on until one has a thin tin thread. Then the tin thread is twined around a thread made of reindeer sinews by means of a kind of distaff. The fabrica-

53

tion of sinew thread is described later on. There are two kinds of tin thread—round, and flat. The flat thread is made by pressing a piece of bone against the thread when it is pulled through the last hole. The embroidering is performed in the same way as gold embroideries; the thread is arranged on the material according to the design and attached with fine untwined sinew thread or thin wool. Tin embroidery was used for decorating dickies, belts, caps, and stiff collars. This kind of embroidery became obsolete in most regions towards the end of the last century, when people began to use glass pearls. In our days this craft has been revived among the southern Lapps.

As a rule there are no pockets in the Lapp frock. Usually there is a pocket on the inside of the dicky. In some regions the men used to have a small bag attached to the belt, like the Scotsmen; in this bag one kept the spoon which earlier was a strictly personal implement. The whole front of the frock above the belt functions as a gigantic pocket, in which almost anything can be carried.

There are three kinds of belts, namely yarn belts, stuff belts, and leather belts. In the northernmost lappmarks the men use only leather belts. They are made of ox leather, black and about four to six inches broad, decorated with silver or brass in the form of round buttons or with linings around holes pierced through the belt. The young elegants of these regions place their belts very low so that the head-part of the frock bulges very much in the front. The Lule Lapps use belts which are woven or plaited by means of a kind of weaving reed. The material is woolen yarn of blue, yellow, and red. Such belts or sashes are about two inches broad and so long that they can be wrapped three or four times around the waist. They have tufts at both ends. The belts that are used in the southern regions are made of reindeer shammy covered on the outside with pieces of cloth in appliqué. The pieces of cloth are usually of the same colors as the decoration of the garment. The appliqué is ornamented with tin-embroideries in more or less complicated zigzag designs. The women used to have their scissors, needlecase, thimble, and even

54

keys tied by plaited leather strips or sinew-cords to a little wheel of brass or horn attached to the belt.

Special belts, so-called silver belts, were used at great festivals. They were made of shammy and cloth like the embroidered belts, but the cloth was covered all the way round with a row of square (or occasionally round) silver plates or buckles with thin silver leaves hanging down from them. These belts were used by men and women alike. The women on the same occasions used to wear so-called silver collars. The silver collar is a kind of false shirt or rather false undercoat, that is to say, a piece of cloth made in the shape and size of that part of a frock which would be visible if the frock were worn under a regular frock. It should be added that this false coat had a stiff collar. If a dicky is worn, it is worn under the silver collar. Petrus Laestadius says:

"A lot of silver finery is sewn on to this collar, some of which consists of quite heavy plates, some square, some round, with various engravings, holes, or figures. Others again are globe or eggformed buttons of considerable size and ornamentation. Most of these are gilded and adorned with a multitude of gew-gaws, i.e. small, flat crosses, rings, and the like, fastened by loops to the larger pieces, and jingle slightly."

To this description Laestadius adds the information that such a collar can cost up to fifteen or twenty reindeer.

On long winter journeys the Lapps earlier used scarves made of bear skin or marten skin. On very cold winter days fur capes of bear or wolf skin were used which covered the shoulders and the upper part of the breast and the back but not the arms. In bad weather the northern Lapps still use a kind of poncho made of frieze. In Lule Lappmark a kind of anorak made of the same stuff has been used until recently, especially by women.

On solemn occasions the Lapp women in most regions use big silken kerchiefs, wrapped around the shoulders and fastened to the breast with a brooch.

The Lapps wear narrow trousers which reach to the ankles. For men and women alike they are made without fly or slit. The upper part of the trousers is very low, reaching just above the hips, thus leaving the kidney region rather unprotected, and this is the reason for the tendency to place the belt as low as possible. The trousers are kept up by a drawstring, usually made of plaited leather. The oldest known model is sewn together in three distinct parts, namely, the upper part, which covers the buttocks, the part covering the uppermost part of the thighs, and the close fitting trouser legs or leggings. The upper part seems (according to Gudmund Hatt and other scholars) to have developed in prehistoric time from a hide which was wrapped around the buttocks from behind, drawn up between the legs, and joined on the stomach.

The leggings are not sewn together all the way down. In the lower end there is a slit so that the trousers can hang over the tops of the shoes.

The hard projection under the hind part of the shoe, for which the English language has no other expression than heel, is a comparatively late invention. In pictures from the Middle Ages even royal persons can be seen wearing brogues without heels and with pointed turned-up tips. This tip shoe, although it has neither heel nor sole, is a much more advanced model than the moccasin, which has developed from a piece of skin wrapped around the foot and tied together with a string or thong around the ankle. The tip shoe is still used by the Lapps. There are different models for winter and summer. The summer shoes used to be made entirely of reindeer shammy; nowadays only the upper part is made of shammy, whereas the soft bottom part is made of tanned ox leather, which the Lapps of course have to buy.

The regular winter shoe is made of reindeer leg skins with the hair on the outside. When it is very cold one may wear shoes with the bottom made of the skin of the head of the reindeer. Such shoes are rather slippery. In the early spring even shoes made of the leg skins of cows or horses are used, because such skins do not lose the hairs as easily

56

as reindeer skins, and they are more waterproof and warmer than summer shoes.

There are northern and southern styles of brogues. In the northern type the shoes have protruding pointed tips and the seams are turned inwards. The shoes of the southern Lapps have blunt tips and the seams on the outside, but even in the southern regions the children's brogues are sewn with the seams on the inside, lest the snow stick to them. The northern type seems to be older than the southern type. The bent tip is necessary to the northern Lapps because they use no heel straps on their skis.

From an aesthetic point of view the color is not unimportant in leg skin shoes. Snow white is considered the most elegant color, and soot black comes next.

Instead of shoelaces the Lapps use long ribbons about one inch wide, fastened by means of a short narrow leather strip to two loops on the front side of the shoe and wound many times round the upper part of the shoe and the hem of the trouser-legging (clockwise on the right leg and counter-clockwise on the left). The free end has a tuft on it, which is put under the last turn and pulled hard. The shoelaces are either woven in the same way as the Lapp women's belts, or plaited by hand. The northern Lapps wear only woven shoe laces. The tuft is joined to the woven ribbon by a long plaited string. The patterns are geometric, mostly zig-zag patterns. Plaited shoelaces are worn in Lule Lappmark and farther south. The shoelaces of the men are patterned like the woven laces of the northern regions. The shoelaces of the women are sewn together of plain sections in alternating colors.

The Lapps do not wear socks or stockings. They use sedge grass (*Carex aquatilis* and a few other species of *Carex*) instead. They are particular about collecting the finest and softest sedge they can find; the stiff flower stalks cannot be used. For the children the very finest kind of sedge grass is used. The grass is combed, and softened by beating it against a rock. Having collected and combed and beaten the grass, one twists it into plaits, and in the northern regions one winds the plaits together in big round bundles.

The following lines of an old Finnish popular poem, which has found its way to Lönnrot's *Kalevala*, gives a good idea of how the farmers of southern Finland have looked upon the Lapp footwear:

> *Songs have even the sons of Lappland,*
> *even the hay-shoes chant and chatter,*
> *having drunk some drops of water,*
> *having chewed a piece of pine-bark.*

But the Finnish colonists in Lappland have adopted the despised sedge grass to their own advantage, although they are not able to choose and prepare it as the Lapps do. The sedge grass is superior to socks; for in this imperfect world there are no truly waterproof shoes, and of course rubber boots cannot be worn on a long expedition in summer without spoiling one's feet. On the marshes of Lappland one can seldom avoid getting one's feet wet. When a sock made of any kind of cloth gets wet it feels cold and clammy and hurts the foot. The sedge grass when wet still feels warm and comfortable. When you rest during a walk, you can take out the wet sedge grass, spread it over a forked twig and hold it above the fire; it will dry in a few minutes.

It is no easy task to fit the sedge grass into the shoe. Having untied a plait of grass, one rubs and kneads it gently and lets it fall piecemeal to the ground till one has got a homogeneous, almost rectangular pad of adequate dimensions. The pad is folded around the right fist and then shoved into the shoe. It is important that this layer of grass should be so thick that it gives just enough room for the foot. One has to smooth it and make sure that it is of about the same thickness on all sides. Then the foot is put into the shoe, the hem of the trouser-leg is put around the edge of the shoe, and finally the shoelace is wound round the leg.

Well-made summer brogues are watertight to some extent, having been tarred inside and outside and greased.

They are sewn with reindeer sinews, which swell when they get wet and fill the sewing-holes better than hemp thread can do. One can even wade a little in shallow water if one makes sure in advance that the laces are tightly wound around the leg. For more frequent wading one has to equip oneself with well-greased shammy leggings which are threaded onto the upper of the brogues and then wound with the brogue laces. They reach half way up the thighs, where they are fixed by means of drawstrings.

I have mentioned that the woman's frock is considerably longer than the man's, and that it has no collar. The shoulder section is not so gaily ornamented as on the man's frock, the decoration being concentrated on the sleeves, the hem, and the belt. In the northern regions the women have recently begun to wear multicolored cotton aprons. The prevalent color of the women's dress is dark blue everywhere.

I ought to add a few words about the belts of the women. In the southern regions they wear the same kinds of belts as the men. In the northern regions the women's belts are made of reindeer shammy covered with pieces of cloth appliqué, in zigzag patterns. In the extreme north woven bands are used instead of appliqué.

As early as the seventeenth century the Lapps used Dutch broadcloth for their frocks, but there was a time when they were clad in hides in both summer and winter. One might object that skin clothes must be too warm in summer, but this is not quite to the point. First, a wide fur coat (or rather frock) made of the thin short-haired skin of reindeer fawns is rather cool in summer. I have seen a Lapp wear such a fur coat in the streets of Stockholm on a hot summer day without perspiring visibly. And second, the Lapps like warmth and stand it much better than most Scandinavians do.

The Lapp fur coat is of the same cut as the frock. Usually they are made of the skins of reindeer fawns which have been slaughtered in August. Half a dozen skins are required for one fur coat, and they should be chosen carefully so that they are all of exactly the same dark brown color. Snow white is an exquisite luxury, seldom to be seen.

The fur coats described above are beautiful and light of weight, but not very strong or very warm. In their daily toil the Lapps prefer fur coats made of the skins of reindeer which have been slaughtered in the late summer or the early autumn of the second year of their life. For inactive occupation in piercing frost fur coats made of the longhaired skins of older reindeer are used. Such fur coats have also been used by the Finnish army.

In the northern regions there are still a few old men who wear an inner fur coat. This article served as a shirt for the ancient Lapps. It had the hair inwards, otherwise it was like a regular fur coat of fawn skin. Of course it was worn over the trousers.

The traditional winter trousers, which are still used in the northern parts of Lappland, are made of two different materials; the upper part is made of reindeer shammy, and the leggings of leg skins, with cloth hems.

To complete the description of the winter equipment I should also mention the longhaired leg-skin gloves, which are extraordinarily warm. Sometimes one improves them by putting sedge grass into them. The winter gloves of the children are even lined with leg skin.

If a reindeer fur coat is used for years it gradually loses its hair. In prehistoric time the Lapps probably wore such coats in the summer, and they still do so to some extent. But clothes made of reindeer shammy are also used. They have the same cut as the woolen frocks and trousers which I have already described.

There are two methods of unhairing a hide. The first method is to put the skin in a brook until the hair comes loose. The other method is more complicated. One makes a paste of water and rye flour and a small quantity of train oil and smears it on the fleshy side of the skin. Then one rolls it up and puts it under the twig flooring of the tent. This procedure is repeated a few times so that the skin keeps moist all the time. By this method the hair comes

60

loose in three or four days. This method is used in the southern regions; it is supposed to produce a better skin.

Then comes the barking or tanning by a decoction of alder bark or birch bark. The birch bark is usually collected in spring, when the bark comes loose easily from the tree. The bark is boiled in water till one gets a strong dark-red extract, into which the unhaired hide is then put. Now and then the hide is taken out of the decoction and scraped with an iron scraper on the fleshy side to remove sinews and membranes, and rubbed and kneaded in order to make it soft. The procedure is repeated several times. By using alder bark one gets a still better result.

Shoes and skin garments are sewn with thread made of reindeer sinews. The sinews are taken from the legs or the back of the reindeer. Such thread as is made of the dorsal sinew is softer, and is used for sewing fur coats. After the sinews have dried, they are split into strings. Then they are bundled together and wrapped in birch bark to keep them moist. They are stretched and moistened by pulling between one's teeth. The next step is to spin long threads out of these short strings. This is an archaic procedure performed without a distaff or any other implement. The joint ends of two strings are pressed against the cheek and rolled in this position till the ends are spun together; then a third string is added by the same technique till one has got a thread four feet long. Then the thread is folded in the middle and the two halves are twisted together by rolling them on the knee.

The headgear is very much differentiated. As a rule the cap which the Lapp wears clearly shows from what region he comes. The fashions have changed rapidly, and the Lapps have been prone to adopt foreign cap styles, just as they are in these days in Västerbotten. Even religious points of view have influenced cap fashions. It should be noted in this context that the Laestadians, especially the western branch, are averse to luxury and showiness in matter of clothes. On the whole the Lapps are exempt from this religious taboo, but there are two articles which the Laestadian preachers of the last century did not like, namely, first and foremost the decorative if not practical bright red woman's hood of Finnmark with its protruding helmet-crest, and second the cushion-like man's cap from the same region, with its four salient angles (obviously a Slav model). The preachers characterized the cumbersome helmet-comb as "the devil's horn." Even the four points of the man's cap agitated the lively imagination of the western Laestadians in an analogous way, if to a less degree. Both fashions were seriously prejudiced by this semi-clerical indictment, and the devil's horn has disappeared altogether.

As an instance of a vanished style I may mention the biretta which Linnaeus wears in the pictures where he appears in Lapp attire. This biretta was a woman's head gear as far as we know; now it is no longer used.

The oldest of the Lapp cap styles is no doubt the conical cap, which occurs in several variants all over the Lapp territory. Often the tip is decorated with a tuft or pompon of red woolen yarn; in Tornio Lappmark the pompon grows visibly bigger almost from year to year, so that nowadays it almost covers the whole cap and makes it look as if it were flat. If you meet such a Lapp on a mountain plain, the first thing you see is the pompon, which is visible at a mile's distance, looking like a red street-light. In this region they have also provided their caps with a leather peak, which is practical, if not decorative.

With few exceptions the women's caps do not protect the ears, and the men's caps never do except for the four-pointed Finnmark cap. But in some regions the forehead, at least, is protected in cold weather by a loose edging which is fixed around the cap with a drawstring. In Gällivare this edging is made of the middle part of the skin on the forehead of reindeer fawns, which is regarded as the tightest and warmest part of the whole hide of the reindeer. This piece is about half the size of a post card, and as each fawn provides only one piece, a dozen of fawns must contribute to one single edging.

It may be that such accessories have in the course of time been adapted for decorative purposes. This development seems to have resulted in three different types. The first is a transversal, broad, tin-embroidered piece of cloth covering the front edge of the woman's cap and tied around the cap by means of a plaited woolen string fastened to each of its ends (from Jockmock). The second is a similarly ornamented cloth casing almost to the whole height of the cap (from Västerbotten). The third consists of four stiff rectangular pieces of cloth, each surrounded by a narrow red edging, sewn together and fixed to the border of the cap but not joined to the cap at their upper edge (the prevalent man's cap in Jämtland and Härjedalen). This last style, however, has probably a foreign origin.

In many districts the women wear silk kerchiefs under the cap in cold weather.

The men's caps are blue. The women's caps are blue or red. In Tornio Lappmark the women's caps are decorated with multicolored ribbons.

CHAPTER VI

LAPP DWELLINGS

THE habit of living in tents is inseparable from full-nomadism. The tent is the only kind of dwelling which the Lapps are known to have had a thousand years ago or still earlier. The Lappish word for tent, *goatte,* is inherited from the Finno-Ugric parent language, but it cannot be traced back as far as Primitive Uralic; it has no correspondent in the Samoyed languages. It seems to be an ancient Iranian loan-word, identical with the Avestic word *kata,* which means a kind of storehouse or cellar (*kad* in Modern Persian means "house"). Incidentally, it may be that the Scandinavians at an early epoch borrowed this word from the Finns or the Lapps, giving it the signification of "a poor, humble hut or shed": English *cot.*

The conic tent, with a framework consisting of a dozen straight poles with forked upper ends to keep the poles together at the top, and with a wide opening for the smoke, is known from almost all regions where Lapps live, but the typical tent of the Scandinavian full-nomads is of another structure. The principal frame of this tent consists of two pairs of curved birch poles shaped like hockey sticks, with a hole at the curved end. One joins the curved poles by threading them on to a straight transversal pole, two of them at each end, so that one has a frame that reminds one of the lower part of a saw-horse. Two other transversal poles parallel to the one just mentioned are fastened to the curved poles about half-way up. This forms a stable frame, which is so firm that it can support the weight of a full-grown man. The first-mentioned transversal pole (called *suovvamuorra* "smoke-pole"), which keeps the frame together, has also another function; when the tent is ready one fastens to the smoke-pole an iron chain with a hook at its lower end, on which the cooking-pot or the kettle is hung. The height of the smoke-pole above the earth is about two yards. There are in addition three straight poles which belong to the stable frame of the tent, each with a round hole in their upper end so that it can be fixed to one end of the smoke-pole. Two of these, the door-poles, are put with their lower ends on the earth so that they form an inverted V. The third pole is attached to the opposite end of the smoke-pole. Thus there are ten poles in all, seven of which touch the earth with their lower ends, forming a heptagon inscribed in an imaginary ellipse, with a diameter of about four yards. Now a dozen slender straight poles, about three yards long, are put in oblique position around the stable frame to form a kind of cone. Sometimes the loose poles are tied to the frame with ropes.

The tent-cloth consists of two halves, which are fastened together at the pole which is opposite the entrance. The free edges of the tent-cloth are fixed to the door-poles. The tent-cloth is of different material according to the season. The summer tent is usually made of sacking, with a broad frieze-border at the upper edge. In winter warmer material is needed; the winter tent is made of thick woolen rugs. Earlier the summer-tent cover was made of birch-bark moistened in hot water and sewn together with sinew-thread, and the winter-tent cover was made of reindeer-hides. The tent-cloth does not reach very high; it leaves at the upper edge a circular opening about four feet in diameter to let out the smoke. The door is a triangular piece of sacking or some other material, with transversal wooden ribs to stretch it, and with a pierced piece of wood at the upper end. It is hung over the entrance and can easily be shoved aside by the dogs. If there is a threshold it consists of an oblong board with two holes at each end, and is fastened with straps to the door-poles.

Now let us look at the "floor" of the tent. In the center is the hearth, consisting of a ring of stones. There are two parallel logs or sills which run from the door-poles to the hearth. Between them there is a heap of fuel. Beyond the hearth there is another pair of parallel sills, reaching to the part of the tent-wall which is opposite the door. This part of the tent is called *boaššo*. It functions as kitchen and scullery. Earlier the *boaššo* faced the north and the entrance faced the south. According to some authors there was an extra door on the *boaššo* side, this door to be used when a dead man was carried out of the tent or quarry brought in. I think it would be more correct to say that at such occasions an opening was made at the back of the tent.

It will appear from this description that there are two rooms in the tent, separated by the sills and the hearth. These two segments are called in common by the name *loaido*. They form the veritable floor, covered with a thick layer of birch twigs (or, in winter, spruce twigs) which are laid once a week from the wall to the sills, with overlapping ends. The Lapps find it comfortable enough to sit squatting on this carpet, but they decidedly prefer the recumbent position. In the angle between the floor and the lower edge of the tent-cloth there is an elevation chiefly formed by rolled-up hides and other stored bedclothes, which one can lean one's head against. Nomad Lapps as a rule find it inconvenient to sit on a chair, and this position is nearly as tiresome to them as squatting is to us. A stranger who comes into a Lapp tent may be invited to sit on the low oval wooden chest which the Lapp uses for a safe, but if he accepts this suggestion he will soon regret it, because the smoke then badly irritates his eyes. The only means of avoiding the smoke is to be sitting or lying on the ground.

The Lapps have not much furniture or other household articles. The food is served in flat wooden bowls or on oblong wooden trays. Everybody has his own wooden cup, or rather scoop, for drinking and his own knife to cut the meat. Formerly everybody carried his own spoon in his pocket. Forks, plates, coffee cups, and saucers are recent luxuries among the Lapps.

The bed consists of a reindeer hide, the cushion (in conservative homes) of a rolled-up fur coat. For quilts the Lapps use woolen rugs or in the winter sheepskin rugs, with a pocket at one end for the feet. Sheets have not yet been introduced. When it is very cold in the winter one has to wrap oneself up carefully, and for this purpose even blankets may be used. In many regions they use a kind of canopy, or in other words a small prismatic tent of thin cotton tied to the tent-poles. Such a tent is just big enough for two persons. The canopies are arranged in two rows from the *boašo* to the door, so that the nocturnal tent presents much the same aspect as a Pullman car. In summer the advantage of this arrangement is manifest; if the lower edge of the canopy is carefully folded around the edge of the reindeer hide, there is no chance for a midge to penetrate and disturb the sleepers.

The Lapp cradle is made of a hollow piece of wood, covered with leather, with a hood to protect the baby's head. On each side of the cradle there is a row of loops, and a thong is threaded through the loops crosswise from the foot to the head. The free ends of the thong are so long that they can easily be tied together when the baby is lying in the cradle; this prevents the baby from falling out. Instead of a mattress the cradle is lined with peat moss or the sawdust-like powder which is to be found inside the bark of a birch tree which has decayed standing on its root. Sometimes pulverized peat is used. This absorbent substratum is thrown away when it gets wet, so that the baby always is kept dry and warm. This old idea has recently been brought into the market by a non-Lapp merchant, and is protected by patent. I hope the Lapps will not be prosecuted for violating the patent right of the inventive merchant. A narrow knitted ribbon is fastened to the foot of the cradle; towards its other end the ribbon is split into three parts which are fastened to the edge of the hood at some distance from each other. This simple contrivance makes it possible to protect the baby from insects or sunshine by covering the cradle with a cloth, without making it too warm or stuffy. By means of a strong thong or rope which is fastened to both ends of the cradle one can hang the cradle on a peg in the tent or on a branch in the open air and rock it at pleasure. In winter, when the baby is well covered, the cradle can occasionally be put into the snow in vertical position. On journeys the mother carries the cradle with the baby in it on her back if she walks or goes on skis. On longer trips the cradle is often hung on one side of a pack reindeer, with an adequate counterpoise on the other side.

There is nothing primitive about the Lapp tent. Let us take into consideration the requirements that such a movable home should fulfill. It should be easily transportable; no single part of it should be too heavy or too cumbersome to constitute one half of the burden of a pack reindeer (maximum weight forty pounds). In case any part of it is lost or damaged during a migration, it should be possible to replace or repair it. It should be stable and strong enough to endure a gale. It should be easy to heat, as tents go. It should be big enough for a numerous family to eat and sleep and entertain guests in. I do not know whether the military experts of the western world have managed to meet these requirements better than the Scandinavian Lapps have done.

A primitive home is sometimes thought of as a scene of disorder and want of design. The Lapp tent is a little cosmos. All the different utensils and other household goods are put in their place after they have been used; nothing is lost or spoiled by neglect. The tasks and occupations of the different members of the household are regulated by ancient usage, and so are the places which they and the different categories of guests occupy when sitting down or lying down on each side of the tent floor, nearer to the *boašǒ* or nearer to the door. A tourist who enters a Lapp tent thinking to observe barbarians may commit a dozen *faux pas* in a few minutes without noticing it. Whatever he may do or say his hosts make no comment. When he has left the tent its inhabitants go on with their previous conversation without taking the least notion of the interruption.

In the winter the fire burns in the tent all day and as long as anybody is awake at night. Of course it consumes a lot of fuel. In the night, after the fire has gone out, the temperature sinks to much the same level as the outdoors, since the smoke hole at the top of the tent has a diameter of one yard or more and it is usually not covered for the night. When it rains or snows the windside of the smoke hole is usually covered with a cloth which, in some regions, is put on a wooden frame made for that purpose. The outdoor temperature may go down to sixty degrees below zero Fahrenheit. This means (especially in such regions where canopies are not used) that one cannot take off anything when one goes to bed, except shoes. Under such circumstances a guest who comes from a milder climate cannot help thinking, like the Ecclesiastes, "How can one be warm alone?" In the morning another inconvenience may present itself. It happens that the whole sleeping party is covered with a thick layer of snow, and the housewife has to dig herself out before she can make the morning coffee. But such an incident is hardly worth mentioning compared to what occasionally happens in a stormy night; you may wake up to realize that the tent is somewhere far away in the impenetrable darkness! Even in summer the tent may be uncomfortable in bad weather, when it is filled with smoke right down to the floor.

I have already said that the hearth of the nomad consists simply of a circle of stones. The Lappish name of the fireplace, *arran*, is a Scandinavian loan-word, and probably the Lapps took over the construction from the Scandinavians in a remote past. The contrivance for hanging the pot or kettle above the fire has also obviously come to the Lapps from their Scandinavian neighbors, although it is by no means a Scandinavian invention. It consists of an iron hook and an iron chain fastened to the transversal smoke-pole. This construction is identical or almost identical with the construction prevailing in finds from Uppland in Sweden, dating from the seventh century, whereas the kettle chains found in Swedish dwelling places from

69

the Viking epoch are of a different construction. The old Lappish name of the chain is of Scandinavian origin, but the word is not found in any Scandinavian language. In the whole Germanic world it is known only from Old High German, and with the same meaning (Lapp *awle*, O.H.G. *hāhala*, *hāhila*). This fits in very well with the archeological dating of the construction. As Professor Sune Lindqvist of Uppsala has pointed out to me, there is nothing to show that this construction has ever been used by the Norwegians, and moreover, a special kind of fork, which the Lapps have used to take out pieces of meat from the cooking pot has an exact Swedish counterpart which has been found in Swedish dwelling places and not elsewhere in Scandinavia. Professor Lindqvist thinks that these circumstances indicate prehistoric relations between the Lapps and the Swedes.

It has been suggested that the tent form which we have described above might have had a prehistoric Scandinavian construction as its model or prototype. It seems natural to think that this tent construction, which is used only by the Scandinavian Lapps, should be of Scandinavian origin; but nothing is known about the alleged Scandinavian prototype. (It has also been suggested that this tent construction might go as far back as the Stone Age, but this is a mere guess without any foundation in facts.) And the loan theory is hardly necessary. Dr. Ruong has found a sheep hut with a transversal pole supported by two pairs of poles which are forked at their upper ends, and he regards this as a kind of intermediary between the conic tent construction and the structure with curved poles. He adds that in the upper part of the birch zone it is so difficult to find straight birches that the curved form of the poles presents itself. The only detail which sharply distinguishes the transportable Lapp tent with its curved poles from all other tents is the circular holes which are bored through the curved poles at their upper end. If one is inclined to think that the Lapp tent has had a Scandinavian model, the first thing to look for should be a tent rather than a house. Actually, the Scandinavians used tents on board their ships in the Viking period, and the Lapps must have seen such tents when they visited market places in northern Norway. The wooden frame of the Ancient Scandinavian tents as we know them from the fragments found in the Viking ship from Gokstad in Norway, is like the basic framework of the Lapp tent, except that the two pairs of crossed poles are straight and that their upper ends are formed into decorative dragons' heads. It is easy to imagine that the Lapps might have got the idea of combining this structure with the conic tent. The result of such a combination would have been the Lapp tent as we know it.

The conic tent (with straight tent-poles forked at their upper end) is still used by the Russian Lapps and by the Fisher Lapps in Finland. In Finnmark and to some extent in Tornio Lappmark it is still used in summer, and farther south such tents are found here and there where it has been convenient to have the framework standing at some place to which one regularly returns. Herdsmen who move around in the mountains without vehicles or pack reindeer cannot take any tent poles with them; they raise a conical framework where they can find the necessary material for it, and wrap one piece of tent cloth around it. In Härjedalen herdsmen have used a portable framework, consisting of three or four slender poles with a hole in their upper end and a ring to connect them.

The custom of living in tents the whole year is restricted to the region north of Torneträsk and the adjacent parts of Troms Fylke and Finnmark in Norway. The custom of living in huts made of birch wood covered with birch bark and peat has spread from the sedentary Lapps of Finnmark to the nomad Lapps in Norrbotten. At the dwelling places in the zone of the great lakes, where the nomad families nowadays spend the greatest part of the year, most of them live in peat huts. These are of two kinds: the open hut which has about the same form as a Lapp tent, with a big smoke hole, and the roofed hut, which as a rule is provided with an iron stove. The open hut is much darker than a tent, without being much more

71

comfortable. The roofed hut has all the inconveniences of a poor cabin, without any of its advantages. It is humid and stuffy and usually it rots down in about fifteen years. The reason why the Swedish Lapps have adopted this kind of architecture is mainly that they were not allowed to build regular wooden houses west of the limit of cultivation. Perhaps the Swedish authorities were right in maintaining that stable houses are incompatible with full-fledged reindeer nomadism, but they pursued this policy in a half-hearted way and in the long run they did not achieve anything. Their aim was to force the nomads to keep on migrating together with their herds and their families, but this aim could not be attained by preventing the Lapps from building wooden houses. Nor could it be attained by keeping the nomad schools on an antiquated standard. I have seen Lapp communities where the children were taught in a tent during the summer and the teacher was the only one to live in a tent. During the winter the nomad schools were situated in church villages or other big villages, but the children had to live in small pyramid-shaped huts. It is easy to understand that the motives of this housing policy were good. Today the Swedish nomad Lapps are allowed to build regular wooden houses for themselves, and the children are kept in big boarding schools with all the amenities of modern comfort and hygiene. It is impossible to foretell how this change is going to influence the fate of reindeer breeding in Sweden.

In the region south of the railway from Sundsvall to Trondheim the Mountain Lapps nowadays live in timber houses or in pyramid-shaped wooden huts all the year. The Forest Lapps of Pite Lappmark do not use any tents; until recently they have lived in pyramid-shaped huts made of boards on a low substructure of timber.

Along the arctic coast of Finnmark the Fisher Lapps earlier lived in miserable peat-covered huts, where people and cattle and sheep were crowded together. (Earlier relations from Finnmark about people living in partly subterranean dens or huts made of whalebones may be apocryphal.) Lately housing conditions among the Norwegian Sea Lapps have substantially improved.

A few words must be said about the so-called *Stallo*-housegrounds, which have been found in southern Lapp-land (Västerbotten). These are circular or elliptic flat depressions in the ground; they may have been originally about a half yard deep. The late Torkel Tomasson, who investigated some of these "house-grounds," thought that they were places where Lapps had pitched their tents in olden times. He thought that the Lapps had dug out the ground in order to be safe from the spears and arrows of enemies in the night. It is easy to see that an enemy who did not venture to come so close to the tent that he might arouse the dogs had no good chance of hitting people who were lying in such a depression. Tomasson thought that these tent grounds are of medieval origin, and he connected them with the legends about Chude roving invaders.

In another chapter I have spoken about the winter villages of the Russian Lapps. Apparently there were in ancient times such winter villages in all parts of Lappland, even if we do not know what the buildings looked like.

There is another kind of Lapp community, known by the name of "Lapp towns." These are big clusters of wooden huts and storehouses built by the Lapps in the vicinity of churches and chapels, to be used during church festivals and fairs. The "Lapp town" of Arvidsjaur in Pite Lappmark, still in use, has recently been put under the supervision of the King's Custodian of Antiquities, in accordance with a law concerning the protection of old buildings.

A few words ought to be said about the dwellings of the Russian Lapps. According to Charnoluskij, the Kola Lapps nowadays live in tents only when they are travelling. The tent poles are straight (they have the same name as in other Lappish dialects); the tent cloth is made of pack cloth or sacking. For one person five or six tent poles and one or two pieces of tent cloth suffice; for a company of six persons sixteen to eighteen poles and five or six pieces of tent cloth are required.

The word *goatte* (or rather its Kola Lappish equivalent) is used for a kind of hut which resembles the wooden hut of the Forest Lapps of Pite Lappmark: a pyramid made of horizontal boards, with a smoke hole measuring a square foot, on a low quadratic substructure of battens. The whole hut is covered with moss and turf. According to a popular tradition, there has been a time when the Ter Lapps had no winter villages, "the *goatte* epoch"; then the huts were usually transported from one place to another when the Lapps migrated, or at least the boards that form the upper part of the hut. The *goatte* is now almost obsolete among the Ter Lapps.

The *barta* (this is a loan-word, Finnish *pirtti*) is a simple plank cabin, with one to four windows, and a stove. A shed for fuel and implements is added to the cabin, which is constructed so that it can easily be pulled down and then be built again on another place in one or two days. The stove is more complicated, and requires an expert to build it in one day. The *barta* is the normal dwelling of the Kola Lapps nowadays.

The *izba* (this is a Russian word) is bigger and more stable than the *barta*, and it has a big stove of the usual Russian model. A still larger kind of a house, called *dom* (Russian) is found only in the winter villages.

There is still a kind of movable building, namely houses built on runners. The Russian Lapps in the Kola peninsula have small wooden houses which stand on runners and can be drawn by reindeer from one fishing station to another. In Lule Lappmark some people have small storehouses on runners. They are drawn by the owner himself on the snow, and they are kept so secret that only a few people know of their existence.

In old times the Lapps did not believe in banks. Every well-to-do Lapp had his own safe, consisting of a brass kettle which he dug into the earth at a place which nobody else but himself knew about. In many cases the owner died without having any opportunity to tell his heirs where the hiding-place was situated. I know of a rich Forest Lapp who had a stroke of apoplexy and lost his faculty of speech, never to regain it. Before he died he pointed at his forehead and then spit in the hollow of his hand. This seemed to mean that he had hidden his treasure at a place where there was a well beneath a roundish rock. For many years his heirs searched for a locality of this description, but the treasure has not been found yet. It should be added that one cannot be quite sure that a man who had hidden his silver dollars intended to tell anybody about the hiding-place. He might also have thought that he could use the money in *nubbe aibmo*, "the other world."

Buildings made for the reindeer are known from Russian and Finnish Lappland and from Jämtland in Sweden. These buildings were made in order to protect the reindeer from midges and from sunshine in summer. Väinö Tanner gives the following description of the reindeer shed used by the Skolt Lapps in the Petsamo district: "A twenty meter long roof is raised by the Lapps to something over a man's height, and against the long sides of this roofing ridge they lean long props which are covered with birchbark, sprucebark, or sod, so that they form protective walls against both the scorching sunlight and the rain."

In northern Jämtland the Lapps made a kind of narrow clearing or path through a dense birch wood. The tops of the birches standing next to the path were bent and plaited together to form a kind of pergola. Such a refuge was called *lanuo*, which Dr. Ruong has shown to be an ancient Scandinavian loan-word, identical with English *lane*.

The peat-covered goat sheds which are found at Lapp dwellings are of recent date.

I have already mentioned a few of the different kinds of storehouses and other receptacles for food and household goods. One of the oldest kinds of storehouses is no doubt the *njalla*, a small thing, often not much bigger than a pigeon house, but solidly built of logs, usually

75

standing on a single thick pole or a rooted tree. In most regions the *njalla* is now obsolete.

I have not spoken of the *suonger*, which consists of three birch stems, with a few twigs left on them, and put together at their upper ends like so many rifles. On this structure one hangs different provisions to keep them out of reach of the dogs. Four or more such structures may also be used to carry a raft-like roof, on which provisions are stored, usually wrapped up in a tent cloth.

The Forest Lapps have elaborate storehouses, which probably were made after a Scandinavian model.

As the storehouses are usually built on a substructure of up to man's height, one needs a ladder to enter them. Two kinds of ladder are generally used: one is a log with steps cut into it; the other has the shape of a tuning fork with a few rungs on it.

CHAPTER VII

FOOD AND DRINK

SAMUEL RHEEN (see Chapter XVIII, p. 221) gives the following account of the gastronomic habits of the Lapps of Lule Lappmark in the seventeenth century: "The food of the Lapps consists chiefly of reindeer, game, fowl, and fish, which they eat winter and summer without bread and mostly without salt. The Mountain Lapps are not great fishermen; they eat meat, cheese, and milk; in autumn and winter they eat little else than meat without salt and bread, except on Fridays, when all the Mountain Lapps keep their fast-day, and if they cannot catch any fish themselves they buy it from other Lapps; and if they cannot even buy fish, then they eat milk and cheese. They boil the meat over a slow fire and hardly longer than fish; nay, often they boil fish and meat together. In spring they mostly eat dry meat and cheese, in summer milk and cheese and whey. They also prepare gruel of reindeer blood boiled in water, which is a frequent kind of food. They keep the blood in firkins and in reindeer stomachs, and it is bought and sold by weight. All the food must be prepared by men and not by women, except if a woman is travelling and there are no men present; otherwise no women cook, but their work is to make clothes, shoes, gloves, fur coats, and harnesses for draught-reindeer. . . . And when they eat meat or fish they drink the broth in which the meat or the fish has been boiled. The Forest Lapps live on fish and game which they catch in the forest and eat winter and summer, in autumn and spring, partly fresh and without salt and bread. They live partly on dried fish, which they dry in the air and the sun, in springtime and in summer; they eat it instead of bread, sometimes boiled and sometimes unboiled. They preserve the reindeer milk, which they milk late in the autumn, in big bowls and let it freeze into ice, and they cut it into pieces like cheese and eat it frozen. They also make butter out of reindeer milk; this butter is white like tallow. They salt a little and keep it in tubs. . . .

"The Lapps take the stalk of the Angelica-plant before it runs to seed, and eat it in the following manner: they peel off the rind, and they roast the pith on embers and eat it. All Lapps take an extreme delight in this food. The Lapps also cut off the stalk, when it begins to run to seed, boil it in whey a whole day, till it turns red like blood, and preserve it for the winter and other seasons of the year. This is a rather bitter food, and sometimes they use it as a medicine. In the mountain regions there also grow plenty of cloudberries in the marshes. They boil these berries together with fish in the following way: they boil the fish and remove the bones, and pound the fish and the berries together with a wooden pestle and eat it with spoons. They do the same thing with red whortle-berries, crowberries, and blueberries. The Mountain Lapps mix berries and milk together, all kinds of berries that are to be found in their districts. Sorrel also grows there in plenty; they boil it with milk. They pick the cloudberries when they begin to ripen and are quite red. They make them seethe without water in their own juice over a slow fire. They sprinkle just a little salt on them and preserve them then in well-tied birch-bark boxes, which are put in the ground and covered with earth to be taken up in autumn or in winter, and then they are as fresh as if they had just been picked. The Lapps also use pine-bark for food, especially those Lapps who live in the forest region. They strip the bark of big pines, preferably that which is next to the root, scrape it well so that it looks like fine linen, dry it a little in the sun and then split it into narrow slices and put it in big birch-bark boxes, which they dig down into the earth and cover with sand. Then they make a big fire there and let it burn a whole day. When they take up the bark it is red and sweet and they eat it like candy."

The above description given by Samuel Rheen was still accurate sixty or seventy years ago; now it is partly antiquated. But reindeer meat has remained the chief food of the Scandinavian Lapps, at least in the winter.

The Lapps usually do not slaughter any reindeer in spring or summer. In August they may kill a few fawns, not because of the meat, but because of the furs. The meat season begins in September and lasts until the time immediately before the spring migration.

In some parts of northern Lappland the Lapps kill the reindeer by piercing it with a knife in the breast right to the heart. Nowadays this method is regarded as cruel, and the Lapps are giving it up. The southern Lapps have from time immemorial used another method; they press a long knife through the occipital pit into the brain, thus rendering the reindeer unconscious before it is killed in the way which we have just mentioned. A Swedish veterinary surgeon has constructed a curved knife which makes the stroke easier to deliver, and this is now in Norway the only legal method of slaughtering reindeer. In Sweden experiments have been made with slaughtering masks, but the Lapps have grave objections against the application of this method to the killing of reindeer.

When the heart of the reindeer is pierced, all the blood accumulates in the breast cavity. The Lapp pours the blood into the turned out paunch and then keeps the blood frozen. When he needs blood for cooking, he cuts a bit of the frozen blood with a knife or a hatchet. The fresh blood is used for sausage. Another kind of sausage is made of the blood plasma. Almost all the parts of the reindeer are used for food, or for the preservation of food. In some regions the lungs are usually given to the dogs, and the same is true of the spleen.

There are (or were) minute precepts as to which parts of the reindeer should be eaten by men, by women, by the housewife, by the servants, and so forth. The old rule that the preparation of food was the task of the father of the family has been relaxed since the seventeenth century, but has not faded altogether.

Nikolai Kharuzin says in his great work on the Russian Lapps, published in 1890: "The Lapps, in general, eat much and often. At six o'clock in the morning they begin their day by eating salted fish and reindeer cheese, and he who can afford it drinks tea or milk. At noon they have their lunch, consisting of soup, and salted or boiled fish. At four o'clock they start eating again, and they end their day at nine o'clock in the evening by having supper, for which they have the same food as at lunch."

The Scandinavian Lapps used to have one regular repast, namely the supper. The Lappish word for supper, *males*, is a loan-word from Primitive Scandinavian, the equivalent of the English word *meal*. And to the Scandinavian Lapps supper is really the meal *par excellence*. If a reindeer has just been slaughtered, the supper is a banquet. The reindeer saddle is cooked in a big kettle together with the tongue, the liver, and the scut, and the sausage is boiled in the same kettle. Before the meal begins, the marrow bones, of which there are eight in each reindeer, are put into the boiling water. After a quarter of an hour or so the head of the family takes a marrow bone and carves in it with the point of his knife; if the trace of the knife is white, he takes the bones and splits them with his knife, so that the marrow can be picked out and eaten. It is preferably eaten together with the liver.

The appetizer of the banquet consists chiefly of marrow, sausage, and tongue; the fat scut is handed round, so that everybody can cut a bit of it.

The reindeer broth is delicious. It is covered by a layer of pure fat. The head of the family puts a spoon to the surface of the broth in oblique position and blows towards the spoon so that the fat accumulates in the spoon. The fat is put into a frying pan and is used instead of sauce, because the boiled reindeer meat is rather lean.

The only drink that is served at the meal is a cup of broth, and if you are offered another cup you should decline the offer, because in most regions the broth by custom belongs to the dogs.

This ample appetizer does not prevent the Lapps from enjoying the subsequent boiled meat to the full. The Lapps have a remarkable appetite, but they are not more gluttonous than their Scandinavian neighbors were fifty years ago, and corpulent Lapps are pretty rare.

The suet of the reindeer is kept in rennet-bags or similar natural receptacles. It is very useful as frying fat, in spite of the rancid taste it gets by being preserved for weeks and months. The Lapps do not fry big pieces of meat, but cut the meat into small slices and fry it in a pan, adding a considerable quantity of water.

In the summer the Lapps still eat dried reindeer meat, just as in the time of Rheen. The Swedish and Norwegian Lapps also used to smoke reindeer meat after rubbing it with salt. Dried or smoked meat is indispensable as provision for journeys.

The Lapps are very fond of bear meat. The soles of the bear's feet are considered an exquisite delicacy.

The hare has hardly any gastronomic value according to the Lapps.

There are plenty of fowl in the forests of Lappland, including capercailzie, woodcock, hazel hens, and ptarmigans, but the Lapps do not eat much fowl, except for the Russian Lapps, who, in spite of their orthodox religion, are allowed to eat hazel hens during their 150 days of fasting.

All the Lapps are fish eaters, but this is especially true of the Fisher Lapps of Inari and in other parts of Lappland, as well as the Russian Lapps and the Sea Lapps in Norway. The Mountain Lapps of Swedish Lappland enjoy the privilege of fishing in the lakes above the limit of cultivation, and the Skolt Lapps have perhaps the best fishing waters of the world. The Lapps usually boil the fish, but they also broil them on a spit. There is another method of preparing fish. Once when I had gone about fifteen miles on skis with three Lapp herdsmen, we came to a little isolated homestead where the housewife was of

Lapp extraction. She asked the Lapps in their vernacular, "Does your companion eat our food?" They said, "Yes, he does." I made up my mind not to disappoint them, whatever we might be served. The housewife then took a few samples of whitefish, cut them across and put the pieces on the table. It turned out to be so called "sour whitefish," which all the inhabitants of Swedish Lappland like very much. The preparation of this kind of food is simple. The fish is salted slightly, or I should rather say insufficiently, and then it is put into a keg and left there for months, until it becomes rather gelatinous and emits a characteristic smell. It may be a severe trial to anyone who is not accustomed to it.

Milk is not abundant in the Lapp household. A reindeer doe does not yield more than a half cupful at a time, which in nutritive value is equivalent to a pint of cow milk. The Lapps were accustomed to put the reindeer milk into a rennet bag; there it curdles and can be used as a substitute for cream in coffee. The reindeer butter has a high melting point and is therefore good to use on journeys.

Nowadays reindeer milk and reindeer cheese are rarities, and reindeer butter is practically nonexistent. Instead of milking their reindeer, the Lapps keep goats or, in the northeastern regions, sheep.

Regarding butter, I should like to mention a curious evidence of the natural sagacity of the Lapps. When margarine first was brought into the market the Lapps readily bought it because it was much cheaper than butter, but after a few years they returned to natural butter. When asked about this, they answered that margarine spoils the eyesight. This was before the physicians had found out that margarine had to be vitaminized in order to provide the same nourishment for the eye as does natural butter.

Today the Lapps eat a good deal of bread. The Russian Lapps used to build big outdoor ovens, and this fashion has found its way even to Enontekiö in Finland. Most of the Scandinavian Lapps still stick to the conservative method of baking unleavened bread, chiefly made of barley, on embers or hot flat stones. They eat much porridge and gruel; to the latter they often add some reindeer blood or slices of dried meat.

Bark bread, made chiefly if not exclusively of the soft and juicy inner cortex of the pine (*Pinus silvestris*), is an old kind of food, which had a revival in northern Sweden and Finland during the famine in 1867 and 1868. Gruel and other dishes prepared from bark meal are well known to the eastern Lapps and also to Swedish Forest Lapps even today.

Most of the vegetables mentioned by Rheen are still in use among the Lapps, and a new kind of vegetable has been added since his time, namely potatoes, but the nomads do not eat many potatoes, except perhaps in winter.

The nomad Lapps usually make a point of pitching their tents at places where good drinking water is to be had. In the winter they are often forced to melt snow in a pot or kettle in order to get water.

In some regions the Lapps have thought it unwholesome to drink water directly from a well, and therefore they have made drinking tubes, usually from the shin bone of a wild goose or some other bird. According to the folk tales the wife of the man-eating Stallo (see Chapter XVII) had a drinking tube of iron.

The Scandinavian Lapps drink a lot of coffee, and they regard it as an absolute necessity. Coffee is the first thing which a guest is served, but the Lapps as a rule do not have coffee after their meals. They are particular about the quality of their coffee; they seem to prefer a mixture of Mocca and Liberia. Old Lapps think, as the Scandinavians did two generations ago, that a grain of salt should be put into the coffee pot, otherwise the coffee gets a watery taste.

The Russian Lapps drink tea to the same extent as their settled neighbors.

The Lapps prefer loaf sugar to lump sugar, not from conservativeness, but because loaf sugar is superior in quality.

Many travelers have accused the Lapps of drunkenness. I think this is chiefly because they have seen intoxicated Lapps at fairs. But it would be as unjust to judge the Lapps on such observations as it would be to infer from a visit to a sailors' pub that all sailors are drunkards. Actually the nomad Lapps usually drink strong liquors only on special occasions, such as weddings, and in some regions liquor is not served even on these occasions.

Petrus Laestadius gives the following picture of the hyperborean Bacchanalia at the famous winter fair at Arjeplog:

"It is small wonder if the poor Lapp (now at the end of the fair) makes a regular day of it, after having done all his errands, and no serious mishaps having occurred, and so forth. . . . We should consider that relatives and friends are now going to part and that they will not see another again for months, perhaps for years, or forever. We should furthermore consider that there is another separation, namely, from the noble nectar of Life, the corn-brandy, which does not flow in the mountain rivulets, which cannot be ladled from the forest wells, but can be got only when one comes back to the church village after two or three months, and then it will be more expensive than it is now. Thus the Lapp buys brandy and drinks with his relatives and friends; now the song sounds from all huts, storehouses, and snowdrifts. Everyone sings. Here you see people holding their arms around each other's necks; one sings, the other listens attentively and answers by singing in his turn. . . . People sob and weep in the embrace of parting, friendship, or love. . . . There again you witness jesting laughter, joy, and mirth. Here somebody sits with his hands on his hips, singing in proud tunes about his 'rocky ground' (hidden riches), his 'antlers' (his numerous reindeer herd), and other poetical figures. These Saturnalian scenes sometimes are interrupted by violent rows."

Such is the eating and drinking of the Lapps.

PLATE I. The land of the Lapps — snowy mountains, vast forests, rivers rushing to the sea. A summer midnight in Lapland.

PLATE II. Lapp tents in summer, in the foreground, pitched by a glacier-fed stream.

PLATE III. A Lapp from Jukkasjärvi.

PLATE IV. Lapp children in Tornio Lappmark.

PLATE V. An aged Lapp from Jukkasjärvi.

PLATE VII. Mother and daughter.

PLATE VI. Two young men.

PLATE VIII. Father, children, and dog, with sledges drawn up to the camping ground.

PLATE IX. Fisher Lapps. Fish are an important part of the diet of all Lapps.

PLATE XI. Straw inside the shoes makes easy walking, and is quickly dried if it gets wet.

PLATE X. Cleaning the fish.

PLATE XII. Pitching Lapp tents.

PLATE XIII. Detail of the interior of a tent, showing door poles and door. Note the smoke pole with fish attached for drying and smoking.

PLATE XIV. The Lapp tent, with storage poles in the background.

PLATE XV. The Lapps do not sit in chairs, but lie below the smoke on a bed of twigs and branches.

PLATE XVI. Inside the tent.

PLATE XVII. A "Lapp town" in the church village of Arvidsjaur. The pyramids are dwellings, the other buildings are storehouses.

PLATE XVIII. A Lapp, with skis, draught reindeer, and sledge.

PLATE XIX. A pack reindeer must be loaded equally on both sides. The normal load is about eighty pounds.

PLATE XX. Reindeer nomads following a migrating herd in winter. The reindeer must spend the summer in the high snowy mountains, to get away from the heat and flies of the lowlands.

PLATE XXI. In the highland in summer. The man on the extreme left is a Swedish ethnologist.

PLATE XXII. A sieide in a lake. Such idols were worshipped and received offerings supposed to bring luck.

PLATE XVIII. Communion in a Lapp church.

PLATE XXIV. The congregation.

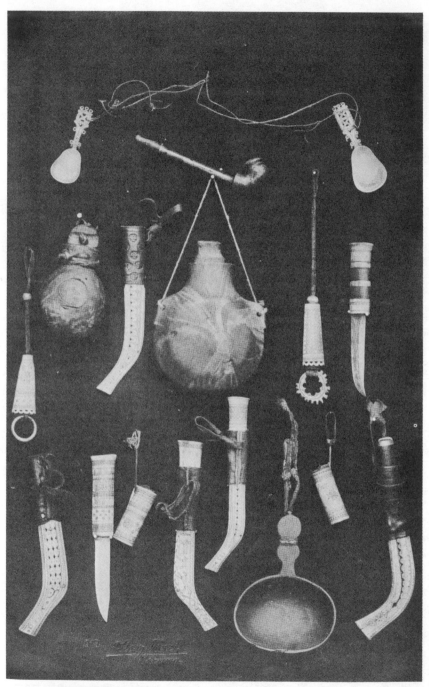

PLATE XXV. Knives, scabbards, bowls, and pipes, carved by the Lapps.

CHAPTER VIII

THE REINDEER AND ITS DOMESTICATION

THERE ARE two typical systems of reindeer breeding, namely full nomadism and half nomadism. The first kind implies wide periodical migrations on the part of both the reindeer and the herdsman. The latter kind implies a lesser degree of migration. If we take the Mountain Lapps in the extreme north of Swedish Lappland, they move in the spring from the spruce region, not very far from the Bothnian Gulf, northwest all the way to the Norwegian sea coast, covering a distance of about two hundred miles. They would hardly do it if they did not think it necessary. In their opinion, a big reindeer herd never becomes domesticated; to some extent the reindeer can be driven in a certain direction or even kept from moving, but now and then they will take the lead and go where they wish to go, and the owner has to go with them if he does not prefer to lose control of his property. It is impossible to check the migratory instinct of the reindeer, because it is a necessity for them to move from one region to another according to the seasons of the year. This opinion is shared by some competent naturalists, and it is the orthodox opinion. But according to other scholars those far-reaching annual migrations have come about chiefly because the Lapps do not like to live in the alpine region during the winter, and it is suggested that in most parts of Lappland they will cease sooner or later, because nowadays the Lapps do not like to live in the alpine region in summer either. When the adherents of the orthodox view allege that there are two races of domesticated reindeer, namely, the moun-

tain race and the forest race, and that the mountain reindeer cannot live without spending the summer in the
snowy mountains and the winter in the spruce forests,
their adversaries reply that reindeer herds have sometimes
subsisted quite well in the mountain region during the
winter when the weather has hindered them from going
east in the autumn, and also that, for instance in the
eighteen eighties, some Mountain Lapps chose to stay for
good with their reindeer in the Tornio valley beneath the
Lappmark frontier, without any detriment either to themselves or to their reindeer.

It is far beyond my competence to take a stand in this
controversy. In the following account I shall start from
the orthodox view and stick to it as far as possible.

In prehistoric time reindeer lived in many parts of central Europe and even in the Pyrenees. In modern times
wild reindeer have lived in the arctic and subarctic parts
of the Old World; nowadays they are scarce everywhere,
and in Scandinavia there are wild reindeer only in the
mountain desert of Hardanger, and a few other places in
the alpine regions of southern Norway. The extirpation of
the wild reindeer is chiefly due to the trade of reindeer
breeding.

Wherever reindeer have existed they have apparently
made annual migrations. The wild reindeer which spend
the winter in the conifer forests of Canada east of the
Rocky Mountains and in the region between Hudson Bay
and the Great Lakes used to move toward the northern
tundras in the spring. The does hasten in advance right
to the sea coast, where they bear the fawns. Towards the
summer they join the bulls, and in the autumn, after the
end of the rutting, the whole herd returns to the winter
grazing grounds. In a similar way the wild reindeer used
to wander in Alaska, in Newfoundland, Siberia, and the
island of Sakhalin. The chief cause of these migrations is
the conditions of nutrition. In the winter the food of the
reindeer consists chiefly of lichens, especially one or two
species of *Cladonia*. Thanks to its broad spade-like hoofs
the reindeer is capable of digging through the snow, but

when the snow is very deep or tough or the ground is covered by ice, it must subsist on beard lichens (*Alectoria, Usnea*) and crust lichens (*Parmelia*), which are not very nourishing. It is much the same in the early spring, when the snow is covered by a hard crust. Towards the end of the winter the reindeer therefore are apt to move to the birch zone or to the tundra, where the surface of the snow hardens later and spring comes more suddenly than in the conifer zone. When the melting of the snow has come to an end the lichens soon get dry and hard so that the reindeer do not eat them. Then they go preferably to the marshes and glens of the conifer zone and birch zone, where there is plenty of tender grass and herbs which constitute their principal food in the summer. But this is true only if the reindeer have persisted in the conifer forests during the difficult change from winter to spring. If they have once chosen to escape the snowcrust and are then overtaken by the sudden arrival of early summer, there is no return; they go on moving up to the cool regions above the tree-limit or at the sea coast. In those regions there are plentiful grassy pastures, and a tolerable protection against the midges and the gadflies, which are the more or less inevitable tormentors of the reindeer. In the autumn when the grass withers and snow begins to fall even beneath the forest limit, the reindeer begin their retreat to the lichen grounds, and when high winter comes the reindeer go to the conifer forests where the snow at this time is not so hard as on the stormy plains and in the alps.

The reindeer which dwell in the conifer zone are called forest reindeer, the others are called mountain reindeer or tundra reindeer. Some scholars are of the opinion that these are two different races, at least in Europe.

It is not easy to say whether there is any racial difference between wild and domesticated reindeer in Fennoscandia. The wild reindeer are bigger and have longer legs than the domesticated reindeer, but the inferiority of the latter may be due to domestication.

Reindeer breeding exists along the whole arctic coast

of Europe and Asia, and it has existed for about one thousand years at least. Some scholars think that it has a common origin in the whole territory; but there are no facts to prove this except for earmarking, which is practised also by sheep-breeders in Scandinavia and elsewhere, and the habit of castrating males by biting. It is not even probable that reindeer breeding is a very ancient profession. It may have come about in two different ways. On one hand it is easy to domesticate single wild reindeer if they are captured as tender fawns, and such reindeer may be broken in and used as draught animals; at least this is true of the castrated males. This may or may not have been the first stage in the development of reindeer breeding. On the other hand the domestication, or rather semi-domestication, of whole herds of reindeer may have developed from a kind of game-protection. As long as the Lapps were hunters and there were plenty of wild reindeer, it would not make sense to follow the annual migrations of the reindeer. In summer it must have paid better to dwell at the lakes and live from fishing. The best time for reindeer hunting must have been late in the autumn, when the reindeer came in more or less compact herds on their way from the summer pastures to the conifer forests. This was a very easy form of hunting, and everywhere, in the Old World as well as in North America, it has resulted in thinning out or even annihilating the reindeer stock. It is easy to imagine how the hunters of a certain region may have realized the danger of exacting a too high ransom from the big game and made up their mind to follow the reindeer on their wanderings in order to protect them from other hunters and from beasts of prey. Gradually the reindeer got accustomed to the presence of man. Or to be more exact, some of the reindeer shunned man and remained in the wild state, while in the others the herd instinct prevailed, so that they kept together even when the movements of the herd were checked by their human companions. In regions where there were good grazing grounds and little or no competition on the part of other hunters, a group of families would go on living in this way for generations without interfering very much with the life of the reindeer. This means that the domestication of the dog is not an indispensable prerequisite of reindeer breeding. There are still in Siberia reindeer-breeding tribes without dogs. But, as conditions are in Lappland, the nomads cannot do without their dogs.

It may be that the milking of the reindeer does (in the summer and the early autumn) is the last phase in the development of reindeer breeding; it is unknown among some Siberian tribes, and most of the Lapp nomads have ceased milking their reindeer. The name of the milk in the Lappish language is an old Scandinavian loan-word, and from this it might be inferred that the habit of milking the reindeer is also of Scandinavian origin, but the word for milking is genuine Lappish.

About a thousand years ago and still earlier there were probably three different main groups of Lapps in Fennoscandia, namely, the Eastern or North-Eastern, the Central or Western, and the Southern groups. This distribution is still reflected in the dialects of the Lappish language. Eastern Lappish is spoken by the Russian Lapps and by the Fisher Lapps of Inari in Finland. The idioms of the Fisher Lapps along the coast of Finnmark have a few conspicuous features in common with Eastern Lappish. Central Lappish is spoken by the Mountain Lapps in Finland and by all the Lapps in Norway and Sweden down to Lule Lappmark and the Northern half of Arjeplog in Pite Lappmark inclusively. Southern Lappish is spoken by the indigenous Lapps of the South; but the dialect of the Forest Lapps in Lule Lappmark shares a few peculiarities with Southern Lappish.

These three groups of Lapps must have been isolated from each other for a considerable time. In their mode of living the Fisher Lapps of the North-East and the Forest Lapps of the South, who can both be characterized as seminomads, are more conservative than the nomads of the Central region. It is probable that reindeer breeding never was essential to the Lapps of the Kola peninsula. Like the Southern Lapps, they have been earlier hunters and fishers and reindeer breeders, but probably they have never depended so much on their reindeer as the Mountain Lapps did and still do. Centuries ago the Forest Lapps paid their taxes chiefly in valuable wild skins, whereas the Mountain Lapps chiefly delivered reindeer hides. This simply proves that the Forest Lapps did more hunting, and it cannot be inferred that reindeer breeding is a comparatively recent trade among the Forest Lapps. On the contrary, one might think that the distant migrations, as they are practised by the Northern Mountain Lapps, are a late phase in the development, brought about by dire necessity when there were no longer enough wild reindeer to make big-game hunting profitable.

According to Israel Ruong, the nomadism of the Northern Mountain Lapps may draw its origin from collective game protection, whereas the half-nomadism of the Southern Forest Lapps may have come about by domesticating wild reindeer fawns to be broken in and be used as draught animals. This would account, says Ruong, for a characteristic difference in the customary right of these two groups of nomads. The Southern Lapps think that it is ignominious to steal reindeer, and according to a historically unreliable but symptomatic popular tradition it was earlier even regarded as a capital offence. In Finnmark and in Tornio Lappmark even the most scrupulous Lapps think that the stealing of reindeer can be tolerated to a certain extent. This basic difference in the sense of justice may be due to the twofold origin of reindeer breeding. In a distant (perhaps not very distant) past the Mountain Lapps regarded the reindeer as the collective property of the tribal community, whereas from the beginning, in the opinion of the Forest Lapps, any single reindeer was the private property of an individual owner.

To the Lapps, as to many Scandinavians, the "taming" of an animal means breaking it in for driving. The Lappish word for this proceeding (*dabmat*) is a Scandinavian loanword, but it is not certain that the Lapps have learned this art of taming from their Scandinavian neighbors.

Both sexes of the reindeer have antlers; hornless females are rare exceptions. The reindeer shed their antlers, and the shedding begins after the rutting, but the pregnant females keep their antlers till they have calved, so that they are able to defend themselves and their tender fawns. During the first day of its life the fawn walks a little stiffly, but after two or three days it is able to run after its mother. The fawns and their mothers call each other by a peculiar sound that reminds one of the grunting of pigs. The fawn usually accompanies its mother wherever she goes, and so it is easy to distinguish between the fawns of different owners even in a mixed herd. But there are cases when a doe does not allow her newborn fawn to suck her; sometimes the fawn of the previous year goes on sucking his mother, excluding his younger brother. There is a special term in the Lappish language for a female reindeer which does not care about her fawn.

Most of the fawns are reddish during the first six weeks of their life; the Lapps usually make fur coats for small children out of the furs of such red fawns, if they are slaughtered, which seldom occurs. In summer all the reindeer change their coats; the new coat of the fawn is usually brown (if it is not white) and before the fur has grown out to its full length the skin is excellent material for elegant fur coats.

In summer, or at least in early autumn, the fawns should be earmarked. The marks are cut with a knife into the edge of the ear and consist of a combination of a few cuts of different form. There are about a dozen of such different elements, and as most of them can be put in the front or in the back edge of the ear, and both ears are usually not marked in the same way, there is an almost endless variety of possible combinations. These owner-marks are registered by the courts of justice, and each owner has an inviolable legal right to his proper earmark. The law even stipulates that nobody is allowed to adopt an owner-mark which by any manipulation can easily be confounded with the owner-mark of anyone else in the same judiciary district. When an inheritance is divided, each of the heirs usually has to make an addition to the previous owner-mark. Incidentally a Lapp boy's career as a reindeer owner usually begins when he gets his first tooth; this an old custom which reminds one of the *tannfé* or tooth-gift of the Old Norsemen. Obviously the nomad Lapps could not do without providing their reindeer with owner-marks. Many Lapps show a remarkable skill in "reading" earmarks. A Scandinavian who sees a reindeer at some distance without being able to make out whether it has any earmarks or not, must be surprised when a Lapp can tell him the name of the owner. Most of the old nomads know all the owner-marks of their own district and the adjacent districts; and if the reindeer should happen to be from a distant region, they usually can tell at least from what region it came. And they can describe any earmark so that no mistake is possible.

On the whole, the terminology of the nomads Lapps is admirable. Linnaeus could not imagine how the Lapp women in Jockmock managed to distinguish between all the different individuals of a reindeer herd. The secret lies in the system of designation. The Lapps do not give their reindeer proper names such as we give to our dogs and horses but they describe the individuals of their herds in an ingenuous way. Linnaeus in his *Systema naturae* used a binary (dual) nomenclature: each plant or animal has a genus name and a species name, for instance *Picea abies,* "spruce," or *Perca fluviatilis,* "perch." The Lapps have a nomenclature which enables them to denote a reindeer by a term which consists of three or four members. The main categories of division are the following: (1) sex and age; (2) color; (3) the form of the antlers, or absence of antlers.

The fawn gets its first name when it is newborn, the second one when it is able to run, the third when it sheds its hair, the fourth when the change of fur is completed, the fifth when the coat is grown out to its full length; but it is still called by the generic name *miesse* (fawn). When it is one year old it is no longer a *miesse,* but a *chærbmak.* These names are common to both sexes. A little later the male (*vares*) starts assuming a series of names which do not apply to the female reindeer. He gets a new name in the summer of his second year, another in his third year, till he is called in his seventh year by the definitive name of *namma-lappe*, i. e. "he who has lost his name."

The special names of the castrated male (*hærge*) chiefly depend on whether he is broken in or not and what special functions he performs; there are also two terms which refer to different degrees of incomplete castration.

The female reindeer gets its final designation in its fifth year, but on the other hand the category of fertility makes for a special distinction. The word *aldo* means an adult female reindeer, but it especially denotes a female which fulfills her normal functions, whereas *rodno* (plural *ronok*) means a female which actually has not become pregnant or has not a calf, and *stainak* means a sterile doe which never gets a calf. As Professor Lid has shown, the two latter words are of Scandinavian origin. *Stainak* contains the same word-stem as English *stone;* according to a popular belief, sterility in cattle may be due to a kind of petrification in the uterus. *Rodno* is of the same root as the verb *run;* as a matter of fact, such cows as have not become pregnant may be in heat for a considerable time after the end of the normal season. At first sight it is rather puzzling that such terms of reindeer breeding should be of Scandinavian origin. It can hardly be assumed that the Lapps have learned anything from the Scandinavians in so far as the peculiarities and habits of the reindeer are concerned. It might be added that there are also a few other similar terms of the same origin in the Lappish language, for instance the designation of a female reindeer which gets only one horn, a rather rare phenomenon. It is obvious that the Lapps cannot have felt any need for borrowing such terms from the Scandinavians. Probably such words came into the Lappish language because the Scandinavians had to speak to the Lapps about reindeer and did not know the Lappish expressions. In many regions the farmers own reindeer which are tended by Lapps and kept in herds together with the Lapps' own reindeer. This is an old institution, which probably existed as early as the ninth century in northern Norway. A Lapp who tends reindeer for a farmer is called in Lappish *raide.*

This is no doubt a loan-word from primitive Scandinavian, and from the beginning it seems to have meant "he who gives account." From the point of view of the settled reindeer owner the annual account was, as it still is, the most important aspect of his relationship to the *raide*. His interest concentrated upon the increase of his reindeer flock, and it is easy to understand that the Lapp now and then had to inform him that this or that doe was sterile or had not got any calf in the last calving season. On the other hand it must occur that the reindeer owner asks the Lapp about a reindeer which he remembers because of its characteristic appearance. In that way a few Scandinavian terms belonging to cattle breeding and reindeer breeding may have been adopted by the Lapps.

Now we come to the question which puzzled Linnaeus. How is it possible to distinguish between a lot of reindeer and give them different designations according to the color, notwithstanding that most of them are grey, and that the color varies considerably from one season to another? This is a difficult problem, but the Lapps have solved it.

Our horsemen have a good many more terms to characterize the color of a horse than other people have. And the names which they use do not solely refer to the color of the body of the horse. A horse which a man in the street characterizes as yellow has two different names according to whether the mane and the tail are black or light. And then there are special names for a mixture of different colors, for patches of different size and configuration, and so on. The Lapp reindeer nomenclature is of the same kind in principle, as far as colors are concerned, but it is much more differentiated. The Lapps divide the reindeer in four, five, or even seven classes according to the color of the body (the barrel), from black through brown, grey, and yellowish grey (dark isabel) to light grey, whitish and snow white. The brown class is divided into subclasses according to the more or less light color of the belly or the sides, and the color of the neck gives another basis of subdivision. Most of the other classes are also divided into subclasses; and in addition there are a good many names for spots and patches of

94

different shapes and colors. The reindeer has about fifty different names according to the color of its coat.

The antlers make another category of classification. The form of the antlers as seen from the side or from the front, the density, the direction, and the magnitude of the different ramifications, all such features have called forth different names. Even the absence of antlers is characterized by different terms according to circumstances of which the uninitiated do not know anything. I have mentioned already that there are female reindeer which never get antlers. Second, all the reindeer shed their antlers every year. Third, midges or other insects may cause a kind of scurf which hinders the new antlers from growing out. Fourth, a reindeer buck may loose its antlers in a fight. Fifth, the Lapps sometimes cut or saw off the antlers of unsuccessfully castrated males before the rutting begins. This means that there are at least five different designations for hornlessness.

Now, if there are about fifty different color names and almost as many names referring to the antlers, and dozens of names according to sex and age, it is easy to see that by combining these three bases of classification the Lapps have a system of nomenclature which would enable them to distinguish between tens of thousands of reindeer. Such systems are known also among other nomadic peoples, for instance the Samoyeds, but it must be admitted that the Lapps have carried it very far, and I should think that in matter of classification of their chief domestic animal they are second to none, except perhaps for the Bedouins.

A migrating reindeer herd has the form of a triangle. First comes a castrated male which is led by a Lapp who walks or goes on skis. Then comes a reindeer ox which is broken in to accompany the first-mentioned ox without being led by anybody. This "follower" is perhaps the most valuable animal in the whole herd, because he sets an example to the other reindeer. After him there comes a small troop of tame oxen and does. After this troop of volunteers follows the main body in broadening files, driven more by the herd instinct than by obedience or sense of loyalty. The base of the triangle chiefly consists of such individuals as follow more or less unwillingly, and there is always a rear guard of recalcitrant reindeer, driven by dogs and herdsmen. It will appear from this description that a reindeer herd is partly a kind of organization kept together by an élite of individuals which in force of training and temperament are on a higher level of domestication than the others.

The draught reindeer form a group of their own. Nowadays only castrated males are used for this purpose. According to a popular tradition sterile does were earlier used as draught animals, and were swift runners. It takes a long time to break in a reindeer for driving, and such a reindeer is first tied to the last sleigh in a caravan in order to function as a kind of brake in going down steep hills.

Most draught reindeer are at least as tame as horses, as far as driving is concerned. Ordinary bridles cannot be used on reindeer because they would not tolerate a bit in their mouth. Instead a halter of a rather simple construction is put around the head of the reindeer, and the animal is directed by a single rein. In driving, the rein is kept on the right side of the animal; in order to stop the animal you have to shift the rein to the left side. This arrangement does not give the driver much possibility of using compulsion upon a refractory animal. If you add to this that the sleigh is joined to the harness only by a broad leather strap, it must be admitted that it would not be easy to keep a lively colt under control with such a contrivance. As a matter of fact, the draught reindeer are mostly easy to handle, but there are exceptions, and it can even happen that the reindeer goes mad and attacks his driver.

The old Lapp sleigh has the form of a small boat or canoe cut off in the middle. The ordinary freight sleigh may or may not have a stern board; in a sleigh used for driving this contrivance is of course indispensable. Some driving sleighs are half-decked, i.e. the fore half is covered by a hide nailed to the edges in order to protect the driver from snow. There are also "full-deckers" for the transport of valuable and fragile goods.

The boat-shaped sleigh is now going out of fashion everywhere except in Norwegian Finnmark, where it is indispensable. It may be uncomfortable, but is no doubt the best vehicle in a rocky and stony terrain where there is much snow and no roads. The Kola Lapps have learned from the Samoyeds to drive with teams of three reindeer; this makes it possible to use sleighs with runners even in summer on the heaths. The most primitive kind of sleigh (still in use) is a reindeer hide in which the goods are wrapped up.

Driving from one dwelling place to another, the Lapps put their vehicles together into caravans, so that the halter of the second draught reindeer is tied to the stern of the first sleigh, and so on. Usually each family has two such rows of vehicles, and each of them consists of half a dozen vehicles. At the front of the first caravan goes the head of the family, leading the first draught reindeer. The housewife usually sits in the first sleigh of the second caravan.

When there is no snow the baggage must be packed on the draught reindeer. It is important that the weight is the same on both sides of the pack animal. The normal load of a reindeer is about eighty pounds. In the matter of drawing sleighs, four reindeer have about the same capacity as one horse.

Except for children, the Lapps never ride on reindeer.

The reindeer are good swimmers, and narrow fords do not cause any difficulty to them. But they do not like to swim very far, and it is quite safe to keep reindeer herds unguarded on islands at some distance from the coast in summer.

CHAPTER IX

THE DOG AND THE ENEMIES OF THE REINDEER

THE herdsman's dogs of the Lapps are spitz dogs. In some regions they are kind and gentle, in other regions they are decidedly uncivil towards strangers, so that it is not advisable to come alone to a Lapp camp in the darkness or when no adults are present. The Lapps do not use dogs to draw vehicles. They are educated only to assist in tending the reindeer and in hunting. According to the Lapps there are great individual differences in the natural aptitudes of herdsmen's dog. The training of the dogs is not very hard; but the Lapps do not fondle their dogs, and the pups are promptly punished when they try to pilfer food in the tent or elsewhere.

Reindeer breeding would be rather difficult without dogs, and dogs are indispensable for keeping the reindeer herd together during migrations. The dogs pursue lazy or fugitive reindeer and drive them to the herd. Some dogs are unreliable in that they are apt to chase fawns and even grown-up reindeer if they are let alone. In order to prevent such a dog from doing harm, the Lapp ties a hobble to its collar. The same contrivance is used to keep the farmers' dogs from harassing the reindeer herds. Incidentally, the farmers have to keep their dogs tied or indoors when the Lapps pass their dwellings on their annual migration.

The reindeer often seem to be conscious of the authority of the dogs and also of the limitations of their powers. If a dog, after having driven a reindeer back to the moving herd, does not stop at the margin of the column, the reindeer may turn angrily threatening the dog with his antlers, so that he has to flee.

When the selective separation of a mixed herd of reindeer (belonging to different owners) is being performed in an unfenced place, the dogs are usually kept at some distance, lest they frighten the reindeer. But if one reindeer after another tries to escape from the herd, so that the completion of the separation seems threatened, an old dog may take command and circle around the herd two or three times at a high speed, loudly barking, till the order is restored.

The Lapps have a high opinion of the intelligence of their dogs. I will illustrate this by an episode which I myself witnessed. One summer day a herd of about five hundred reindeer had been driven to a ring fence, where the women were waiting in order to milk the does. When the reindeer, immediately followed by herdsmen and dogs, arrived at the funnel-shaped entrance of the fence, they suddenly turned and rushed in the opposite direction, so that men and dogs had to leap aside, and a few minutes later the whole herd had scattered and disappeared. There was nothing to do about it, and we sat down to have some coffee. In the meanwhile a terrible tumult arose among the dogs, and when we looked we saw that one dog had been attacked and trodden down by the other dogs. Then one of the Lapps remarked, "This is because they think that it is the fault of this dog that the reindeer escaped."

Immanuel Kant speaks of a "world of rational purposes," and by this he means a community of rational beings united by a bond of solidarity. I do not know whether he gives the dogs a place in this community, but I am sure the Lapps do. I once lived for a week in the tent of an old widow who had the most decrepit dog I have ever seen. She told me that she had allowed the dog a pension, promising him to live as long as he pleased. The dog had belonged to her son, who had died during a journey. The dog had not accompanied him on that journey. And after some time the dog had formed the habit of standing motionless for hours every day, looking in the same direction where his owner had disappeared, and he did not desist from this habit till two years had elapsed.

Johan Turi in his book *From the Mountains* relates the following story:

"Once a Lapp family tended their reindeer on the mountain Movsovardo during the winter, and the herd was high up in the mountain three miles from the place where they lived. The reindeer were out without a herdsman, since no wolves had been reported seen in the vicinity. But the wolves came during the night, as is their wont. Now the Lapps had a dog so sensitive that his instinct told him that the wolves were abroad that night. He ran out from the tent alone, and got to the herd at the same time as the wolves. The wolves seized a reindeer and killed it, and began to attack the entire herd. But then the dog began to gather the herd together all by himself, and then the wolves became frightened. They thought that there were human beings around also. And the dog collected the herd and drove it to the tent. But the Lapps heard the commotion, and took a gun, intending to kill the dog who, they thought, had run out alone to molest the reindeer, but it was dark and they could see nothing. But the servant girl in the tent got hold of the dog and began to beat him, although he begged for mercy. He lay down and wagged his tail, but the girl had no mercy on him.

"When daybreak came, they saw what had happened. And nearly all the people cried, when they saw what the dog had done in saving the herd from the wolf pack. Well, now the herd had to be watched, and the girl was sent out in the woods to tend the reindeer. She had with her the dog she had beaten, although he had begged for mercy. But now it was the girl's turn to ask him for forgiveness because she had beaten him, and she cried when she asked him to forgive her. While she and the dog were together with the herd, it suddenly became frightened. The dog ran out to the spot where the herd had shown fright, and barked fiercely and once again frightened the wolf pack away from the herd. Then the girl's conscience began to hurt her, because she had beaten the dog, and she threw her arms around his neck and said: 'Dear dog, forgive me for beating you.' The dog let out what seemed like an understanding sound, and then

100

the girl finally believed that the dog had forgiven her sin, and they became good friends from that moment."

Everyone who takes part in reindeer breeding has a dog of his own which usually follows him wherever he goes.

According to the Lapps the most humane way of killing an old dog is to hang him.

The Lapps say that next to the dogs, the midges and the gadflies are their most efficient servants; and there is a reason for that. There are two kinds of reindeer-gadflies, namely *Hypoderma* (or *Oedemagena*, or *Oestrus*) *tarandi,* and *Cephenomyia trompe.* The *Hypoderma* lays its eggs here and there in the coat of the reindeer. The larva pierces the skin, leaving a hole which later on gets covered with a thinner membrane. A reindeer hide with more than nine such scars is regarded as second-rate. The *Cephenomyia* lays its eggs in the nostrils of the reindeer; when the larva grow out they cause a large secretion of mucus, which causes vehement coughing. Like cattle, the reindeer and even the fawns are instinctively afraid of the gadflies.

The midges appear in Lappland about midsummer and flourish until the beginning of August. This is also true of the ordinary mosquitoes; in August they are followed by two or more smaller relatives, which in spite of their infinitesimal size are hardly less irritating. To say that the midges are frequent in Lappland would be a gross understatement. On the other hand, there is no malaria in those Hyperborean regions, and the midges do much less harm than the flies, even though they are extremely annoying.

Beasts of prey do a good deal of damage to reindeer herds, even though their number has been considerably reduced during recent generations. The Lapp regards the wolf as his worst enemy. The wolf runs much faster than the reindeer and is strong enough to kill any reindeer. The wolves usually move in flocks of half a dozen or more. They preferably attack the reindeer during the night. The reindeer get easily frightened when they smell the wolves, and if the herd scatters a good many reindeer may be killed.

Anta Pirak says that if a wolf comes into a quiet reindeer herd at night, he kills ten reindeer or more. "Earlier old

101

people said that one single wolf can kill thirty reindeer in a night. Ten I have seen with my own eyes." Turi asserts that in the winter, when the snow is deep, a single wolf is able to kill up to forty reindeer or even seventy. (Turi was a hunter by profession.) The wolf can be caught in iron traps or killed by poison (strychnine). Nowadays people hunt wolves from the air in Norway and Finland, but this method is not allowed in Sweden. There are still hunters who pursue the wolf on skis. This requires a very high degree of sportmanship, and it can be practised only in the winter, when the snow is loose and deep. The hunt may last for several hours or even for a couple of days almost incessantly. Even if it is very cold, the hunter gets so hot and sweats so badly that he is forced to throw away one piece of clothing after another and, if he has not a man to ski after him and collect his clothes for him, he may run the risk of freezing to death when he has killed the beast. Anta Pirak has told a story of a wolf hunter who had stripped to the waist in pursuing the wolf; having killed the wolf he flayed him and put on his skin for a fur coat, thus causing no little sensation when he arrived at the next settlement.

In pursing the wolf the Lapp usually has no other weapon than his staff and his knife; the gun would be too cumbersome. The hunting goes on till the wolf is so tired by jumping in the deep snow that it cannot run any longer. Then it turns its wide-open mouth towards the hunter, and when the hunter tries to beat him he may manage to catch the staff with his teeth. The hunter may fall to the ground, and then his situation is not easy; even if he succeeds in killing the wolf with his knife he may be bitten so badly that he cannot move. Turi says that if the wolf gets hold of one's hand, then one must push the hand right into the throat and squeeze the bottom of the pharynx so that the wolf cannot bite, and if one is swift in handling the knife with the other hand, then there is no danger. The first thing to do when you have overtaken the wolf is to hit him hard with the staff right on the muzzle or just above the tail. Some Lapps use a good deal of profanity in killing their hereditary enemy, but Turi says that an experienced hunter does not bully the wolf and does not curse either, because he knows that the wolf is only acting according to its nature.

J. A. Friis gives the following lively account:

"If the wolf is absolutely starving, he cannot be scared away, not even by rifle shots; but otherwise he keeps at a distance and attacks when it suits him, because he knows the Lapps, and realizes that he is no match for the Lapp on skis when the snow is deep. But just as soon as the herder has crept into a snowcovered shelter to take cover from the snowstorm, and has lain down to rest for a while, it often happens that a commotion starts in the camp. The dogs, who have stretched out over his legs and for a little while lent him their warmth, suddenly spring to their feet and rush out, barking furiously. The reindeer, who also sense danger, first cluster together in a tight pack. Then they begin to scatter and run aimlessly around, until they get the scent of the beast, but then they set off at a terrific pace, usually against the wind, followed by the wolves, who try to scatter the herd so that they then in pairs can attack the lone reindeer. Now the herders (often children of around fifteen) must act quickly. One of them must race with the dogs after the herd, the other has to throw himself on his skis and dash away to the tent and arouse the family, or families, if many are camped together, crying *'Gumpi lae bottsuin'*—the wolf is in the reindeer herd."

It is characteristic that a few years ago the Lapp schoolboys of a community in Swedish Lappland refused to enroll as Boy Scouts, because in Sweden the junior scouts are called wolf cubs. They added that they would be glad to join the movement if they were allowed to call themselves lemmings.[1]

---

[1] The lemming, a not too distant relation to the gopher, is one of the most heroic creatures on the earth. Although they cannot hurt even a rabbit, the lemmings defy men and reindeer alike, barking like diminutive dogs. The lemmings are very prolific and their great problem is overpopulation. When the situation becomes acute they start big migrations, causing a good deal of damage when they pass through cultivated regions. They move in broad columns, literally covering the ground, followed by beasts of prey which take their toll all the time. When they come to a river or lake they swim across it instead of deviating from their line of march. The journey's end may appear in the shape of a torrent which pulls the badly decimated remainder of the crowd into a swirling cataract.

The wolverine is not so frequent as the wolf, and it hunts alone. It has a technique of its own. When it has overtaken a reindeer it jumps up on its back and bites through its cervical tendon. The wolverine is a wanton killer, and the Lapps hate and despise it intensely.

The bear does less harm to the reindeer than the wolf or the wolverine. Although he is much swifter than a man he cannot overtake a running reindeer. And it should be kept in mind that most bears are vegetarians, even if they are fond of ants. Some bears occasionally kill reindeer calves in the summer and they may even lie in ambush in order to kill fully grown reindeer. The Lapps are not afraid of the bear and they do not hate him either. Turi says that if you are courageous and approach the bear from the lee side so that he cannot get the wind of you, you can shoot him as you shoot a ptarmigan.

The reindeer fawns have also three other enemies, namely the arctic fox, the eagle, and the raven. The raven is dangerous only to fawns which have been left alone by their mothers. The eagle now and then flies away with a fawn.

Of the infectious diseases which may befall the reindeer, anthrax (also called the Siberian reindeer pest) is the most dangerous; in Lappland it occurs rarely, if ever. Hoof-rot is well known in all the parts of Lappland, but nowadays it is not so frequent as it was earlier.

Hydatic disease (caused by a kind of tapeworm) is rather frequent in reindeer and dogs in some regions. Occasionally it spreads to human beings. The Swedish physicians try to extirpate this disease by keeping the Lapps from throwing the lungs and livers of reindeer to the dogs.

Among noninfectious reindeer diseases vertigo and lumbar paralysis are the most frequent, apart from strangury, which comes about if a draught reindeer is driven too hard and not allowed to urinate in time.

CHAPTER X

REINDEER BREEDING

THE life of the reindeer nomads is regulated by the migrations of their reindeer. The calendar of the nomads is determined by the breeding habits of the reindeer, such as calving and rutting, as well as by the seasons of the year.

The winter is the most quiet time of the year from the point of view of the Mountain Lapps, but the early spring is dramatic. As soon as the snow begins to melt, a crust is formed on the surface of the snow in the night, and a little later the crust remains also during the day. As soon as the crust becomes thick enough to carry the reindeer, they move toward the mountains, and the nomads have to join the reindeer and try to organize the migration as well as possible. This means that they must have their draught reindeer ready and their baggage packed in sleighs. Such migrations may be very tiring. It is no easy thing to walk up to two hundred miles in a few days in a difficult terrain without roads. And in addition the herd must be watched and kept together the whole time, day and night. Sometimes there is a dense fog and sometimes snowstorms. In the high mountains it may be very cold at this time of the year, and the fuel is scarce and bad if there is any. Often the Lapps are in such a hurry that they cannot even afford to make regular night quarters, and sometimes storms blow the tents away.

This description is especially true of those Lapps in Tornio Lappmark who dwell in Norway during the summer. But the spring migration means a heavy strain even in those regions where the families are in the habit of staying in the subalpine zone and send only the herders to the calving places in the mountains.

The does calve in the month of May. They usually run in advance of the rest of the herd to their customary calving places. In most regions the calving does not take place in the alps or at the arctic sea coast, but in the lower mountain region, where the tree limit forms a zigzag line. In this region the nomad Lapps spend spring and autumn; there they nowadays have permanent turf huts or even log cabins or regular houses. Some old people who are not able to migrate stay there even in the winter, living chiefly from ptarmigan trapping. In most parts of Swedish Lappland, which is still the stronghold of full nomadism, the families nowadays spend the whole summer in their spring dwellings, where the old men do a good deal of fishing. Here the Lapps feel at home; here they have clustered together in villages. Here a development is going on, which in the long run almost inevitably will lead to a settled agricultural mode of life. All the Swedish nomads are allowed and encouraged to keep goats, five for each household. In winter these goats are tended by farmers in the spruce region, but in the other seasons of the year the Lapps keep them at their dwellings. Some Lapps even keep one or two cows, and this is not a recent phenomenon. In this way a more or less primitive nomad camp, which from the beginning was intended only for a temporary periodical use, can develop into a regular farm village. In the southern lappmarks, where the soil is fertile and the climate propitious, most of the indigenous nomads are at the same time farmers. This is no doubt one of the reasons why they have been superseded to such an extent by the immigrated Northern Lapps in the last decades. The settled life of a farmer can of course be combined with reindeer nomadism only if sons and herdsmen are detached for tending the reindeer far from the farm. In summer it is very difficult to keep the reindeer in the woods, chiefly because they are harassed by midges and gadflies. It is true that the Forest Lapps keep their herds in the forest region even in summer. Some people say that the forest reindeer can stand the heat and the insect plague better than the mountain reindeer, which are of a different race. As a matter of fact, the Forest Lapps in many districts have to protect their reindeer from insects by burning smoke fires, and in some places they even have spacious sheds for the same purpose. The reindeer of the Mountain Lapps like to escape the insects by running right up to the glaciers and snow fields of the high mountains. In the region of the great lakes reindeer lichen is scarce, or rather cropped, because it has been excessively grazed. It may be said that the maximum limit of reindeer breeding is determined by the capacity of the lichen grounds of that zone. Therefore it is vital to the Lapps to economize with these lichen heaths. Even if the reindeer do not eat the dry lichen in summer, they spoil it by treading on it while they move up and down in search for tender grass and other green vegetables of which their summer food consists. Thus it is an economic if not a biological necessity to keep the reindeer in the alpine region or at the arctic coast in summer. The camping life in the mountains is a heavy strain on the herders, who do not even enjoy the modest comfort of a regular tent, and this is one of the factors which make reindeer breeding in Scandinavia more and more difficult.

The summer food of the reindeer consists chiefly of such grass as grows in the mountains, and osier leaves and the like. The summer is a good season for the reindeer, but the herdsmen must often keep watch over the herd day and night. In many places the terrain is dangerous; in the glaciers there are deep crevices covered with snow, and whole herds occasionally slide down on steep mountain sides. The following passage in Anta Pirak's book, *A Nomad Lapp and His Life,* especially refers to the summer season.

"There are three different ways to keep reindeer. To let them roam about in freedom is the easiest and best way. If, in places where the Lapps remain for a long period, there happen to be natural barriers which prevent the herd from straying off to other mountain slopes, then the herd is left to roam free.

107

"Such barriers can consist of large lakes and rivers on one side, and on the other creeks with such slippery stony beds that the reindeer will not venture across them; sometimes there are cliffs, high mountains and rugged peaks. But in some direction there is probably an opening, and there a keeper has to go now and then and drive the herd back. Lucky are those Lapps who have such land to turn their reindeer out on all summer.

"Another way is to round up the herd during the day, let it go free around midnight, and then drive it together again early in the morning, let it range alone during the night again, and so continue in this way. The herd must be tended in this fashion when it grazes on flat ground, where there are no natural barriers or shelters, otherwise, if left alone to range free for a few days, it will be hopelessly scattered. During the time the Lapps herd their reindeer in this manner, they usually milk for a day or a week, in late summer. Perhaps we should milk for a longer time, but the hoof disease generally comes during this season, at least if one milks for a longer time, because the herd must remain in the resting ground then. And a reindeer doe does not give much milk. When the herd begins to get hungry it wanders off to graze, and the dogs must be sent out to drive it back to the resting ground. Then it may turn about and take off in another direction, and in this way it runs first this way and then that. During such a milking period the reindeer fatten very slowly. Therefore the owners are anxious to let the reindeer roam about in freedom, for then they thrive best of all.

"The most strenuous way to tend the herd is to keep watch day and night without rest. Nobody watches a herd so closely, however, unless it is absolutely necessary, either before migrations, so that the reindeer won't get lost and left behind, or on crusty snow. Then the reindeer gets wings on his feet, especially in the springtime, when he moves from the forests up towards the mountains. That kind of watch is necessary also during the time in summer when the Lapps separate their herds and group them according to communities. And when the wolf comes, then the same close watch is kept, day and night."

I have already pointed out that reindeer herds are not domesticated, and cannot be domesticated to the same degree as herds of cattle. When a reindeer herd is grazing together or lies ruminating or reposing, the reindeer feel safe and are not easily frightened; the herdsman can go quite close to the herd if he is not accompanied by his dog, and he may even move into the middle of the herd if he is careful and moves slowly. But if he tries to get hold of a single animal, it moves away. Usually there is no other means of catching a reindeer than the lasso, and every nomad Lapp wears his lasso over his shoulder when he is herding reindeer.

Whether the reindeer breeding is "intensive" or "extensive," it is necessary from time to time to separate the herds in order to single out such reindeer as do not belong to the owner of the herd. If very extensive breeding is practised, the reindeer of many different households may graze pell-mell; a nomad may have a substantial part of his reindeer scattered over three or more districts. But even in regions where the reindeer are scrupulously tended, reindeer belonging to different owners may stroll together, for instance in the beginning of the autumn. Thus the separations belong to the routine of reindeer breeding. Such a separation may be an easy procedure if only a small or medium-sized herd is to be divided, especially in winter when the snow is deep and loose. Then the Lapps often use a simple method called "separation with the staff." The reindeer are driven slowly to a convenient place, for instance a small land tongue, a clearance in the forest, or a slope where there is much snow. Stretching his staff before him, a Lapp walks through the flock, dividing it gently into two parts, which we will call A and B. Then they try to transfer one by one from A to B those reindeer which belong to the Lapp who owns the majority of the reindeer in the group B, and vice versa. All this is done chiefly by touching the reindeer with the

109

staff and without letting the dogs into the neighborhood of the reindeer. It is not so easy as it may seem from this brief description.

Johan Turi in his *Muittalus samid birra* gives a detailed account of this kind of separation. The case which he describes is fairly complicated, and according to him the procedure takes two days. The second day he describes in the following way:

"When the weather is good, then the tenders can keep the herd together; and when day breaks they return with the herds and then the separating starts again in the same way as on the first day. First as many as possible of one's own reindeer are separated from the herd, and when the herd gradually becomes smaller, then it is approached from two directions to separate those that are of mixed ownership, and then the little mixed flock stays in the center, and now comes the difficult part. If the people who separate are calm and skilled, then the whole business is done quickly and easily, but if they are impatient and clumsy, and if a few start running after their animals, the others must do likewise, and then the reindeer may begin to mix with each other again. Then it may happen that they begin to send the dogs on them, and after that it sometimes so happens that they get mixed up again. And if there are some unmarked animals, or some that during the summer have been marked wrong, then arguments begin when others claim to recognize their own reindeer, and these then run around in spite and spoil all the work of separating that has been done. If a fight begins among the men, there is so much more work to do the next day, and the men get so angry that they may even start slaughtering one another's reindeer. But in olden times the Lapps kept their herds so distinctly apart that reindeer from other herds never got mixed in; and if a reindeer from one flock strayed to another, he was soon brought back again."

Nowadays the Lapps use big circular wooden fences or corrals for collecting and separating their reindeer. In many

110

places each reindeer owner who is present at such a separation has a small fence of his own, attached to the big corral (on the outside). A big fence can receive a herd of many hundred reindeer. The entrance is flanked by two straight wings which form a kind of a big funnel. This funnel has the same name in Lappish as a contrivance which was formerly used by the Lapps for catching wild reindeer. This reindeer trap was built according to the same idea as a bow net. It had gigantic dimensions. It has been suggested that the ring fence has developed from that hunting contrivance. As a matter of fact, the ring fence has recently spread from Finnmark and Tornio Lappmark to the southern parts of Lappland. Dr. Ruong thinks that the ring fence is one of the characteristic features of northern extensive nomadism.

In the ring fence the herd usually moves incessantly counter-clockwise, raising a dense cloud of dust, mixed with reindeer hair. The Lapps stand with their lassos inside the moving circle of animals and try to catch their animals one by one. As soon as a reindeer has been caught by the lasso it is dragged, often by its hind legs, into the fence of its owner or to some quiet spot in the big corral where it can be earmarked or otherwise treated according to the season or the circumstances. All this cannot be done without violence, and some reindeer almost inevitably are hurt or damaged. The reindeer are more or less afraid of the corral, and sometimes it is difficult to drive them into it. The less domesticated the reindeer are, the more they suffer from this rough treatment. Those Lapps who have been employed as reindeer-breeding instructors in Alaska have made an invention which might be advantageously applied in Scandinavia. In their corrals the exit has the shape of a long and narrow passage, about a foot at the bottom and considerably broader higher up, so that there is room even for the big antlers of old bucks. As the reindeer can pass through this exit one by one, they can easily be collected by their respective owners. Now this construction would not be sufficient for the purposes of the Scandinavian Lapps; but it might easily be completed by a contrivance which is used by the sheep farmers in Australia. In the Australian sheep corrals there is a swinging door at the farther end of the narrow exit. By means of this door the sheep can be distributed into either of two pens. The man who handles the door has only to look at the earmarks of each advancing animal and make up his mind as to which of the pens it shall be admitted. No doubt this invention could be introduced into Scandinavian reindeer breeding if the authorities were not as conservative as the nomads.

From an economic point of view there are, broadly speaking, three kinds of reindeer in a herd, namely breeders, reindeer for meat, and such reindeer as are trained for some special function, such as draught reindeer, bell oxen, and reindeer which are trained to be led in front of the herd during migrations. The last category is the most valuable. Then come the breeders, and especially the does. As only a few bucks are needed for breeding, most of the males are slaughtered or castrated. The castration usually takes place in the early autumn, before the rutting begins. The Lapps perform this operation by biting and chewing the testicles with the intermediary of a piece of cloth; only the Russian Lapps use a knife. This may seem rather crude, but the Lapps insist that it is the most wholesome way of performing the operation.

The rutting of the reindeer begins in the second half or at the end of September and for each buck it lasts for about three weeks or more. Of course the reindeer must be let loose more or less during this season. The old males have the advantage of power (there are no decrepits in a herd of domesticated reindeer) and the half-grown bucks have to bide their time till the end of the season. The old nomad Mattias Persson Allas from Jukkasjärvi has given the following account of the rutting season:

"The rutting begins in September, at about Michaelmas, about a week before St. Michael's day. And it is thus: it begins little by little, and the rutting lasts a month and a half. The reindeer bucks rut and pursue the does; and they may even kill the doe by prodding her so that she expires. And they do not allow the small bucks in the neighborhood of the does. And the bucks fight so hard that their antlers break. If there happens to be a flock of forest reindeer in a region and a man comes there, then the forest buck will attack the man. If there are no trees he puts an isolated man in danger, and the man must put his dogs onto him, so that he can hide away or climb a rock, so that the buck cannot reach him. He keeps the man on that rock and watches him, and the man cannot go away from there; he has to stay there for a few days. But it is rather lucky however that I see people coming, and then that reindeer buck advances towards those men. He goes to attack them. Now they must take their lassos and undo them before he comes close to them. And then both of them must throw their lassos onto the buck's two horns, and then they pull their lassos in two directions and hold him firmly. Well, they hold him till that third one comes, the one who has been on the rock for two days. And he comes to assist the others, and he takes his lasso and puts it on the hind leg of the buck, and he suddenly pulls the buck by the leg, and so they turn the buck over. Then they castrate the buck and cut off his antlers. And then they let the buck loose; now he is quiet indeed, after he has been castrated.

"Now, when the main rutting comes to an end, the small bucks start rutting; before that, they dared not move. And when the big buck gets exhausted, he may even expire. And he is so very thin that he is well-nigh breaking off at the groins."

The full nomads of Swedish Lappland usually migrate to the conifer zone a few weeks before Christmas. As a rule the supply of lichen is much richer in this region than in the birch zone, and the nomads have wide areas to move in. The choice of winter pastures is more or less free in the whole district as far down toward the sea coast as the Lapps have a customary right to migrate. Speaking of the so called tax lands, I have mentioned earlier that each Lapp probably had a hereditary exclusive right to a certain strip of land, at least in southern Lappland. Among the half-nomadic Russian Lapps this institution is still alive. A certain part of the territory of the community is allotted to each nomadic household. The position of the reindeer owner is compar-

113

able to that of a hereditary tenant; his right to the pasture grounds could be modified or reduced, if not abolished, by the community.

This state of affairs was left untouched by the Russian authorities till the end of the nineteenth century, whereas in Finland, Norway, and Sweden it did not remain anywhere later than the eighteenth century. This means that the Scandinavian nomad has a certain *embarras de richesse* in disposing of the winter grounds for his reindeer. He needs a ripe judgment, for the usefulness of the terrain depends very much on the weather; a tract which has been excellent in the last year may be unusable in the coming winter. The reindeer dig in the snow with their broad hoofs (not with their antlers, as some people think); they can dig even through a thick layer of snow, provided that the snow is fairly loose. But if the snow melts, then the ground is covered with a coat of ice which often makes it impossible for the reindeer to get hold of the lichen, and if they do the ice-covered lichen causes indigestion and sickness. Sometimes the snow becomes tough and doughy to a thickness of several inches or even one or two feet; this is still worse than the ground crust. If one or the other of these evils occurs in a wide area, as is often the case, the Lapps must fell spruces so that the reindeer can get hold of the beard lichens. The Lapps are allowed to do this under certain circumstances, even on private lands, but the beard lichen is a poor kind of food, and often the Lapp must ask, like Alexander the Great when he was offered a cup of water in the Indian desert: "How could this suffice for so many?" As a last device he may scatter his herd and leave his reindeer to take care of themselves as best they can. Such a winter may be ruinous even to a rich reindeer owner.

From the point of view of tending the reindeer, reindeer breeding may be "intensive" or "extensive." The chief characteristic of intensive reindeer breeding is that the herdsmen keep the reindeer in control in spring and summer. During the summer the does are milked daily or twice a day, and they come of their own accord to the vicinity of the tent to be milked. The fawns are partly kept from sucking by putting a gadget into their mouth or by smearing the udder of the doe with reindeer excrement. The herd of each family is usually kept apart, at least in spring, summer, and autumn. The herds are comparatively small, seldom more than five hundred animals.

The extensive form of reindeer breeding implies that the reindeer at certain times of the year, especially in spring but partly also in autumn, are given much liberty to move within the boundaries of the nomad district in order to find their pasture for themselves. The more free the reindeer are, the more they are apt to spread into small flocks, and one of the consequences of extensive reindeer breeding is that the different herds get mixed up. One might even say that this form of breeding is by definition more or less collective. The reindeer grow wilder; the milking of the does can take place only at exceptional occasions, so that goat milk must be substituted for reindeer milk.

The extensive reindeer breeding has manifest advantages. The fawns get all the milk their mothers can yield, and the freedom of movement is advantageous to the adult reindeer too. The spreading of epizootic diseases is reduced when the much-trodden muddy milking places are abandoned.

On the other hand, the extensive mode of breeding easily makes for disorder. The herds get out of control and many reindeer wander far away into foreign districts. For the owner of a small herd it is often difficult or impossible to get hold of his draught reindeer when he needs them. In the long run this system unduly favors the owners of big herds.

Formerly the intensive form of reindeer breeding was prevalent almost everywhere. In these days there is not much left of it. Its disappearance is at least partly due to the fact that the lichen has been cropped too hard in the subalpine zone. But even if the lichen should be allowed to grow ankle-high again, there is not likely to be any revival of intensive reindeer breeding. It requires the collaboration of all the adult members of the family to such a degree that it no longer seems socially practicable.

Full nomadism with its far-flung migrations, may be a relatively recent phenomenon in Fennoscandia. It is unknown in Russian Lappland, and it is not even practised in all the districts of Swedish Lappland. Many of the Mountain Lapps in Härjedalen migrate only about thirty miles in each direction. They might be called Mountain Lapps *par excellence*, because they spend practically all their life in the mountains. The reindeer breeding practised by them is a kind of intermediary between full nomadism and half nomadism. Half nomadism means relatively short migrations between relatively few dwelling places, and the combination of reindeer breeding with some other important means of livelihood, especially fishing, or, in earlier times, hunting. The Russian Lapps are true half nomads. In summer they are chiefly occupied by fishing in the lakes and at the mouths of the rivers. Since the spawning time is different in different lakes, the fishermen have to move a good deal in the fishing season. During this time they cannot pay much attention to their reindeer herds. They use their reindeer only as draught animals and for meat, and they never keep very big herds. In the winter the whole district community lives together in log cabins, each family in a cabin of its own. This winter residence is the scene of the administrative and judiciary life of the community. There all the common questions of the community are treated and settled by the district council (*norraz*), which consists of the heads of the households (a household often comprising two or more families, because married sons who live together with their parents are not regarded as being of age and are not admitted to the council). The council even functions as a court of justice, judging on such minor offences as are rather against good manners than against criminal law. Earlier the councils also treated criminal cases, and it is characteristic of the policy pursued by the Russians towards the Lapps that the judicial competence of the Lapp community councils was restricted as late as 1517.

The habit of living in winter villages has survived among

the Fisher Lapps in Finland, and seemingly there are remains of such residences from the Middle Ages. In Swedish
Lappland a few places called *Dalvadis* (from Lappish *dalve*,
"winter") still give evidence of the same old custom; these
places have long ago become centers of the Swedish colonization, being situated nearer to the lappmark frontier than
to the limit of cultivation. In our days most of the Swedish
Mountain Lapps have begun to lead a life which resembles
half nomadism in so far as the families spend the greatest
part of the year in one place (namely, where they earlier
had their dwellings in spring and autumn), but the reindeer
and the herders still keep up the full nomadic mode of life.
Some scholars think that full-fledged nomadism, as it is still
practised in Karesuando and Jockmock, is only an episode
in the history of Fennoscandian reindeer breeding. The
difficulty is to find out how long this episode has lasted.

The most conservative and characteristic form of half
nomadism is no doubt that which is practised by the Russian Lapps (in so far as they have been able to keep up their
old standard of living) and the Fisher Lapps of Inari.[1] The
Forest Lapps of Pite Lappmark and the adjacent districts
in Swedish Lappland now all live in regular farmhouses;
two or three generations ago they lived in small open huts
or tents and lived chiefly from reindeer breeding and secon-
darily from fishing. Three hundred years ago they were
more or less prosperous hunters and paid most of their taxes
in wild skins. Petrus Laestadius gives the following account
of their life as it appeared to him at the beginning of the
nineteenth century:

"The Forest Lapp dwells in the forest region of Lappland during the whole summer and does not make any wide
migrations there. Each of these Lapps has his tax land,
where he dwells. Here he has several wooden huts, built in
convenient places two or four miles distant from each other.

---

[1] In Sweden the term Fisher Lapp usually means a Lapp who has been
forced by economic difficulties to quit nomadism and has settled at a lake
in a region where agriculture is impracticable, or a descendant of such
settlers.

At each hut there is an open larder[2] and an enclosure, into which the Lapp drives his reindeer in order to milk them in summer. In the larder he puts the cheese to dry. At some of the dwellings he has a small storehouse. I will begin his history at springtime, when he comes up from the lowlands. As soon as he has arrived on his land, in the beginning of May or at the end of April, he lets his reindeer loose; they are allowed to run where they want to. Then he has no care for them till the end of June. During this vacation he is occupied with hunting and fishing, which is a subsidiary livelihood to all Forest Lapps. Just after Midsummer, when midge time comes, they begin to go and look for their reindeer and collect them. Everyone searches the woods of his own tax land and collects all the reindeer he finds there. There are certain places where the reindeer go on their own account, when they are tormented and chased by the midges, namely, such places as are open to the winds so that the midges are blown away. The Lapps know these places and go there first, get hold of a reindeer and put a bell around its neck. Then they take with them the reindeer which they have found, and the flock steadily increases; for wherever they pass they are joined by those reindeer which are in that region. Instinct drives them to cluster together. The midges are supposed to torment them less when they are close together. When they hear the bell they run in that direction in order to find other reindeer."

Having described in detail the separation of reindeer, Laestadius continues:

"In one or two weeks' time this whole procedure is brought to an end and everyone has only his own reindeer herd to tend. During the whole of July and the first half of August the Forest Lapp has his herd in his care and custody. In this time the does are milked. They are driven into the mentioned enclosure twice or thrice every day. Here several fires are lighted and covered with moist turf, so that they give plenty of smoke. The smoke keeps the midges from the reindeer so that they can rest and ruminate. The

[2] A horizontal board, supported by two or more poles, with a roof above it.

does are milked once a day. In the middle of August the reindeer no longer like to keep together. Then the Lapp is forced to let them loose again. Then he has six weeks' vacation, and during this time he is occupied with fishing and hunting. He sets wooden traps and shoots fowls in the forests. At Michaelmas when the rutting season comes, the Forest Lapp starts collecting his reindeer again. Then he keeps them in his custody during the whole winter and migrates to the lowlands in the same way as the Mountain Lapp."

The total territory of reindeer breeding in Fennoscandia is about as large as New Mexico, or twice the area of England and Wales. The area in which reindeer breeding is the most important means of livelihood is perhaps no larger than Holland and Belgium together. The number of the Lapp households living exclusively or chiefly from reindeer breeding is about one thousand, rather less than more. The total number of reindeer is about 500,000. It fluctuates considerably; thus two decades ago the reindeer stock in Swedish Lappland decreased from 300,000 to less than 200,000. This was something of a catastrophe, but it was by no means unprecedented. It seems safe to apply a special "catastrophe theory" to the conditions and developments of full nomadism in Scandinavia. I am not speaking of ground crust, wolves, and hoof rot, but of a fatal periodicity in the basic conditions of nomad economy. The factors which make for a temporary decrease of the reindeer herds are insignificant in the long run, because they are counterpoised by the fertility of the reindeer, and if all the reindeer owners of a district should be ruined and forced to quit the trade, there is always (or at any rate, there has been up to these days) a reserve from which the gap can be filled. There is more to fear from the factors which make for prosperity. Half-nomadic reindeer breeding may be intensive or extensive according to the circumstances; but full nomadism, when it prospers and expands, inevitably tends to become more and more extensive. The limit of increase in a given district is reached when the reindeer cannot get enough food in *all* seasons of the year. We have seen that in Swedish Lappland

119

the lichen is severely cropped in the birch region, whereas in Härjedalen and in Idre in Dalarne the lichen reaches above the ankles and the reindeer prosper to such a degree that even one-year-old does calve, a phenomenon unheard of in the northern lappmarks. Those northern Lapps who have been induced by the Swedish authorities to migrate far south during the last two decades believe that the dislocation has done them no end of good. Such a movement towards the south has taken place for centuries on a small scale without, or even against the will of, the authorities. We have also seen that the Mountain Lapps of Swedish Lappland and northernmost Jämtland (Frostviken) have surreptitiously extended their winter migrations far beneath the Lappmark frontier and even right down to the sea coast, nay, to the archipelago, and acquired a customary right to these newly gained territories. In the Swedish part of the Tornio valley and adjacent districts, illegal reindeer breeding has expanded in our own lifetime, and it was sanctioned by legislation only twenty years ago. Nowadays Finland is the only country where Lapp reindeer breeding has any chance of further expansion. And in this context the word "Lapp" should not be stressed. As we know, Finland is the only country where the Lapps have had no place in the sun. And it seems consistent that by now about four-fifths of the reindeer stock in Finland is owned by non-Lapps. In Finland, as far as reindeer breeding is concerned, the future no doubt belongs to intensive half nomadism.

But let us return to the conditions of full nomadism. It is the fate of the nomads, or rather of their animals, to be fruitful and multiply and replenish the earth. Nothing prevents the nomad from increasing his herd till he has reached the point where an excessive use of the grazing grounds begins. And then, if the territory cannot be extended, what follows? The choice of winter pastures becomes more and more restricted, which means that the consequences of bad weather and unfavorable grazing conditions become more and more serious. The impending risks of zoötic diseases may force the nomads to abstain from the intensive tending of their reindeer, and in order to spare the lichen grounds in the birch zone they will let their reindeer loose as much as possible and drive them to the conifer zone as early in the autumn as possible. The reindeer will spoil the hay of the farmers and the nomads will have to pay for this one way or another. Domestication is in reverse; to some extent the reindeer run wild, and they cannot even be kept within the boundaries of the district. It becomes difficult or even impossible for the reindeer owner to get hold of his draught animals when he needs them. All this means that the mechanism of reindeer breeding has lost its elasticity. The system is no longer resistant against the vicissitudes of wind and weather. Two or three subsequent bad winters may lead to disaster, catastrophe, and inevitable ruin. Or rather, ruin for the poor and poverty for the rich. In a few years the reindeer stock of a district may be reduced to a third or a fourth of what it was. Many of the nomads have to give up reindeer breeding altogether and settle as fishermen and trappers under conditions which may be good at the beginning but in many cases deteriorate rapidly in the next generation. And if the descendants of such settlers should prosper, they are often undesirable from the viewpoint of the nomads, because they become a consolidated part of the settled population and move the spearheads of cattle breeding and agriculture deeper into the land of the nomads.

Such a catastrophe, as we have witnessed it lately, has a therapeutic aspect; it reveals something of the healing power of Nature. In order to get their scattered herds under control, those reindeer owners who have survived the cataclysm are forced to adopt a more intensive mode of tending them. As time goes on the lichen grows higher and the grazing-conditions improve. The herds increase, and an era of prosperity has begun, which sooner or later will lead to another catastrophe.

Whatever may be said of this theory, it seems certain that the full nomadism of the Lapps, apart from its ups and downs, is steadily declining in the long run from a quantitative if not from a qualitative point of view. In view of their vast extension, the reindeer-breeding territories cannot be improved by any sort of cultivation. And they cannot easily be widened either. The last expansion took place in the nineties of the last century, when the Swedish Government bought from the private owners the controversial territory in Härjedalen where there had been such a bad conflict between the nomads and the settled population. Almost everywhere agriculture expands to the detriment of reindeer breeding. Rapidly growing mining centers interfere with the migrations of the reindeer herds and considerably reduce their grazing grounds. Even the big power dams, as the Suorvadam in the Great Lule river, intrude upon nomadism to some extent. We have seen that in northern Norway the possibilities of reindeer breeding have been reduced in the last decades. It may be that these territorial reductions are not essential, but there remains the fact that the soil on which the reindeer live can neither be extended nor improved. To this there comes another factor which is decisive: the basic reindeer number, that is to say, the minimum of subsistence as expressed in number of reindeer, steadily increases.

Earlier the Lapps produced most of their necessities, and there was not much need for money. They paid their taxes in skins and the like. The wages of a hired herdsman consisted of a few female reindeer, a set of clothes, a pair of skis, and so forth; after fifteen years of service he might have a small reindeer herd of his own to start with. In our days the Lapps wear cotton shirts and rubber boots, and they buy much more material for clothes than before. In many regions the women do not sew summer shoes any longer, but they have to be bought. Their diet has been enriched by many articles which are now regarded as necessary. Traveling is much easier than fifty years ago, but it costs money. The Lapps move on the lakes with outboard motors and for their migrations they often use automobiles. Four years ago a nomad Lapp asked me how much it would cost to hire an airplane in order to bring his family and twenty hundredweights of provisions up to the mountain region in spring. There may come a time when this means of transportation is also regarded as a necessity. The nomad needs a lot of money to pay his taxes and to pay the wages of his servant, if he can afford to hire one.

It stands to reason that the basic reindeer number depends on the price of reindeer meat, which fluctuates greatly. About thirty dollars is a good average price for a reindeer; fifteen years ago the price was a third or a fourth of this amount. In Norway the demand for reindeer meat is fairly good; in Sweden it is much smaller. Efforts have been made to promote the trade by forming organizations, building freezing factories, and so on. But it seems safe to predict that the price of reindeer meat will not rise more rapidly than the general cost of living.

From all this it can be inferred that the number of households subsisting on full nomadism will continue to decrease.

To this a dynamic demographic feature should be added. Formerly all the adult members and even the half-grown children took part in the different phases and performances of reindeer breeding. Nowadays the tending of the reindeer becomes more and more the specialty of middle-aged reindeer owners, aged sons, and hired herdsmen. The wives spend most of their time in the settlements in the birch zone, where the Lapps earlier used to pitch their tents in spring and autumn. In many districts these settlements can hardly be distinguished from ordinary farmers' villages. The children are kept in boarding schools for six or seven years, and during this time they get accustomed to the amenities of urban life. In Finland and Norway the young men have to interrupt their nomad activities for military service. (The Swedish nomads are exempt from conscription in peacetime.) The girls become estranged from the profession of their parents; they can easily get appointments as housemaids, nurses, shop-assistants, and clerks, and to a substantial extent they are absorbed into the urban population. Mr. Carl Johansson, who is a Lapp by birth, having watched the development in one of the biggest parishes of Swedish Lappland for twenty years, says that the young men in the ages from eighteen to forty years have stuck to reindeer breeding, ". . . and the oldest of these are well-to-do reindeer owners, each with one hundred to four hundred animals, but unmarried. How could they, anyway, compete with large institutions and factories and wealthy business men in the cities for women workers? They cannot pay a hundred dollars a month in salary and provide a room with modern conveniences, an eight-hour working day, regular free time, and such, for women helpers. And what is there to do about it? I refrain from making any suggestions, because to try to look for all the whys and wherefores and change the makeup of a people is nearly as difficult as to try to find the secret of the infinite universe."[3]

[3] *Samefolkets Egen Tidning*, No. 4, 1948.

CHAPTER XI

FROM THE CRADLE TO THE GRAVE

IT IS not to be wondered at that infant mortality is high among the nomad Lapps. In his autobiography Anta Pirak says that he was born in a tent in early winter; he has been told that it was so cold that the upper ends of the tent poles were white from frost above the smoke hole. When he was two months old he accompanied his mother to the coastal town Piteå, a distance of about 150 miles. "My mother had, of course, to take me out of the cradle many times, put it across her lap and nurse me. And I have myself seen how one must take a babe from its cradle, no matter how cold it may be, or how heavily the snow is falling, rock it in one's arms when the infant begins to cry and wimper, especially if it is a new-born child. And the reindeer caravan must keep going in the meantime. The woman with the child drives in the lead sleigh, and the caravan follows."

The Lapps have a lot of obstetric tricks and practices, some of them sound and rational, some disgusting and superstitious. As a specimen of both I will quote a note made by Rector Qvigstad among fishing Lapps in the province of Tromsö:

Old Inger Solheim, who died in 1880 in the age of nearly one hundred years, functioned as midwife for more than sixty years and had not a single casualty. She used dead men's bones, which were sewn into a black catskin. When the newborn baby did not breathe, she put it quickly into a bucket filled with cold water and gave it a heavy slap on its bottom. Then the baby started breathing. When a child had died in its mother's womb, she took it out piecemeal; the head made the greatest difficulty.

The following treatment of puerperal fever seems to be a borderline case between rational and superstitious therapy. One takes a fat reindeer doe, ties its feet and pierces its breast in front of its fore legs, so that the blood spurts. The woman drinks as much as she can of the spouting blood, two or three cups.

The Lapps are very fond of children, and their way of rearing them is usually mild, or even slack. In this respect there is a striking resemblance between Lappland and the United States. In both countries there seems to exist an interaction between the educational system (or lack of system) and the prevailing keep-smiling-even-if-you-should happen-to-be-crucified attitude of the adult, although it must be admitted that this attitude is not quite as frequent among the Lapps as among the amiable Yankees. Anyhow the results of this Rousseauan education are encouraging (just as they are in America). The Lapp children are often outspoken, self-indulgent, and irreverent towards their parents, but their behavior towards strangers is usually irreproachable, and at school they readily learn all kinds of polite manners. As boarding-school alumni they are easy to handle, and they learn a little quicker than Swedish children, at least in the first school years.

In another chapter I have spoken of the well-intentioned efforts of King Carl IX in the field of Lapp education. His successor Gustavus Adolphus was more successful. The so-called Skyttean school for Lapp boys was founded in 1631. It was named for the king's former tutor Johan Skytte, a learned and skillful statesman, who during a diplomatic mission to England was dubbed a knight by King James I. The aim of this school was to prepare a restricted number of Lapp boys to be teachers and even to open an academic career for them. The school did not fall short of this modest ambition. In the years between 1633 and 1722 at least thirteen Lapp students wrote their names in the album of Uppsala University. A few of them will be remembered in the history of Lapp civilization. In 1672 came Olof Sirma, whom I shall speak of in the chapter on Lapp literature; in 1688 Lars Rangius, who made the first Lappish translation of the New Testament.

In the middle of the eighteenth century there were, besides the Skyttean school, seven schools in the Swedish lappmarks. The instructors were clergymen. The boys who had passed these schools could then function as teachers and missionaries in their own communities. Nicolaus Lundius, who was the son of the first Lapp priest in Sweden and who came to Uppsala University in 1674 after having passed the Skyttean school, says in his *Descriptio Lapponiae* (written in Swedish and handed over to Schefferus):

"In the Lapp district of Umeå live the most sensible Lapps under the sun; the reason for this I know, because when the Lapp children come from the Lapp school at Lycksele (the Skyttean school) then they teach their parents a little about God. I have often myself taught the Umeå Lapps about God, creation, and how the earth was created, and they willingly listen—but they are so made that they do not remember things very long, but forget about them quickly, and neither do they take these teachings very much to heart; they believe that the world has always been. They also say that there will never be a new heaven and earth, but they say, 'As it has been, so it will be eternally.' "

In 1735 the first step was taken to introduce ambulatory schools, so-called catechete schools. In the sixties of the same century there were in the Swedish lappmarks twelve "catechetes," who went from one nomad camp to another and stayed about six weeks at each place to give the children the most indispensable rudiments of profane and religious instruction.

In 1818 the stationary schools were reduced to three and the number of catechetes was increased to twenty-seven. Two ambulating "missionaries" were appointed to supervise the catechetes. The famous *Diary* of Petrus Laestadius gives us an insight into the lives of these missionaries.

During the nineteenth century the stationary Lapp schools were transformed into ordinary Swedish primary schools. In the third quarter of the century the Lapp educational system reached its low-water mark; the catechete system was abolished without being replaced by anything else. Toward the end of the century the ambulatory educational system was introduced again.

In 1916 the educational system was put on a new footing. Special nomad schools were established under the supervision of a nomad school inspector. There are two kinds of nomad schools, namely, ambulatory summer schools for the first three school years, and stationary winter schools for the subsequent three school years. Most of the teachers are Lapps, but the instruction is chiefly given in Swedish. Lappish as subject of instruction has hitherto been treated in a stepmotherly fashion, but it will soon get a regular status.

The aim of the new nomad school system is to give the children of the nomads the same educational possibilities as other Swedish citizens, without estranging them from the trade of their fathers. To that end the children have to learn Swedish thoroughly; but on the other hand a special stress is laid upon such topics as nomadism and the history of the Lapps. K. B. Wiklund wrote a reader for the nomad schools in three volumes; the third part is an excellent handbook on Lapp subject-matters, perhaps even better suited for adults than for children. The publishing program for the next years comprises a Lappish grammar (Finnmark Lappish), two Lappish readers (one in Finnmark Lappish, the other in Southern Lappish), and a textbook on nomadism (including the history and ethnography of the Lapps).

In the southern lappmarks the nomads never approved of the ambulatory summer schools, and even in Norrbotten they were not a complete success. Now they are abolished, except for the two northernmost of them. The unsanitary old winter schools are now only a memory. As has already been hinted at, practically the whole Swedish system of Lapp education has been concentrated in ten boarding schools fitted with every modern convenience. But this evolution has not yet come to a standstill. A seventh school year will be added to the curriculum, and the program of this additional year comprises topographic-biological field-studies under the joint direction of the ordinary teacher, a naturalist of academic rank, and an expert nomad Lapp.

There is also a modest high school in Jockmock for Lapp boys and girls.

In Norway, on the other hand, the boarding school system is of long standing. Recently the Lappish language has been introduced in the curriculum, and a beautiful Lappish primer has been printed in the new orthography which has been accepted both in Norway and in Sweden.

People who have heard about the conflicts between "fennomanes" and "svecomanes" in Finland may be surprised to hear that the rights of linguistic minorities are most scrupulously taken care of in Finland. The Swedish-speaking population of Finland is not a "minority" in the legal sense of this term. The law concerning the use of minority languages in the schools is worth quoting literally:

"In primary schools where there are at least twenty per cent children of Finnish citizens with another mother tongue than Finnish or Swedish, these children shall have oral instruction in their mother tongue, as occasion requires. In primary schools where there are only children of Finnish citizens with another mother tongue than Finnish or Swedish, the instruction shall be given in the mother tongue of the children . . . ."

In accordance with these stipulations, the Lapp children in Utsjoki and Inari are usually instructed by Lapp teachers.

In the Kola peninsula a remarkable work has been done in the field of public instruction during the last two decades. From the handsome Lapp primer, published in 1933, I take the following passage:

"Eight years ago there was not a single educated Lapp. Eight years ago, the young man Ivan (Osipov) went to distant Leningrad to acquire knowledge. Then the Northern Committee opened for the first year the Institute of the Northern Peoples. Now many young people of the North study in the Institute. The Lapps alone amount to twenty-two people. Ivan learned much. Now he has passed the

129

Northern Institute and works in the Lapp parishes. He is the first Lapp teacher."

The Lapps have many games, toys, and pastimes for different ages, beginning with the metal rings and glass pearls which are hung on the ramified ribbon that extends from one end of the cradle to the other, and ending with more or less modern card games and simple variants of chess (Lule Lappish *dablo* = Old Norse *tafl*, English *tables*). As far as is known they have no genuine dances, at least not what we should call by that name. But in the nineteenth century, if not earlier, the Lapps learned to dance like their settled neighbors. The Skolt Lapps are very fond of dancing quadrille, and they especially appreciate good concertina players. More or less dramatic dance games have also found their way to the Lapps. Among the children's games there are a few which have a particularly Lapp character, as the bear game (in which the "bear" plays the dominant role) and the bear-hunting game (in which the bear is killed and carried home). The most frequent pastime of the boys concerns reindeer; they make reindeer of twigs or chips, or put antlers on their heads and act as reindeer themselves.

Skiing is practised at a very early age. Very small children prepare for this sport by sliding down the snow wall on the outside of the tent, sitting on a dog's food dish. The next phase is sliding downhill sitting on a ski. When a little older, the child starts skiing downhill in the regular way.

When the Lapp boys are strong enough to hold a reindeer fawn by the rein, says Anta Pirak, then they put a halter on its head and break it in and "tolk" (a Lappish loan-word in Swedish, meaning in English "skijoring") along a ski-track or along a way trodden by the reindeer herd. Sometimes several small boys "tolk" after the same reindeer.

Through such pastimes the Lapp boys by and by get acquainted with their future trade. I have already mentioned that their career as reindeer owners begins when they get their first tooth.

In olden days marrying was not quite as easy and simple as it is now. Among the Lapp nomads, as among the nomads of the old Testament, the marriage did not only concern

130

the young couple but also their families, in particular the parents of the bride. According to the ancient customary right of the Lapps, the bridegroom had to give considerable presents to the relatives of the bride, especially to her parents. The amount of silver dollars which he had to give was sometimes explicitly determined in the negotiations that accompanied the formal proposal. In the southern lappmarks these presents were designated by the term *rutta*, which in the northern lappmarks is the word for "money." (This word may be of Scandinavian origin; in the jocose Edda song about Thor's stolen hammer the word *brūðfē* "the bride's fee, or money," is mentioned in connection with a wedding, but the context is obscure.) If the marriage was not fulfilled, the *rutta* had to be returned to the young man, and it was often claimed in the court of law. There was a difference in the attitude of the courts. In Sweden-Finland and in Russia regional customary right was accepted to a considerable extent as equivalent to written law, whereas in Norway this has not been the case, as far as is known. The Norwegian courts did not acknowledge the *rutta* as an object of legal claims, but the Swedish courts did, as appears from several verdicts from the seventeenth and the eighteenth century. As a rule the priests seem to have been very much against the *rutta* institution, because they thought that it degraded marriage to the level of a commercial contract; it seemed to them that the bridegroom simply bought his wife from her parents. This interpretation however is not to the point. There are no certain traces of the purchase type of marriage among the Lapps. With better right it might be inferred from the wedding practices of the Skolt Lapps that the Lapps at an early epoch possibly kidnapped their wives, as in Titus Livius's story about the abduction of the Sabine women. Apart from a few isolated statements (chiefly from the sixteenth and seventeenth century) on so-called hospitality hetaerism, the married woman seems to have had a more independent status among the Lapps than among the Scandinavians. As a reindeer owner she had an earmark of her own, and her reindeer formed a distinct unit in the herd of the family.

131

On the other hand, when a well-to-do Lapp girl married, this meant from a strictly economic point of view a gain for her husband in labor and reindeer, and a loss on the part of her parents. Now the *rutta* was an acknowledgement of the sacrifice which the marriage meant to the parents of the bride, and at the same time a guarantee that the bridegroom had a good economic position, so that the girl did not contract a bad marriage. The *rutta* should also cover the dowry. Högström explicitly states, having enumerated the things which the bridegroom or his parents had to give to the bride's parents and other relatives: "But all this is not done in vain, for it is the duty of the bride's parents to provide the newly wedded couple with as many household goods and reindeer as seems fitting, according to the inheritance they will get. And those relatives who have received gifts must also give something in return."

And this is not the whole story. The young man had to "serve for Rachel," even if the Lapp Laban was satisfied with one year and did not demand the service in advance. The young couple usually spent the first year of their married life together with the wife's parents.

During the courtship the young man used to give presents to the girl—silken kerchiefs, a ring, and the like. The girl could accept such presents from two or more boys at the same time; but when she eventually married, the spurned suitors could claim their gifts back, and they were not ashamed of doing so.

The formal proposal was a big affair. The wooer started with a whole caravan, often accompanied both by his father and mother and other close relatives, but the most important figure was the "head of the wooing" or the wooer's proxy, who had to argue the whole case on behalf of the suitor. The wooing party was well provided with corn brandy and other material ingredients of merry entertainment, and asked for permission to enter the tent and distribute some refreshments; an affirmative answer was regarded as a definite encouragement, in view of the purpose of the expedition. Then there often followed a lively bargaining. The "head of the wooing" praised his client in an eloquent manner; but some elderly female member of the girl's family might make disparaging remarks concerning the economic position, skill, or character of the suitor (who sat quite silent during the whole procedure). The "head" defended the wooer as best he could, and he might even start a counter-attack against the poor girl (who did not take part in the controversy).

Judge Solem, who has written a valuable book on the customary right of the Lapps, has remarked that the Lapps have observed certain rules about inheritance which may reflect an earlier tribal organization. There are for instance distinct traces of ultimogeniture or a privilege of the youngest son in matter of inheritance. In Finnmark and among the Russian Lapps the rule has prevailed, and to some extent still prevails, that the youngest son keeps the tent or the house of the parents, and even the soil around the house; he also inherits his father's reindeer earmark. Regarding the Skolt Lapps, Paulaharju says that according to an old custom the youngest son has to stay at home and take care of his parents as long as they live. He has also to provide for his unmarried sisters. As a recompense he gets the owner marks of his father and all the property which the father has left behind him.

Earlier, when the full nomads lived in tents the whole year, it was not easy to provide for feeble and chronically sick old people. The Lapps certainly did not like to "come to the parish," and in some regions the attitude of the settled population towards the Lapps was even hostile. As a rule the old people took part in the migrations as long as they were able to, or still longer.

In June 1930 I witnessed at Övergård near Lyngenfjord a quaint funeral procession. The whole cortège consisted of a single horse-drawn carrier's wagon, and the driver sat astride the coffin. I was told that the deceased was a Karesuando Lapp, who had come across the mountain ridge the other day. When the time for migration arrived, he had made up his mind to go to Norway like all the others. Nobody was willing to have him in his company, because he was obviously too decrepit to walk all the long way. Then he gathered his small reindeer herd and went alone. He arrived at his destination, and late in the evening after his arrival two young herdsmen saw him and spoke to him. He lay on the ground, wrapped up in a tentcloth, and he told them that he was all right. The next morning he was found dead on the same spot. This was a death fitting for an old nomad.

Like the Norse vikings, the ancient Lapps seem to have thought that they had better prospects beyond the grave if they died with their boots on. According to a popular tradition from southern regions (Västerbotten and Jämtland), decrepit Lapps were often killed by their younger relatives, with their own consent. As far as I know, there is no concrete evidence to back up this tradition. Professor Arbman, who has collected a good many testimonies, thinks that they are quite sufficient. One of the best items comes from a Lapp who lives in the northernmost tip of Jämtland.

"When a Lapp in the olden days became so old and infirm that he could not care for himself and go along on the migratory journeys, his days were ended by his people. One way was to take the aged person in the wintertime and drive him up on a precipitous mountain, there put him in a sleigh and then push him down the worst precipice—this is called *såålekeskoute,* which means, roughly, "blessed journey." Another way was to chop a hole in the ice on a lake and then put the aged one down in the hole and leave him to drown under the ice. It was felt that in such cases the one who put an aged person to death was not responsible for taking a life, for that was done by the spirit of the mountain or of the water. The old Lapps, who were brought up in the belief of their forefathers, did not see anything dreadful in such an end, rather were they glad when their time came. They were freed from their struggles and in a way which assured them of bliss after death."

The Lapp who gave this information (to Dr. Levi Johansson) added the following remark: "Nothing like this has happened in my time or that of my parents, but the old folks in my youth recorded it from their ancestors as a fact and I have no reason to believe that they made it up."

These Lapp traditions have a Scandinavian counterpart. According to an Icelandic saga (probably from the thirteenth century), steep rocks had been used in southern Sweden (Västergötland?) for old men's suicide in the time of paganism. Similar traditions about suicide and homicide have been noted in southern Sweden in modern times. In the opinion of some scholars these traditions are apocryphal.

The old burial customs of the Lapps and their attitude towards the dead are well described by Rheen, Lundius, and Tuderus. According to Tuderus, the Lapps of Kemi Lappmark in olden time used to put the dead between two trees in the forest, covering the body with pieces of wood. Nowadays, he says, they lay them in coffins, and if they can avoid it they do not like to bury them in the wild forest, lest wolves and bears dig them up, but they take them to small islets where there are sandy slopes, to bury them there; and in the winter the priest has to go to those distant places to conduct the burial according to the Christian ritual.

The oldest Lapp cemeteries seem to date from the beginning of the seventeenth century.

Nicolaus Lundius, whose father was a priest and a Lapp by birth, says of the Umeå Lapps:

"When someone dies, they put in the coffin of the deceased a little sack with various kinds of foods—cheese, fish, butter, tallow, and other things which I cannot all remember. They also put in fire-making implements and an axe, saying that the dead must have his sustenance when he comes to the people who inhabit the nether regions of the earth. The Lapp does not know whither the soul goes after death, which I have often questioned him about. He says: 'I do not know, but you, be a good friend and teach me where my soul will go.' The Lapps do not often bring the bodies of their dead to church, for they mostly bury them where they die."

135

Samuel Rheen gives a detailed report concerning Lule Lappmark, which I think is well worth quoting:

"Many are the Lapps who persist in the erroneous belief that the dead shall not rise again, but that something is left after death they believe, and therefore they have a dread of the dead. For when someone dies they leave the room at once. And when the deceased is about to be placed in his coffin, which usually is a hollowed out tree or log, the surviving husband or wife, father or child, must give to him who places the body in the coffin a brass ring, to be worn on the right arm. This ring he must keep on his arm until the body has been lowered into the grave, so that in the meantime no harm shall befall him. All of the clothing worn by the dead person is brought to the grave or churchyard and left there, as is the sled which carried the corpse. The laying out is done so that if the deceased was a man of position and wealth he is dressed in linen, covering his whole body and head like a shroud; but if he was a poor Lapp he is laid out in old frieze.

"Three days after the corpse has been buried, the reindeer that pulled the funeral sled to the graveyard is slaughtered in honor of the dead, and the relatives and kinsmen eat the meat; however, all the bones are gathered together in a chest which is dug down into the earth. Then an image of wood is made and placed upon the casket, and this image is large or small, according to the stature of him who is dead. If they can get hard liquor to drink they do so in honor of the dead and call it 'the blessed wine.' If the deceased was rich or well-to-do, they sacrifice and slaughter reindeer in his memory one, two, or three years after his death, and bury the bones down in the earth in like manner. Through the right ear of this reindeer which is sacrificed a piece of black thread is sewn."

CHAPTER XII

PAGANISM AND SUPERSTITION

MANY of the pagan beliefs and superstitions of the Lapps are of Scandinavian origin; some may have come from the Finns. There are also, as one should expect, traits which the Lapps had in common with the Samoyeds and other northern border-peoples in European Russia and Siberia. It would be precipitate to think that everything that the Lapps have had in common with the Scandinavians is due to Scandinavian influence. Dag Strömbäck may be right in supposing that the shamanistic practices which are known from Old Norse literary sources by the name of *seiðr* are an instance of Lapp influence on the Norwegians in the Viking age. It is well known that the ancient Norwegians regarded the Lapps as their masters in sorcery, and that people were reported to have visited Lapp wizards (which was explicitly forbidden by law) not only to consult them, but also to learn the trade from them. If we assume (as Gustav Neckel and Strömbäck have suggested) that the shaman drum was used by Norse magicians, it seems natural to ascribe this to Lapp influence. On the other hand, this and other traits may well be survivals from an ancient community of ideas which in prehistoric times comprised most of the northern half of the European-Asiatic continent, as has been shown by Uno Holmberg-Harva.

Is there still anything left of the pagan religion of the Lapps? Yes and no. No pagan gods are worshipped, but old superstitious beliefs and practices still exist among the Lapps as well as among the settled population of many rural districts in Scandinavia.

137

In 1844 Lars Levi Laestadius wrote a polemic preface to the second part of his "Lapp Mythology,"[1] in which he said that he did not know of any remnants of paganism among the Lapps and he did not believe in the rumors that magic drums were still to be found in Lappland. He added that the Lapps were not more superstitious or credulous than the rural population in the neighborhood of Stockholm who believed that the freemasons used to eat children. About a hundred years later there was a controversy in the Swedish newspaper *Svenska Dagbladet* on the same topic, and the arguments were much the same. It seems that Laestadius was not well informed about magic drums, because there is good evidence of drums having been used in southern Lappland and Jämtland at least forty years after Laestadius wrote his mythology.

In this context I think we have to distinguish not only between religion and superstition, but also between theoretical and practical superstition. In 1943 it was mentioned as an evidence of pagan cult that Lapps occasionally had put big sums of money in the alms bag. I would not call that paganism. I suppose these were votive offerings, given because of a promise made in mortal danger. A few decades ago it occurred that such votive offerings were not put into the alms bag, but in a joint in the floor of the church. This is superstition, but is it contrary to the Christian religion? There is no doubt but that certain rocks were smeared with reindeer fat in order to promote the trade of reindeer breeding at Laestadius's time, and reindeer antlers, indeed entire reindeer, were immolated at a much later epoch. But even in these days there are professors who will spit three times when they cross the path of a black cat!

Johan Turi was of the opinion that archeologists had caused a good deal of adversity to reindeer breeding in Jukkasjärvi by taking coins and other things from ancient tombs. They should have left something there instead, as Mrs. Demant-Hatt did. On the shore of a lake in Arvidsjaur there is a pyramid-shaped stone to which the Lapps earlier used to sacrifice. Some fifty years ago a Lapp fisherman, who

[1] Manuscript in Yale University Library.

had been unsuccessful in his fishing, hit the idol with his oar and decapitated it. It is not easy to say whether he believed in the idol or not.

In a village in the parish of Gällivare a farmer of Lapp extraction, who was born in 1840, told me about his grandfather who lived at the time of the American Revolutionary War. He was the first Lapp in Gällivare to buy a Bible and he was active in fighting against paganism. At that time there was a stone idol near Lake Sakajärvi. People used to sacrifice to that idol, and women were not allowed to approach it. The man who owned the Bible openly defied the idol and one day he resolutely turned it upside down. But the idol was still so influential that the man got a fit of mental aberration and did not recover for a whole year. I had the impression that my informant believed every word he said.

In the summer of 1943, during an excursion in the mountain region of northwestern Jämtland, I was one day accompanied by an old nomad Lapp. As we rested near a small lake the old man told me that once many years ago when he was tending his reindeer, he took a rest at exactly the same place. Having fallen asleep, he was awakened by a voice telling him that the reindeer herd had escaped. He woke up just in time to be able to overtake the herd. He did not see the being that had warned him, but he knew that it must have been one of the fairy people, who live under the earth, but otherwise live in the same way as human beings. He told me a little more about those fairy people. He and his wife once had happened to pitch their tent just where a subterranean family lived, and the subterraneans did not like that. Once he had seen one of those fairy people with his own eyes. It was an old man, dressed as the peasants of Jämtland were in olden time, wearing yellow breeches and a red woolen cap. He had big dark eyes and a strange, almost lunatic look. All of a sudden he disappeared. That much my informant told me about the fairy people, and then he added: "But you see, there are people who tell all kinds of stories about the fairy people, even such things as are not true."

139

In the same summer in Arvidsjaur I had a phonograph record about a Lapp woman who lived not very long ago and who had tended in her own herd reindeer belonging to the thunder god and I was also told what the earmark of those reindeer was like. Now the question arises whether my informant believed this story. I cannot tell.

When the Finnish linguist Arvid Genetz visited the Kola peninsula in 1876 there was still so much left of the old mythology of the Lapps that he could get a list of no less than sixteen divinities, not to speak of such minor deities as the spirit of the house (or the tent), water spirits, and mountain spirits. But among these divinities we recognize Christ and the Virgin Mary in disguise, and also Saint Gabriel appears as the "secretary" of Christ. *Tava(j)*, the god of fishing and hunting, is according to Genetz identical with Saint Stephen or with the Finnish forest god *Tapio*. Number sixteen in the list of gods and goddesses is, in all probability, the genius of the magic drum, no doubt a relatively late creation. A divinity called *Sied-vun* was, according to Genetz's informants, the uncle of Christ (a brother of Christ was also a member of the Kola-Lapp Olympus), but Genetz thinks that we have to deal here with the mother-in-law of *Sieide*, the Lappish word for a stone idol.

A few of the divinities mentioned by Genetz may be old, as *Tīrmes*, the god of thunder (Finnmark Lappish *dierbmes*) and *Rāz-ajk*, "the grass-mother." The latter was important to reindeer breeding, and Professor Lid may be right in identifying her with the *Rananieida* of Swedish Lappland, who was the goddess of the fresh verdure of spring.

The information gathered by Genetz is scanty, but it is valuable because he got it at a time when Lapp paganism was dying away. Most of what we know about the divinities of the Lapps comes from the reports of Norwegian and Swedish missionaries who lived at the beginning of the eighteenth century. The most successful investigator in this field was the famous Norwegian clergyman Thomas von Westen. He brought about a true religious awakening among the Lapps, and he was a skilful confessor. He was one of those Christians of the old stock who believed not only in God but also in the Devil. To his mind the pagan gods were real; they were evil spirits doing the work of the father of all Evil. Using an old method which in our days is erroneously ascribed to Sigmund Freud, he healed the contrite hearts of his converts by making them confess all their previous errors. At the same time he had a scientific mind and he collected a good deal of material for a treatise on Lapp paganism which never was written. Most of the old sources of our knowledge of the pagan religion of the Lapps have been published recently by Qvigstad and Reuterskiöld.

It is not my task here to define the notion of religion, but it is important to distinguish as far as possible between religion and magic. Religion is an emotional attitude towards a subjective reality (i.e. something that is thought of as being real) which is outside the regular course of events constituting our daily life. Religious worship tends to influence beings or "powers" more or less unknown or inaccessible to our daily experience. Religion is a metaphysical state of mind whether you look at it with the eyes of the devout believer or with the eyes of the infidel. On the other hand, magic in its typical form has a metaphysical character only as looked upon from outside. Hypnotism was a magic practice until it was authorized by medical science and assimilated with the stock of common knowledge. To stanch blood without touching the wound (or even without being in the presence of the wounded person) is regarded by some people as a magic practice, but some people think that it is no more magic than killing a dog by potassium cyanide. As a matter of fact no one can account for the psycho-physical mechanism of hypnotic influence, nor can anyone explain how it comes about that a simple chemical compound of carbon, nitrogen, and potassium infallibly paralyses the organs of respiration. To the mind of the child and the philosopher our whole life is full of miracles. The average adult takes everything for granted as soon as he has got accustomed to it and rejects everything that does not fit in with the stock of ideas which he has accepted once and for all.

141

In 1687, the Lapps of Lule Lappmark stated in the court of justice that

". . . because their forefathers have had such superstitions, they have also followed and observed their customs in this respect; and they confessed that (1) they have until now used drums, but they have not done any evil with them, but used them only to make out what bad or good would happen to them, and what success they were going to have with their traps and fishing tackle, and animals; (2) that they have sacrificed on their old places and in the same way as their forefathers have done, namely, first, to Thor, or the thunder, whose images they have formed of wood with axes, as best they could, and then erected them on their old sacrificial places. (3) The Lapps said that some of them have searched out, in order to worship them as idols, stones which are of a peculiar shape or resemble some rational or irrational being, and then they have erected such stones or images at their sacrificial places, pretending (4) that some of them are Thor's sons and some are Thor's man-servants, and to them they used to offer especially the antlers of their reindeer bucks which they slaughter in the autumn, and they have also (5) sacrificed the bones of other animals, according to the indications of the drum, such as foals, pigs, hens, he-goats, sheep, etc. They do not have these animals at their dwelling-places, and they have to travel a long way to Norway and elsewhere to negotiate and buy such animals. (6) The Lapps also said that some of them had made offerings of the blood of the killed animals, pouring it into birch-bark baskets which they deposit at their usual places of sacrifice. (7) The Lapps also confessed that they always have, in accordance with the conviction of their forefathers, commemorated and honored the old sacrificial god Thor with plentiful offerings to the end that he should give them fair weather. (8) They have also made offerings to the dead, in the simple belief and intention that such dead people should not so soon abduct them or take them to their tombs. (9) Some of them have also offered to the evil Satan, lest he cause them any damage according to his power. (10) Others have also offered to the Sun, the Moon, and the elements. Now the Lapps were asked whether they all are equally implicated in this, or only some of them, who have not yet been wholly converted to the Christian faith. To this most of them answered "yes" so loudly that their murmur drowned the voices of the others, namely, the Jockmock and Sjoksjock Lapps, who live nearer to the church and have given up their idolatry."

It may be that this record gives the essential of the pagan cult of the Lapps. They worshipped the thunder, the sun, the moon, and the "elements," that is to say the earth, the water, and the air.

The thunder god has been known and worshipped under several names in all Lapp regions, and he is perhaps the only one of the old gods who has survived up to these days in popular tradition. Probably the Lapps worshipped him before they came to Fennoscandia. When they became acquainted with the Thor of the Scandinavians, they identified him with their own *Dierbmes*. The *Horagalles* of the southern Lapps is nothing else than Old Man Thor. (The Lappish word *galles*, "old man," is an old Scandinavian loan-word, identical with Old Norse *karl*, "old man"; incidentally, English *churl* and Scottish *carl* is the same word.) Samuel Rheen says that the Lapps thought that Thor's office was "to kill and slay all trolls, which they believed to be everywhere in the mountains and in the lakes, and pictured him therefore holding a hammer in his hand. This hammer they called Thor's hammer, and the rainbow they called Thor's bow, with which he would slay all trolls who might want to harm them. This same Thor they also invested with power over men's health and well-being, life and death. Therefore all Lapps dread to hear the sound of thunder." Rheen says that the Lapps made images of Thor; they made the head of a birch root and the rest of the stem of the birch. They erected the images on a kind of altar or table, six feet high, behind the tent. When they sacrificed to Thor, there should be one image for each reindeer they offered. On the drawing which Rheen presents there are four

143

images. Three of them have a hammer in each hand. It has been supposed that this trait belongs to an earlier stage of Scandinavian Thor worship than that which we know from Snorri Sturluson and other Icelandic authors.

When Rheen says that the second of the gods of the Lapps is *Storjunkaren* (this was a recent Scandinavian word, which might be rendered by "His Excellency"), he is not quite to the point. Without being too sophisticated we can safely assert that there was only one Thor, even if he could be represented by many images at the same sacrificial place, whereas *Storjunkare* means a local genius or spirit (connected in one way or other with a mountain, a lake, or some other locality), impersonated by a rock or stone. In a word, *Storjunkaren* is hardly anything else than the *sieide,* which we shall soon account for.

The third god of the Lapps, according to Rheen, is the Sun. They think that she is the mother of all animals. To her they offer young reindeer, preferably does. A white thread is sewn through the ear of the victim to show that it belongs to the Sun. From other sources we know that the thread was only a poor substitute; the best offering was a white reindeer. Having slaughtered the reindeer, they cut a slice of flesh from each of its limbs and put all the slices on a slender (birch?) twig, "as wide as a half barrel-hoop," which they hang on the same altar on which they sacrifice to Thor. The principal bones are arranged in a circle on the altar.

According to other authors, the Lapps used to offer to the Sun a ring made of wood, with a handle on it. The ring should be kept so that the Sun could shine through it. A similar object was offered to the Moon, but this was rather a disc with a small round hole in it than a ring.

In 1946 an Enontekiö Lapp gave Dr. Toivo Itkonen the following information about Sun worship. At the beginning of February, when the Sun began to be visible for a considerable part of the day, the housewife baked a little round loaf, a little bigger than a (coffee) saucer, of flour, reindeer blood, and reindeer fat, with a hole near to its edge, and fixed it on the outside of the tent above the door as an offering to the Sun, which was then greeted by singing

144

on the part of all the inmates of the tent. This offering was good for the reindeer breeding.

We are told that a hundred years ago the Skolt Lapps used to say after sunset: "Now the god is not visible any more."

A peculiar form of Moon worship has recently been practised among the Skolt Lapps. Antti Hämäläinen relates how a Suonikylä (Suenjel) Lapp "let the Moon loose" when there was a moon eclipse in 1936. He took a kettle in his left hand, and watching the moon intently, he beat the kettle three times with a poker. "Do not beat a fourth time," he warned Mr. Hämäläinen, "for then it goes wrong!"

Now to the "elements": earth, water, and air. It is obvious that the ancient Lapps offered to their *sieides*, in order to influence the hunting grounds and grazing grounds. No doubt they worshipped certain localities. But whatever the *sieide* may have been to them, it was not a god on the same level as *Dierbmes*, the thunder-god.

We are also told about a "Water-man" (*Čacc-olmai*) and a "Wind-man" (*Biegga-olmai*); both received sacrifices. They may have represented the two elements water and air respectively, but little is known of them.

The Lapps have a generic word for god: *Ibmel*. This may be a Finnish loan-word, and the notions which it stands for may be relatively recent acquirements.

Ibmel marks the highest stage in the religious development of the Lapps. The most primitive stage, as far as theology is concerned, is the belief in so-called momentary gods. According to a local tradition, the Lapps of Sompio (a region in Kemi lappmark, where the Lappish language became extinct in the nineteenth century) were so modest in their choice of gods that they regarded as their god the first object they saw when they came out of the tent in the morning, whether it was a stone, a stump, or anything. The following day the Lapp had another god, depending on what he happened to meet in the morning. As Erik Daunius has remarked, this tradition is corroborated by the explicit statements of Ziegler, Damianus, and Olaus Magnus, referring to the Lapps in general.

145

CHAPTER XIII

SHAMANISM AND ECSTASY

ONCE when the nomads of southern Lappland were told to deliver their magic drums to the Swedish authorities, a mischievous Lapp excused himself saying that the Lapps needed their drums on their migrations because they used them instead of compasses. This was not a complete fabrication. Earlier, at least in some regions, there was a drum in each household, and it was frequently used as an instrument of divination, for instance when one wished to know about the presumable result of a hunting expedition. I suppose that such a procedure was not much more extraordinary to the mind of the Lapps than it is to us if we phone a meteorological station in order to get a weather prognosis. No doubt the situation was essentially different if somebody was dangerously ill and one had to consult a sorcerer and ask him to go to the kingdom of death and fight for the life of the patient. There was something extraordinary and incalculable about such an enterprise, and it was loaded with emotion. On the other hand we must keep in mind that the modern town dweller's feeling of being sheltered in an environment where everything is clear and evident is a recent phenomenon. When Luther suggested that there might be a devil on every tile in Worms, he spoke half in jest and half in earnest. Even a few generations ago the rural population of Scandinavia were fully convinced of the existence of more or less unknown powers which influenced their daily life and which one had to be careful with. In this respect the Lapps constitute no exception, and they even shared most of the superstitions of their settled neighbors.

146

Shamanism was the most striking feature of Lapp paganism and the Lapp shamans were renowned in Scandinavia as early as the viking period. In *Historia Norvegiae,* a Norwegian chronicle from the thirteenth century, there is a detailed account of a shamanistic séance. Some Norwegian merchants, during a sojourn among the Lapps, one day at mealtime saw how their housewife suddenly died. A sorcerer then brought forth an object which looked like a sieve, on which were pictured a whale, a reindeer with a sleigh, and a boat with oars. Having sung and danced, he fell down with black face and with slobbering mouth; his belly burst and he died. Now another sorcerer was consulted, and he succeeded in bringing the housewife back to life. She told them that the first sorcerer had started in the shape of a whale, but another spirit had changed into a sharp-pointed pole and pierced the belly of the whale. According to Professor Harva, this story probably reflects an early stage in the development of the magic drum of the Lapps.

In spite of the zeal of the Swedish authorities in destroying the magic drums, about eighty drums have been preserved up to our days. These have been photographed and described by Ernst Manker in a splendid *Corpus.*

The frame of the magic drum is made of wood. The membrane is elliptic or oval. The wooden frame had either the shape of a shallow bowl or it was shaped like the wooden frame of a sieve. The former kind is usually called the bowl-drum; the latter, which seems to have been more widely used and presumably is the older model, is called the sieve-drum. The sieve-drum has a straight handle fixed to the inside of the frame; the bowl-drum has two parallel slits so that the piece of wood left between them can serve as a handle. The membrane is made of reindeer shammy; according to a tradition preserved in Jämtland up to our time, the skin should be taken from a fawn born by a one year old doe. According to another tradition it was taken from a *stainak* (a sterile doe). On the membrane a good many figures were drawn with alder-bark juice (or reindeer blood?), some of them more or less realistic, others schema-

147

tic or symbolic. There are pictures of (or symbols for) people, reindeer, dogs, the sun, the moon, different divinities, a church, and so on. On the sieve-drums the sign of the sun is usually found in the middle of the membrane. The membrane of the bowl-drums was usually divided by one or more transversal lines into segments, which seemed to symbolize the main parts of the universe (heaven, earth, etc.). The sieve-drums used to be decorated with chains, leaves of silver or bronze, and leather thongs wound with thin thread. The drum was beaten with a T-shaped hammer made of reindeer horn. To the drum there belongs also a triangular piece of reindeer horn or a brass ring (or more rings tied together) or a similar object. This functioned as an "indicator" when the drum was used as an instrument of divination.

Among the Samoyeds and other Siberian tribes the shaman-drum seems to have been used almost only as an instrument of excitation. The same was probably the case with the Lapps in prehistoric time and perhaps as late as the thirteenth century. For this purpose the figures on the membrane, if there were any, obviously were immaterial. The shaman (Lappish *noaide*) beat the drum and sang incantations till he got into a state of ecstatic delirium. After a while he was completely exhausted and fell to the ground in a state of torpor, which lasted for a considerable time, perhaps for many hours. During that time it was considered to be of vital importance that he was not disturbed, not even by a fly. One of the persons present at the performance was probably charged with the task of calling the sorcerer back to life in case of emergency. Having risen from his recumbent position, the *noaide* professed to have visited some distant place in this or another world. He could during his trance move in the shape of a certain animal (for instance a whale, as in the story which I have quoted from the *Historia Norvegiae*) or alternately take the shape of different animals. Such animals (a bear, wolf, reindeer, pike, or burbot) were called the "companions" of their respective *noaide*. But everybody could have such a companion without being a sorcerer. When a man had died the companion might appear to one of his

148

sons and offer him his services, threatening to tear him into pieces if the offer were not accepted. As Harva has remarked, the ancient Scandinavians had the same conception of supernatural companions (Old Norse *fylgja*, plural *fylgjur*), as well as some Siberian tribes. Among the Skolt Lapps, Harva has noted traits which remind one of totemism. Among them a whole family frequently has a species of animal as their common companion. "If somebody sees a sheep in a dream this is supposed to forebode the arrival of a Feodotov, and if this sheep appears to be in distress, then this means that some danger threatens a Feodotov. There is the same relationship between the horse and the family Letov." There are good companions and evil companions. An evil companion can be sent to harass other people or even kill them. There has also been a taboo against eating animals of one's companion-species. The *noaides* are able to send their "companions" to fight each other.

It seems that two different motifs have amalgamated into the traditional conception of the "companions" of the noaides. One is the *fylgja* notion; the other is the belief that the sorcerer could transform himself into any animal in order to move on the surface of the earth, in the water, or in the air, in order to attain his aims.

When the drum was used for divination, the *noaide* started beating the drum so that the "indicator" moved to and fro on the membrane. He went on beating till, *mirabile dictu,* the indicator stopped moving and stayed obstinately on one spot. The figure on which the indicator stayed gave the clue to the solution of the problem. If the sorcerer had been consulted because of a case of illness, for instance, then the position of the indicator showed the source or origin of the disease (an essential circumstance from the viewpoint of therapy), which divinity one ought to propitiate, what kind of sacrifice one should bring, and so on. The drum could answer almost any question, because its membrane was a kind of microcosm or a magic world map.

Johan Fritzner has remarked that the use which the Lapps have made of the magic drum as an instrument of divination to some degree resembles the so-called coscinomancy or divination with a sieve.

In Russian Karelia coscinomancy has been used in order to diagnose a disease. A sieve was put upside down above a bread, after the names of the diseases which one might suspect, had been written on the frame. As indicator one used a small crucifix which one hung on a thread above the sieve.

In a Finnish incantation the indicator is addressed as follows: "If the illness is mortal, then move clockwise; if it is caused by a curse, then move counter-clockwise; if it comes from the water, then go to the lake, if it comes from the earth, then go northward."

Leaving the *bona fide* question out of the discussion, it seems safe to say that the magic drum of the Lapps is a highly developed form of a widespread type of implement of divination. It is related to such a simple device as an axe hung at the end of a rope on the smokepole to indicate the direction in which somebody has disappeared, and the like.

Among some Siberian tribes the shamans used to eat fly agaric (*Agaricus muscaria,* also called *Amanita muscaria*) to intoxicate themselves. There is little evidence of intoxicating stimulants having been used by Lapp *noaides.* In Lappland as in Siberia it was essential that the shaman should be a psychopath, in so far as he was not a mere hypocrite. This was no secret to Tornaeus:

"Some of them are instructed in this craft and become masters by practice, but some of them have it from nature, and this is horrible. For when those whom the devil has chosen for his instruments fall sick in their childhood, then in this state of weakness they have a series of melancholic visions, of which they absorb and keep more or less according to their disposition. If they fall sick once again, new visions appear to them, and they keep more of them than they did the first time. And if they are attacked by illness a third time, then it comes with such a vehemence that it is almost a question of life and death. Then they see all kinds of hellish visions and apparitions, and they grasp and keep so much as is necessary to become a past master in sorcery." Such a morbid disposition may of course be inherited. But if the shaman profession often has been handed over from father to son through several generations, this may partly be due to the influence of the tradition and the whole milieu.

Harva and other scholars think that shamanism is closely connected with the so-called Arctic hysteria, which is so frequent among northern tribes on the European-Asiatic continent. This phenomenon is not restricted to the arctic zone. Kretschmer says (quoted after Äimä): "The same psychomotoric phenomena that appear in the strong and sound civilized man only under the influence of a sudden extreme emotion are evoked in certain individuals with an unstable nervous disposition already by much smaller irritation, so that in the most extreme cases of hysteric degeneration even the smallest everyday emotion . . . suffices to start the most intense uncontrollable mechanisms."

The phenomenon described by Tornaeus has been called "Lapp panic" by the Swedes. Nowadays it is chiefly known from Russian Lappland. The Fisher Lapps of Inari used to tell stories about the Skolt women, who are so silly and so easily scared. The panic of the Skolt women is partly rooted in superstition. If a Skolt woman is frightened by a sudden cry, she may think that a bear is going to attack her (they even seem to think that a bear can appear in the shape of a man). Incidentally, this explains the "exhibitionist" gesture mentioned by Tornaeus (see Chapter XVIII, p. 223); it is known from different parts of Lappland that this gesture makes the bear ashamed and that he will not easily attack a woman if he can help it.

From Swedish Lappland as well as from the Kola peninsula it has been reported that such fits may befall women who have been frequently harassed and frightened by mischievous boys. This nervous disposition must have been more widely spread in old times than it is now. According to Högström it appeared in men and women alike. He says that some Lapps are so easily scared that they suddenly swoon or behave as if they were out of their wits, and he continues:

"In the churches it has not only occurred that one has found the whole crowd in a swoon, but it has also happened that some of them have suddenly risen to their feet and started beating their neighbors. I have seen some Lapps behave in the same way in their tents when somebody has suddenly screamed, or a piece of live coal crackles. When they are thus frightened, they will jump to their feet, and do not mind if they have a knife or an axe in their hands, but hit the person who is next to them. I have also seen some of them imitate any quaint gesture of other people. If somebody else has twisted his mouth, pointed with a finger, danced or the like, they do all that in the same way; and when it is over they will ask whether they have behaved indecently, because they say that they do not know what they have been doing."

It appears from Högström's description that collective (or shall we say contagious?) fits of ecstasy were sometimes called forth by the sermon against the intentions of the preacher, and that in Högström's opinion this phenomenon was characteristic of the Lapps. This leads us to ask whether the ecstatic transports or "motions" (Finnish *liikutukset*, or *liikutuksia*) of the Laestadians have anything to do with arctic hysteria. It is worth noting that the western branch of Laestadianism, which is more extreme than the eastern branch, is chiefly restricted to Lappland. On the other hand, ecstasy is a fairly normal ingredient in religious awakenings, and so it has been since St. Paul wrote his first epistle to the Corinthians. But there is no doubt but that Laestadius provoked the "movements" intentionally and included them in the ritual of his community. I have witnessed such scenes among western Laestadians several times, and I have the impression that they regard a religious meeting as a failure if it does not end in ecstasy. During a sermon one can even feel it in the air when the ecstasy is approaching. Not from the behavior of the audience, because the ecstasy, when it appears, comes all of a sudden; but from the behavior of the preacher. When he begins to speak of the garden of Gethsemane, then one knows what he is driving at.

When I say that the ecstasy comes suddenly I do not mean to say that the whole audience rises simultaneously. On the contrary, I think that there is usually a single woman who starts before all the others; then other sisters and brothers rise one by one, till the excitement has spread so widely that it is impossible to get a survey of all the details. But in the behavior of each individual there seem to be no intermediary stages. An old man who is sitting motionless with a stolid look as if this pious pandemonium did not concern him in the least may in the next moment be seen in the middle of the room with his arm around the neck of a brother or a sister, singing or shouting in visible exaltation. One shifts abruptly from the rigid passivity of an ordinary Scandinavian churchgoer to dervish-like gesticulation and speaking with tongues. The excitement of the believers is so intense that it may influence even an uninterested outsider. But there you see the preacher standing calm and firm, pressing one sinner after the other to his bosom. Frankly and openly they confess their adulteries and reindeer thefts in the presence of the community, but nobody can hear what they say in the roaring confusion. There is a climax in the general excitement, but no fading away. It comes to a sudden end, as if all the partakers had sobered in the same moment. The ecstasy is gone with the wind— nobody speaks of it, nobody thinks of it, it is as if it never had been there. A few minutes later the preacher sits at the supper table, joking with the women and talking about profane things. Or people will sit in the tent drinking coffee; and if it should happen that a single old woman still goes on with her "movements," they do not pay more attention to her than they would if she were a humming bumble-bee.

CHAPTER XIV

TABOO AND THE BEAR

ETHNOLOGY, like charity, should begin at home. Ethnologists are apt to neglect the very field which they know best, because they dig a gulf between ourselves and primitive man, between our society and the so-called inferior societies. Our society is not superior in every respect to all the other societies, and if you make a detailed inventory of the ideas of Mr. John Q. Citizen you will find a good many primitive things which might be interesting to an ethnologist. We see the ivory ring in the nose of the Senegambian Negro chieftain, but we do not see the silk ribbon on the breast of the European diplomat. In dealing with the superstitions of the Lapps we should keep in mind that most of them are more or less identical with the superstitions of our forefathers.

In the *Norse Mythology* of Snorri Sturluson we are told that the thunder god Thor, when he was traveling, sometimes slaughtered the he-goats which he used as draught animals and ate them for supper. The bones were thrown on the hides of the he-goats, and nobody was allowed to break a single bone. Once it happened that one of his guests split one of the thighbones with his knife and ate the marrow. In the next morning Thor flourished his hammer over the hides and the bones, and the he-goats returned to life; but one of them was a little lame on one of its hind legs. Thor got very angry, and it was not easy to propitiate him.

Snorri, who lived and wrote in the thirteenth century, did not believe in Thor or his practices. But the Lapps are so conservative that almost up to our time they have kept customs which seem to reflect the pagan belief in the resur-

154

rection of certain animals. As late as the beginning of the eighteenth century, and perhaps much later, some Lapps at least were particular about keeping intact the bones of the reindeer which were eaten in the honor of a *sieide* or a deceased relative. This ritual reflects a primitive form of the belief in the perseverance of life and the resurrection of the dead. A thousand years ago or earlier our forefathers and the forefathers of the Lapps thought that a living being that was loaded with an extraordinary power might return from death to life. There was such power in sacrificial animals, as in everything that was connected with a god.

Magic power is, by definition, dangerous. It may have beneficial effects, but it may also hurt and damage. Those who can be hurt by it had better keep out of its way.

Among many peoples adult women have been regarded as "unclean," especially during menstruation, and still more so when they were going to bear or had just born a child. In the twelfth chapter of Leviticus we read: "If a woman have conceived seed, and born a man child: then she shall be unclean for seven days; according to the days of separation for her infirmity she shall be unclean. . . . And she shall then continue in the blood of her purifying three and thirty days; she shall touch no hallowed thing, nor come into the sanctuary, until the days of her purifying be fulfilled. But if she bear a maid child, then she shall be unclean two weeks, as in her separation; and she shall continue in the blood of her purifying three score and six days. And when the days of her purifying are fulfilled, for a son, or for a daughter, she shall bring a lamb of the first year for a burnt offering, and a young pigeon, or a turtle dove, for a sin offering, unto the door of the tabernacle of the congregation, unto the priest; who shall offer it before the Lord, and make an atonement for her; and she shall be cleansed from the issue of her blood."

The passage which I have just quoted is the origin of the custom of "churching" women after a childbirth. In the Swedish church this custom is now obsolete, except in the diocese of Göteborg. It was preserved for centuries after its magic background had disappeared.

To the minds of the pagan Lapps the women were "unclean" under all circumstances, as far as sacrifices were concerned. (At the ecstatic performances of the *noaides* they might be present without disadvantage.) They were not admitted to the holy places. Even the big game, at least the bear, was too holy for them. The boiling of bear meat was a prerogative of the men, and according to some sources the women were not allowed to be present when it was boiled. The reason for this prohibition was that there was in the bear a power which might be fatal to the women. Up to our time all the boiling of meat has been the task of the head of the family or a man-servant to whom he has delegated his competence. It may be that this division of labor has likewise a sacral origin.

"Blood is a quite peculiar juice" (*Blut ist ein ganz besondrer Saft*), says Mephistopheles in Goethe's *Faust*. The Lapps used to smear their wooden idols with blood when they sacrificed, according to some authors. We are also told that the alder-bark juice, which they used in certain magic ceremonies, was regarded as a kind of substitute for blood. The Lappish word for "alder," *laeibe,* also means the blood of the bear, and a woman's menstrual blood. The Norwegian missionaries were told by the Lapps that the ceremonies with alder bark were performed in the honor of *Laeib-olmai,* "the alderman," who was the god of shooting (or hunting) and despised all women.

The bear was usually killed in the winter after he had gone into his winter lair, preferably in March or even in April. The man who had early in the winter traced the bear and "ringed in" the hibernating den, acquired by this achievement a right to the bear. But he could not be sure to kill the bear alone; and in old times, as nowadays, bear hunting was teamwork. In the opinion of the Lapps the killing of the bear required more than pluck and physical dexterity. Before one started on such a portentous expedition, one had first to consult the magic drum in order to make out whether one was going to have good luck. If the drum gave a bad prognosis one had better stay at home. Then one should have as little as possible to do with the "unclean" sex before starting. (This is a superstition which the Lapps shared with their settled neighbors; even nowadays Scandinavian and Finnish gentlemen feel unhappy if they meet an old woman on their way to the hunting grounds.) One should avoid mentioning the bear by his real name. This was good policy even in everyday life, but it was of vital importance when one was hunting.

We shall dwell a little on this point. The old Romans spoke of the "wolf in the fable" (*lupus in fabula*), alluding to the popular tradition that the wolf would suddenly appear when somebody mentioned its name. Such ideas are known from many peoples in different parts of the world. They belong to the class of ideas which modern ethnologists characterize by the Polynesian term *taboo*. Taboo is a kind of prohibition or restraint concerning certain beings or things. This prohibition may imply that the name of the being or thing in question cannot be mentioned without momentous consequences. The Polynesians call forbidden things (objects of restraint) *taboo*, whereas profane nonrestricted things are *noa*. This nomenclature has been adopted by modern ethnologists and linguists. Thus, when the adherents of the Mosaic religion read *Adonai* ("my Lord") for the *Yahveh* (YHVH) of the Old Testament, we say that to them *Yahveh* is taboo, whereas *Adonai* is the corresponding noa word. The names of some animals in English are, historically speaking, noa substitutes for words that have been tabooed in the course of time. Thus, *bear* from the beginning no doubt meant "the brown one." In the hunters' jargon there are a good many noa substitutes, not only for animals, but also for different parts of the body of big game. The Lapps have driven this taboo system very far. Fifteen hundred years ago they apparently thought that the bear understood Lappish, but not Scandinavian, and therefore they used a hunting nomenclature which we recognize as being partly of Scandinavian origin: the foot of the bear was called *fuotte*, the nose *nasek*, the intestines *garnok* (Primitive Scandinavian *garnu,* Old Norse *görn* "intestines," the same word as English *yarn*).

Many noa words are doomed to be ephemeral in their

noa function. Any designation of the wolf may prove dangerous in the long run if it is used every day. Many centuries ago the Lapp hunters started calling the bear *bierdna* (Primitive Scandinavian *bernu*), and in many Lappish dialects the old name *guowža* has disappeared. But as time went on, the bear became acquainted with his noa name, and the Lapp hunters had to call him (in Lappish or Scandinavian jargon) "grandfather of the hill" (or simply "grandfather"), "the wintersleeper," "the goodtempered beast," "the thick fur," "the woolly one," etc.

It is small wonder that the Lapps had a high opinion of the bear at a time when there were no firearms. The bear is bigger, stronger, and wiser than all the other animals; at the same time he is very swift and nimble. He can climb trees, and he can walk on two feet like a man. His habit of sleeping during the winter is so extraordinary that there seems to be something supernatural about it. And yet an expert Lapp bear hunter did not fear the strength and dexterity of the individual bear. When the bear was roused from its sleep and came out through the narrow opening of its den, drowsy and bewildered, the hunter had to direct his spear towards the breast of the beast and keep it steadily, pressing the shaft end to the ground and avoiding the grip of the approaching bear. This was a dangerous job, but if he should fail, there were companions present to come to his assistance. The real danger came from the invisible (magic) power which was inherent in every bear. We risk rationalizing the ideas of the ancient Lapps too much if we say that they thought that the bear had a genius or guardian spirit. They did not distinguish sharply between the individual and the species. No doubt in their incantations they invoked the species or the invisible power which was inherent in all the individuals, but they could not help addressing, after the successful hunting expedition, the very sample which they had just killed. When they wanted the bear to come back to be killed again (a wording which they carefully avoided), did they mean that the very same individual bear should return? I think it would be a psychological mistake to press this question.

Now let us return to the hunting ceremonial. We are told that the bear hunters went to the den in a solemn procession. First went the man who had "ringed in" the bear; he carried a staff with a brass ring at its end. (Brass was the sacral metal of the Lapps; almost all vessels and implements that had anything to do with the bear ritual should be made of brass, or at any rate they should be adorned with this metal.) Then came the sorcerer, and next came the man who was charged with the killing of the beast. There were also other distinguished functionaries, for instance the wood-carrier and the water-carrier necessary for the subsequent banquet.

When the procession had arrived at the den, two poles were fixed across the opening of the den in order to detain the bear on its way out, so that the spearman could have time to put his spear in position. The killing, as a rule, was routine work.

Having killed the bear, the hunters (or one of them?) sang a song in which they thanked him for having been gentle enough not to damage their spears. (Maybe they had before the killing asked the bear not to bite or claw the hunter, as the ancient Finns did according to the forty-sixth song of *Kalevala*.) Then they lashed the dead beast with twigs. The purpose of this obviously was to confer vital force upon the bear, to give him a kind of substitute or compensation for the life which he had been deprived of. The jocose habit of rousing the children in the morning of Easter Sunday by lashing them with a birch twig, which has survived up to these days in the Scandinavian countries even among the urban population, has the same magic background, namely the belief that the life-force which is inherent in budding twigs can be transferred to living beings. Professor Harva has cited a much more striking parallel: in a legend from Carinthia (in Austria) we are told that nocturnal ghosts, having slaughtered an ox, wrapped the hide of the animal around its bones and then lashed it with twigs, with the result that the ox returned to life.

The happy hunters also used to shake their spears at the dead bear and put their skis across it. By doing so they im-

159

proved their chances to be successful on later hunting expeditions. The killer would also wind a birch twig around the lower jaw of the bear, attach his belt to this ring, and then repeatedly jerk the beast from its position, singing a cheerful song all the time. It may be that this action was an alternative to the lashing.

The hunters covered the bear with spruce twigs, and leaving it on the spot till the following day, they went home. When they came near to the dwelling place, they sang a song about their feat. The women answered by singing a song, praising the bold hunters.

According to some sources, the man who had killed the bear should keep in his hand a whip plaited of birch twigs and beat with it thrice on the back entrance of the tent or hut. There is some obscurity in the tradition concerning this detail. Probably we have here to deal with the same twigs already mentioned in connection with the killing of the bear, and these twigs seem to have played an important role in the whole bear ceremonial almost from the beginning. The plait was handed over to one of the women (the wife of the killer?) and wrapped up in a linen cloth. During the festival it was decorated with brass leaves and the like. After the banquet the vertebrae of the bear were threaded on the plait in their natural order and then buried together with the other bones of the beast.

The hunters were not allowed to sleep with their wives until three days after they had killed the bear; for the leader of the hunting the celibacy lasted five days. And then they had to undergo a special purifying ceremony. Each of them should run around the hearth, imitating a bear, and when he ran out of the tent, his wife threw hot ashes after him.

In some regions at least, the men and the women ate the bear together, after the meat had been brought into the tent through the back entrance and cooked by one of the men, but there were several restrictions regarding the women. They were forbidden to eat certain parts of the bear, their portions had to be boiled in a separate kettle, and the pieces of boiled meat had to be handed over to them on wooden sticks. And according to a still more strict observance, the men raised a tent or hut for themselves, where they did all the cooking and spent all their time, day and night, as long as the festival lasted. Half-grown children were sent from the men's tent to bring the women their portions.

When the men returned from the hunting ground, the women had to spit alder-bark juice at them through a brass ring. As late as 1943 I interviewed in Arvidsjaur a ninety-two-year-old woman who had done so once when she was a girl of seventeen. This means that the old ritual was still practised at the time of the Franco-Prussian war. In the Oviken mountains in southern Jämtland there was a bear festival in 1885, and in 1942 I heard a Lapp from the same region sing the song which the bear hunters used to sing when they returned home, and the song with which the women used to receive them. The phonograph record of this performance is kept in the Dialect Archives of Uppsala. The old informant had made a tiresome trip in order to preserve this fragment of a dying tradition. He was so particular about keeping vulgar publicity away that he did not even allow me to let his own sister be present at the performance or hear about it.

The alder-bark juice was used (like the consecrated water in the Middle Ages) in order to protect people from noxious powers. The bear should be sprinkled or smeared with it, as well as the hunters, the hunting dogs, the reindeer which drew the bear home, the tent or hut where the bear was flayed, the children who brought the bear meat to the women, and even the women's portions.

The day after the hunting some of the hunters brought the bear to the dwelling place. On their way home they sang incantations. They had to avoid crossing the track of a woman, according to the strict observance. The draught reindeer which took the bear home should not be used by a woman till a year had passed.

Bear meat should not be stored, but everything should be consumed during the festival, which lasted three days. Fjellström says, that the first thing that was cooked was the blood, mixed with fat. We are also told that the hunters

161

used to smear themselves, their wives, and children and even the tent poles with the blood of the bear.

The bear meat was boiled and eaten without salt.

The dogs had to keep off when the bear was cut up. If a dog should pilfer one of the bones of the bear, this was a capital offence, and he had to deliver one of his own bones instead.

In cutting up the bear, the Lapps were careful not only to avoid breaking any bone, but also to keep the arteries and the big tendons intact as far as possible. The throat and the entrails were not separated from the head, and all this was boiled together after the meat had been consumed. The muzzle was cut off before the head was put into the kettle, and the man who flayed the bear's head was allowed to tie the muzzle to his face. (Did he impersonate the bear in the dramatic dialogue, which was included in the program?)

After the banquet, or after the last banquet, each of the women covered her face with a thick veil. Then the men bury the bones, the muzzle, the head, the genitalia, and the tailskin. Before the nose of the bear they put a conical birch-bark scoop, filled with chewed alder bark. (They did the same even before they flayed the bear.)

After the burial the bear's hide was put against a tree or a snowdrift, decorated with brass leaves and rings. The women came out of the tent with veiled face, and they were told to shoot with a bow or throw an alder bough at the hide (which they could not see). If the first woman who hit the hide was married, her husband was likely to be the next bear killer; if she was unmarried, then she would presumably marry a distinguished bear hunter.

The Voguls and the Ostyaks in the northwestern corner of Siberia, who speak Finno-Ugric languages, used to celebrate the killed bear by dramatic performances in which the beast acted as one of *dramatis personae*; and so did the Lapps. We have seen that the hunters addressed the bear when they had killed him; during the banquet they made him speak, even if they did not make him appear in visible shape. A handwritten record from the middle of the eighteenth century gives the whole dialogue as it was sung by

162

Lapps from Åsele Lappmark (southern Västerbotten), from the moment when the hunters come back and tell the women that they have killed the bear, to the end of the banquet. The dialogue consists of no less than forty-eight short paragraphs, each sung to its own melody. There are three speaking parties, namely the men, the women, and the bear. The text is given in corrupt Lappish (it is a pity that the recorder did not understand Lappish) and in Swedish translation. The bear, when he is introduced, first says: "I intended to go to my own place, but these boys overtook me." This was sung by the women. Then the bear is impersonated by the men, saying: "Now I am coming to the settled country from the wide forests where I have been hunting." So it goes on, till the bear says farewell (this time impersonated by the old men): "I withdraw with joy over mountains and hillsides."

CHAPTER XV

SACRIFICES

JOHAN TURI says in his book on the Lapps: "The animals, the trees, the rocks, and other things have lost the faculty of speech, but they have still the faculty of hearing and understanding." As far as the animals are concerned, Turi was right, but we would find it impossible to share his opinion with respect to the trees and the rocks. The basic difficulty is that we cannot imagine rocks as individuals. But under favorable circumstances we may become familiar with them, or even regard them with a feeling of mutual connection. The Swedish poet Verner von Heidenstam, in a nostalgic poem written when he was far from his native land, says that he does not long for any human beings, but for the soil and the stones:

Jag längtar marken, jag längtar stenarna
där barn jag lekt.

This frame of mind, so natural to anyone having a rural background, will make it easier to understand the attitude of the old time Lapps.

The existence of the fisherman depends on the sea or the lake. Sometimes the lake yields lavishly, sometimes it does not give anything. Is it not equitable that he should give some part of his take to the lake? A dissecting modern mind would object that this would be, at its best, a kind of pump priming. But to the uncomplicated primitive mind this difficulty does not appear. And besides, one may also give such things to the lake as it does not itself possess—pieces of bronze, silver, and the like.

The nomad, who drives his reindeer herd from one tract to another in a steady annual rhythm, feels indebted to the

164

pine-clad lichen grounds and the grassy mountain slopes which take care of his reindeer and feed them. Gift claims gift's return, and even reckoning keeps long friends. It seems natural to the nomad that he should now and then give a reindeer to the habitual calving place, or to the glacier where his reindeer used to cool and find refuge from the midges on hot summer days.

Such a customary gift or remuneration the old Lapps called *vaerro*. This word also means "tribute" or "tax." It is not quite to the point if we render *vaerro* by "sacrifice," "oblation," or "offering."

The offerings were presented to mountains, rocks, stones, growing trees, sculptured sticks, lakes, and wells. The sticks were clumsy representations of human beings; they may be of relatively recent origin. The stones were often of such a formation that they might remind one of a bird or a human being, but they might be of almost any form and size. Usually there was only one stone on each place of sacrifice, but there might also be a group of several bigger and smaller stones, as at the sacrificing place of Vidjakuoika in Jockmock, investigated by Eric von Rosen.

Under the holy stones there should always be a carpet of fresh birch twigs or spruce twigs.

It is fair to say that the entire institution of offering was centered on such rocks and stones and wooden sticks. In the northern part of Swedish Lappland such objects were called by the name *sieide*, and the same term has been used also in Finnmark and Russian Lappland.

It is not easy to say whether such stones should be regarded as gods (fetishes) or as representations of a spirit to which the offerings were presented. Probably both these interpretations are inadequate. The old Lapps did not distinguish between spirit and matter as we do. No doubt the stone was to their mind a kind of individual, but this does not mean that they worshipped it as a god. According to some sources, a rock might be inaugurated and invoked as the "god" of the sacrificer. Reuterskiöld thinks that the custom of offering sacrifices to rocks and stones was rooted in the belief that the power of a whole territory or locality could be concentrated in a prominent, protruding, or extreme part of it. Thus if a fisherman put the heads of captured fishes on a rock that was situated on the shore of the lake where he fished, or smeared the rock with the bloody entrails of the fish, it was because he felt indebted to the lake. According to some scholars, these offerings had their origin in the cult of the ancestors. No doubt the holy stones have in some regions been identified by the Lapps themselves with local geniuses or with the fairy people, and these categories of supernatural beings may at least to some extent have been identical with the dead or the ancestors. But the usual Lappish designation of the local geniuses is of Finnish origin, and some of the names of the fairy people are Scandinavian loan-words. Here we have no doubt to deal with foreign elements, which have been amalgamated with the primitive Lapp worship of fishing lakes, grazing grounds, and other localities.

It is no exaggeration to say that the *sieides* were worshiped. The Lapps are reported to have knelt down before the idol and even approached it on their knees. Some *sieides* were so powerful that women could not come in the neighborhood of the place of sacrifice without risking their life or their health.

The habit of worshiping or greeting rocks is not peculiar to the Lapps. Qvigstad has mentioned a few parallels from Norway, Iceland, and southern Sweden. The most striking case is "the Hill of the Prayer-god" (Bönegudens berg) in Östergötland, which men saluted by taking off their hat and women by courtseying.

The *sieide* has played an essential role in the religious life of the pagan Lapps. The places of sacrifice may have been innumerable. There were great and influential *sieides*, common to whole districts or communities, and there was perhaps a particular place of sacrifice for each single household. A single Lapp might have several objects of worship at different places. Qvigstad mentions one hundred and eighty-two holy mountains and rocks in Finnmark. There may have been three times as many two hundred years ago, because Qvigstad knows of eight holy mountains in Lyngen, and von Westen said there were twenty-four. Carl Johansson mentions forty-one from the three northernmost parishes of Swedish Lappland, and three hundred years ago, Rheen knew of thirty from Lule Lappmark. According to Jessen a certain Lapp in northernmost Jämtland owned thirteen sacred places, his wife had six, and their daughter had six of her own.

Many different kinds of sacrifices were brought to the *sieides*. The basic rule seems to have been that fish should be offered for fishing luck and reindeer for reindeer luck. As I have already suggested, this was rather a kind of natural tax than sympathetic magic. Rich reindeer owners used to give entire reindeer, preferably snow-white or soot-black bucks. Often the reindeer was buried alive so that only the antlers were visible above the earth. Wild reindeer were also sacrificed, probably to promote hunting luck. But the Lapps also applied a kind of sacrificial economy which is known all over the world. Instead of sacrificing a whole reindeer one might arrange a banquet at which the whole animal was eaten, and the *genius loci* got the bones, the antlers, the hide, and some tiny slices of the meat. If one was particular about not crushing any bones, there would sooner or later grow flesh on the bones.

There are also reports of cows and hens and other domesticated animals having been sacrificed by the Lapps, but it is not known how old and how widespread such habits have been.

There are also traditions about human sacrifices. Not far from the railway station Vassijaure on the railway Luleå-Narvik there is on the steep slope of the mountain Vassitjåkka a rock where a *noaide* called Kumin sacrificed his own son, according to a still living tradition.

Holy stones or rocks are often found where there is a holy mountain or a holy lake, or both. It also occurs that the *sieide* may be situated in the lake, in shallow water close to the shore. The holiness of the mountain in many instances appears from its name—*Bassevarre* (holy mountain) and the like. The mountain name *Akka, Akkavarre* may indicate a female divinity. In the southern Lappmarks (from Gäl-

167

livare southwards) the word *saiva* means a holy lake. In Gällivare the words *akka* and *saiva* (either, or both together) are of such a frequent occurrence in connexion with places of sacrifice that there can be no question of mere coincidence. The word *akka* means "old woman," and *akko* means "grandmother"; both words have been used in Finnmark as names of holy rocks. The same seems to have been the case in the Kola peninsula. This nomenclature may be of a profane origin. Even Swedes used to call big erratic boulders *Gubben* (the old man) or *Gumman* (the old woman), especially if there were two of them together. But the question is more complicated than that. Castrén says that the Lapps have worshipped *Aije* (*Aije, Aggja*, means "grandfather" and is one of the names of thunder and the god of thunder) in the shape of mountains, rocks, and lakes. He mentions a rock (or rocky islet) in Lake Inari, which has been regarded with religious veneration. Jacob Fellman, who once visited the place and ascertained that it was an old cult place, says that there was a big cave in the rock. According to a popular tradition there was a subterranean passage from this cave to another rock, called *Akko*, or "the dwelling of *Akko*." Fellman adds that Akko was the wife of the thunder god, and that the Lapps used to dedicate rocks and caves to her. They sacrificed to her by smearing the rock and the entrance of the cave with reindeer fat or fish fat.

The name of the thunder god was tabooed among the Lapps. The word *dierbmes, Tirmes*, which denotes "thunder" in Finnmark Lappish, and is (or was) the name of the thunder god among the Kola Lapps, has disappeared in most dialects. It may be that the old Lapps have regarded even the sobriquet *Aggja* as too transparent and thought it safer to deal with *Akko*, "Grandmother," or *Akka*, "the old woman."

But we are not through yet. *Akka* or *akko* was used in southern Lappland in the names of four different female divinities, according to the accounts of the missionaries. First we have *Madder-akka*, who made in her womb the

168

bodies of all the unborn children and then handed the child (henceforth provided with both body and soul) over to her daughter *Sarakka* (or *Sarak?*). *Madder-akka* was supposed to have a husband called *Madder-aija.* The names of this venerable couple are obviously identical with Northern Lappish *maddar-akko* "great-grandmother" or "first ancestress," and *maddar-aggja,* "great-grandfather" or "first ancestor." *Sarakka* was a kind of universal midwife. She had two sisters: *Uks-akka,* who dwelt under the tent door *(uksa* means "door"), and *Juks-akka (juks* is supposed to be *juoksa* "bow"). We are told that the function of *Uks-akka* was to keep the baby from falling and hurting itself in the tent, whereas *Juks-akka* had the faculty of changing girls to boys in their mother's womb. When a child was born *Sarakka* porridge was eaten in the honor of the divine midwife. This corresponds to what was called *norna-greytur* in the Faroe islands; and it has been supposed that the three *akka*-sisters are imitations of the Scandinavian fate-goddesses, called *Norns.* But as Gustav Ränk has shown, the Lapp *akka*-goddesses have counterparts in the mythology of several Uralic and Altaic tribes.

A zealous Swedish clergyman who made a trip to the Lapps in 1686 says that he found at the dwelling of a certain Lapp innumerable wooden gods and idols. Some of them were dug into the earth, and for some a platform had been made.

On the whole, the wooden idols were used either when there was no stone idol in the neighborhood, or made for special sacrificial occasions, for instance, when offerings were brought to the dead or to subterranean divinities.

In Jämtland in the seventeenth century the Lapps used to sacrifice to a tree in the immediate neighborhood of the tent or the hut. They carved the picture of a man or a man's face or the like on the surface of the tree. The same custom seems to have existed in Finnish Lappland. In Kemi Lappmark low columns were made out of living trees which were left standing on their roots. The tree was cut off and stripped, and the top of the pillar was formed into the shape

169

of a funnel and covered with a flat stone in order to keep the tree from rotting. There could be several such pillars together at one fishing place.

Sources from the eighteenth century speak of a pillar or beam which the Lapps used to put on the place where the "man of the universe" or "the ruler of the universe" was worshipped. This pillar was called "the support of the universe," and its function was to prevent the vault of heaven from falling down. The pillar may be identical with a sacral beam which Knud Leem once saw on a sacrificial place in Finnmark. It stood on the earth, with its upper end against a high pointed rock (there were two such rocks or stones close to each other), gently leaning towards the direction of the rising sun. It had an iron nail in its upper end. It seems evident that this column was a representation of the axis around which the world moves, and the iron nail symbolized the Polar star, which, according to the ancient Finns and other peoples, was the visible upper end point of the world axis. Now *vaeralden olmai* (Lappish for "the man of the universe"), in whose honor the genitalia of reindeer bucks were sacrificed and the "support of the universe" was smeared with blood, seems to be identical with the Scandinavian fertility god Frey, whom the Old Norsemen called *veraldar goð*, "the god of the universe." The pillar has been identified with the *irmin-sûl* or "world pillar" of the old Saxons, known from the sixth century and from A.D. 772, when it was destroyed by Charles the Great. The idea of an axis around which the world turns in daily revolution may be native, but the wooden representation of it is to all probability one of the numerous Scandinavian features in the pagan religion of the Lapps. The *Frey*-worship of the Lapps is an instance of the important role which Lapp mythology plays in the investigation of the pagan religion of the Scandinavians and other Germanic peoples, as has been shown by Johan Fritzner, Axel Olrik, Wolf von Unwerth, and other scholars.

Salubrious springs have been known to the Lapps as well as to other peoples. There is even some evidence of offerings, for instance reindeer bones, having been spent to springs. Johan Turi says that there are strong geniuses in deep seething wells, and that the Lapps worship them.

Now I return to the Lappish word *saiva*, which in some parts of Lappland occurs in connection with sacrificial places. This word is an eloquent instance of the influence which the Scandinavians have exercised on the Lapps. In Finnmark, *saiva* means either "fresh water" or "a lake without any (fairly large) river flowing into it." It is a very old Scandinavian loan-word, identical with English *sea* (in Old English, *sǽ* means "lake" as well as sea) and Gothic *saiw(s)* "lake." In western Finnmark and in Tornio Lappmark the word *saiva* is used of small lakes to which people earlier used to sacrifice. Johan Turi says that there are plenty of fat fish in such lakes, but one has to keep absolutely quiet to get anything. Sometimes there is no fish in such a lake, and that is because it consists of two lakes on top of each other, with a hole between them. Tornaeus says that these are holy lakes to the mind of the Lapps, "which they so revere that no one of them dares to defile them." Tornaeus also remarks that such lakes usually have two bottoms, so that the fish often hide, and that the Lapps therefore used to sacrifice there, "still retaining something of their former appalling superstition." This was written two and a half centuries before Turi.

It is true that lakes with two bottoms exist, but most of them exist only in the imagination of the rural population. The idea of double-bottomed lakes is widespread among the Scandinavians too. Carl Johansson, who investigated this thoroughly, says that all the *saiva*-lakes which he has seen are very shallow, so that it is easy to clear them of fish by fishing there for some time. Many of them have a vein of water, and one can see how the spring water bubbles forth from a "mystic" hole.

The *saiva*-lakes in Gällivare were so holy that no women were allowed to cross the lake in a boat or set foot on the place of sacrifice.

There are sacral *saiva*-lakes as far south as Pite Lappmark, even if they are not believed to have two bottoms. But in Arjeplog, and probably in Jockmock too, the word

171

saiva is also used for a place of sacrifice or a holy rock (or heap of stones). According to the Lapp Dictionary of Lindahl and Öhrling, *saiva* means "holy," and can be used to qualify a stone, a lake, a tree, or a fish as holy or portentous. *Saiva* also meant, according to the same authors, a stone of a peculiar shape, looking like a human being or something else. Fishermen who found such stones used to place them on the bank of a river and put green twigs under them in order to get more fish. It was not allowed to broil such fish on a spit, as the Lapps are in the habit of doing, but they should be boiled in water instead.

In Västerbotten *saiva* as a rule means the fairy people, subterranean mythical beings which resemble human beings; but it has also been used of the geniuses of lakes and mountains. In Jämtland the word has the same meaning, but it is also used of mountains in which fairy people live. Jessen has much to say about the *saiva*-people, who lived in certain mountains and under the earth. They have once lived on the earth and been Lapps; now they still live like Lapps, but they are all rich and happy. The Lapps have much intercourse with the *saiva*-people and sacrifice to them. They function as a kind of assistant which one could acquire by sacrificing, but one could also inherit or buy such assistants, and the more *saivas* a Lapp had, the more powerful he was. The *noaide* could not do without such assistants. He was assisted by a *saiva*-bird, a *saiva*-fish, or a *saiva*-serpent, etc.

In Härjedalen *saiva* is still known; it means either a fairy living under the earth, or the echo (it was thought that the echo was the voice of a troll or hag that lived in the interior of the mountain).

Wiklund has shown that these different meanings of the term *saiva* are links in a chain of semantic changes. In the northernmost regions the old Scandinavian loan-word has retained its profane signification and means simply "lake." The idea of double-bottomed lakes, which may be due to Scandinavian influence, has been connected with the idea of magic fishing luck, and so the word *saiva* has got the specialized connotation of "magic" or "holy" lake. Taboo may also have had an influence here. To the Fisher Lapps the lakes were the most important localities for sacrifice. From their point of view it was natural to give the name of the holy lake to the rock where the offering was made.

According to Wiklund, the Lapps had derived their ideas of the subterranean fairy people from the Scandinavians. This is very likely, but how could it be proved that the basic notion of ancestors living under the earth is not genuine? And, as Harva has shown, there is also another source of the belief in subterranean people. When, for instance, the Skolt Lapps assert that the infernals are left-handed, this reflects a widespread belief according to which in the subterranean kingdom everything is the other way round. The source of this belief is, says Harva, that the water mirror gives a picture where right is left and vice versa. There seems to be no cogent reason to assume that the Russian Lapps should have obtained their ideas of subterranean beings from the Scandinavians. On the other hand, it has not been proved that the Lapp *sieides* as such have anything to do with the spirits of the ancestors, either immediately or through the intermediary of the fairy people.

CHAPTER XVI

PRAYERS AND SPELLS

WHEN we take into account the complicated ritual of the bear festival, with its manifold activities and dramatic performances comprising about fifty songs sung to as many different melodies, we must ask ourselves whether it is conceivable that these ceremonies should have no counterpart in other fields of Lapp superstition. And yet, apart from the bear festival, little is known of Lapp prayers and incantations. Probably this is not because there were very few of them, but because they have been kept secret. Both big and little sorcerers have always been jealous of their spells. When Carl Axel Gottlund in 1817 showed the Finnish farmers in Dalarne in Sweden incantations which he had noted down in the province of Savo in Finland and printed, one of the farmers said, "It is too stupid on the part of the Savoans to dispose of their spells." The general rule is that if you transmit a spell to another it becomes useless to yourself, at least if the other person is older than you. That is why incantations are muttered. The rite may lose its magic power if it is revealed to the uninitiated.

Thanks to favorable circumstances, Professor Ravila has been able to take down from the dictation of an Inari Lapp (whose parents were from Utsjoki) a whole series of texts which form a kind of a pagan service-book. These texts are so unique that one feels tempted to ask whether they can be genuine. I shall now give some specimens from this source.

A private wooden idol was inaugurated with the following words: "I baptize thee with my own blood, so that thou shalt think of assisting me." One should start worshipping such an idol at a fox hole or at a stone where many wild beasts have passed, and one should kneel and kiss the idol.

A fisherman who came to a new lake had to search out a rock on or beside an islet and sprinkle it with the slime of fish which he had caught in another lake. He put a birch-bark basket on his head and said, "Now I come to thee to sprinkle thee and ask thee for luck." In his left hand he had a birch-bark bag with slimy water. He said, "Now that I have come to thee, to sprinkle thee, I hope that nobody else will worship thee." He took off the basket from his head, knelt down and put his left hand on the rock, and with his right hand he poured slimy water on three fingers; the water should not come on the thumb and the forefinger. Then he said, "I baptize thee, in the name of the god who rules over this lake, lord of the fish, capable even of destroying everybody in the neighborhood who comes to this lake to use violence. And I hope that thou wilt obey me as long as I live, that nobody will be wicked enough to come and harass me at this lake, and that thou wilt always give me fishing-luck when I ask thee, and every day I will offer thee the fourth part of the fish I get." To the nets he says, "Now we have got a god on our side." In the evening he lays food on the rock, folds his hands and prays, "I pray to thee, god, that thou give me fish . . . I shall fulfill my promise, as I have given thee food, god, in case thou shouldst need it." He asks the rock to watch over his nets, and in the next morning he says to the rock, "I have had a restless night, because I was thinking of these fishes and of thee, and now let me see if a fish-thief has examined my nets." He gives the fourth part of his catch to the rock, saying that he must deliver the best fishes to the god.

The fishermen's prayers are remarkable enough, but they are rather commonplace compared to the "offering for finding lost reindeer." Here we have a lively drama, in which the Devil's advocate plays a prominent part.

The performance takes place at the end of November. The *dramatis personae* are three reindeer owners who have lost more castrated males than anybody else. The scene is a hill with a big stone, at which fuel has been piled up. The *Sacrificer* has the liver of a castrated reindeer buck in his hand; the *Sprinkler* has a cheese mold filled with blood from the same reindeer. The *Defender of the Beasts* stands five fathoms from the stone; "he has only a belt with a knife around his waist." The Sacrificer makes a fire and lays the liver behind his back. The Beast-defender tries to slip along, but the Sacrificer notices him. He loses his pluck, and then the Sprinkler can climb the stone. He sprinkles it thrice with blood, saying, "I baptize thee King of the lost draught reindeer."

The Sacrificer sprinkles the liver with mucus from his nose, saying, "I spit at the Defender!"

The Defender throws his knife at the liver. If he hits it he has a right to defend, otherwise he has no right to defend. The Sacrificer broils the liver on a wooden spit. If the Defender has hit the liver, he takes it and puts it into the fire. If he has not hit it, then the Sprinkler puts it into the fire. In the meantime the Sacrificer turns his back to the fire. When the liver is in the fire he turns his face toward the fire, kneels down, and says:

"This stone the Sprinkler has baptized King, in order that it shall have in itself the power of the Almighty. And the stone can and will destroy this our enemy who is standing behind me, so that his envy and his ugly eyes should not do anything against my offering. But I want to complain to thee, King, and tell thee why I have arranged this sacrifice, that when draught reindeer are missing from our community, thou shouldst act so that they be found, because I am standing here for those wretched people and am responsible for them to the King."

Having risen, he addresses the Defender, "You insolent being, who comes to defend the spirits and robbers of the forest, you shall withdraw at once from the society of men!"

Exit Defender.

Sprinkler: "We have got the force and power on our side."

Sacrificer: "We must honor this King." (To the stone) "Before I was forty years old, I had to stand before the King on behalf of all the people, and I thank thee because thou

176

hast condescended to drive away the enemy, him who intended to spoil my offering and insult thee."

Exit Sprinkler.

Sacrificer (to the stone): "Thou shalt be our King, and we shall keep in mind that we have to sacrifice every new year in honor of this. Now fare thee well, and be firm and stable!"

The Sacrificer goes home. At his arrival he takes a piece of wood with him, and at the chopping block he takes an axe, and goes into the tent. The housewife lays meat on the axe, and the Sacrificer eats. The housewife recites the Lord's prayer.

The Sprinkler (from without): "Here I am."

Exit Sacrificer. Enter Sacrificer and Sprinkler. The Sprinkler removes the *boaššo*-sills to the door and sits down on them. The Sacrificer gives him meat on the axe.

Sprinkler (having eaten): "I thank thee very, very much, King, from whom I wish draught reindeer luck for myself!"

The happy end is celebrated with coffee drinking.

But what happens if the Beast-Defender should manage to steal the liver at the beginning of the play? Then this is the end of Act I, and a new reindeer must be slaughtered. Act II begins:

The Defender hides a hoof or a piece of the antlers of the reindeer beside the stone. Enter Sacrificer and Sprinkler. If they cannot find the thing which the Defender has hidden, then they must look for a new stone and start the whole business from the beginning. If they find it, they can start sacrificing. They have brought with them the lungs and the heart of the victim. These the Sacrificer pierces with pine needles, and then he puts them into the fire which is burning down. The Sacrificer says:

"This stone was baptized King, but the enemy got loose and spoiled my sacrifice . . ., but now our enemy has lost the game, and I complain to thee that draught reindeer are missing from our community, that thou shouldst make so that they come back again. Now our enemy is not to be

177

seen, but nevertheless he has done conjuring in order to frustrate both thine honor and my sacrifice." (Having put out the fire, he says to the Sprinkler) "Now we must go!"

Sprinkler: "We must say farewell to the King."

Sacrificer: "Thou, King, who has been victorious in this offering, we must thank thee for this good thing, and now I depart." (He touches the stone.) "Fare thee well, and may thy power be strengthened, so that evil spirits and envious eyes cannot do us any harm!"

Exeunt Sacrificer and Sprinkler.

There was, according to Professor Ravila's informant, also a thanksgiving festival between Christmas and New Year's Day. There were a good many peculiar precepts about the preparation of the meal, and several omens were observed. If the heart of the boiled reindeer doe (a two-year-old doe which had not calved) was curved after the boiling, this was a bad omen for the fawns, etc. This festival has a less outspoken pagan character than the others. The food is blessed in the name of Jesus, and while the uterus of the calfless doe is burned, the head of the tent says:

"Now that we are together to sacrifice and to praise the offerings of the forest, which we have brought till now, and those who rule over these offerings, as the almighty Spirit of the Wild, and now, when I am speaking for these people, I wish that nobody should do what he has done before, stealing and doing all kinds of sins and infamy against the Almighty; but we must control ourselves, so that we do not commit such things."

When they are through with the sacrifice, the head of the tent says:

"Now that this offering is burnt and the thanksgiving is done, I will finally speak a benediction, to the end that blessing may accompany these reindeer which we have toiled so much with. Now I thank the genius who rules over all the wild beasts of the forest, that they should not do any harm to the beings I have mentioned!"

This is a sacramental repast with a strict complicated ritual. It is obviously connected with the drama which I have just reproduced.

178

There were also other offerings of a similar character. In early autumn a one-year-old fawn was sacrificed in order to promote the earmarking. At Easter one sacrificed a one-year-old fawn and a gravid doe with many quaint and curious ceremonies. Late in spring a sacrifice was made in order to keep wild beasts from killing reindeer. On this occasion a windfallen tree was baptized "the old tree of the forest"; its function was then to prevent the wild beasts from bringing forth young. At midsummer time penises and uteri of reindeer are offered to the *sieide* (probably the private *sieide* of the family). The housewife took part in the sacrifice, but then for two days she was not allowed to eat flesh or even drink coffee; she could only eat fish. And she was not allowed to sleep with her husband for two nights.

In the chapter on the literature of the Lapps I have quoted after Johan Turi a song in which the grassy mountain slopes of Norway are asked to take care of the tender reindeer fawns. The Lapps have a good many songs of this kind, and they are not merely poetical invocations.

I have tried to explain why the Lapps have been so reticent about their prayers and spells. The spell becomes inefficient if you transmit it to somebody else, just as the sacrificial performance is of no use if an outsider is present. And why should one inform the clergymen about such things? The old Lapps knew very well that such practices in which the Spirit of the Wild was involved were a capital offence which might bring the offender to the stake. And even if pardon was promised and one was safe under the seal of confession, was it safe to challenge the revenge of the *sieide* and the Spirit of the Wild? Is it certain that they are powerless, or that they simply do not exist? Why take chances?

CHAPTER XVII

LITERATURE, ART, AND MUSIC

LAPP literature in the most extensive sense comprises everything that has been written in Lappish and everything that has been uttered in Lappish and been preserved in oral tradition. On the other hand, the few literary works that have been written by Lapps in the Norwegian language can hardly be regarded as belonging to the Lapp literature, even if they treat Lapp themes, as is the case with the excellent short stories of Matti Aikio.

Most of what has been printed in Lappish up to our times consists of translations, chiefly translations of religious texts, made by non-Lapps. The first Lappish books appeared in 1619: an ABC-book and a little missal. They are written in extremely bad Lappish. The service book *Manuale Lapponicum,* published by Johannes Thornaeus in 1648, is on quite another level. Thornaeus thought it desirable to work out a literary standard language on a basis common to several dialects, and he employed informants from different districts, in order to arrive at a *dialectum maximam communem.* This program was approved by the Swedish authorities and developed during the first half of the eighteenth century by priests who knew Lappish. The first ripe fruit of these efforts was the first printed Lappish version of the New Testament, published in 1755. The entire Bible appeared in 1811. In this respect the Swedes were far in advance of the Norwegians, who otherwise have been pioneers in the field of Lappish; in Norway the first Lappish Bible appeared in 1895.

The so-called Southern Lappish Book-language was used in Swedish Lappland till about the end of the nineteenth century. In the middle of that century, a new literary language was inaugurated by Lars Levi Laestadius. Laestadius was born in Lappland, and he learned the Lappish language in his childhood. He wrote vigorous sermons in Lappish and published tales of Biblical history in the same language. He was the first prose writer to use Lappish with an approach to literary style. He wrote in the Lule-Lappish dialect, spoken in the immense parishes of Jockmock and Gällivare. About fifty years ago this dialect was adopted as a kind of official language. Not only the New Testament has been translated into this dialect, but also various laws concerning nomadism and, among other things, Rudyard Kipling's story "Ricki-Ticki-Tavi."

An extensive Lule-Lappish dictionary, written by Dr. Harald Grundström, is now in the press. It will contain nearly twenty thousand definitions.

In Norway the so-called Norwegian-Lappish literary language has been used for about two hundred years. This language may be understood by five-sixths of the entire Lapp nation. It is the richest and most developed of all the written forms of Lappish. Four big dictionaries have been published by Norwegian scholars, one in the eighteenth, two in the nineteenth and one in the twentieth century.

In Finland a special book-language has been arranged for the Fisher Lapps, who number about one thousand people. Very little has been published in that language.

In Russia during the Lenin era the commissariat for education applied to the linguistic minorities the principle formulated by Lenin: "Marxist contents in a national form." In 1933 the Institute for the Northern Peoples of the Soviet Union published an ABC-book in Kola-Lappish, abundantly illustrated, and in the following year there appeared a Lappish reader and an arithmetic. The Gospel according to St. Matthew was translated into Kola-Lappish about sixty years ago.

By popular poetry in the most extensive sense of this word (German *Volksdichtung*) we mean all literary productions (irrespective of form and subject matter) that have been conceived or assimilated in the milieu of a socially unstratified population or in the basic layers of a population and have spread by oral tradition so far in space or time that the knowledge of their authors has been lost.

The folk tales and popular legends of the Lapps have much the same motifs as are found among the neighboring peoples. Being bilingual (or polyglot) to a great extent, the Lapps have easily absorbed foreign folklore. During the last generations they have even drawn from printed sources. In 1834 a Finnish translation of the tale of Ali Baba from the *Arabian Nights* was published in the newspaper *Oulun Wiikkosanomat*. In 1886, A. V. Koskimies took down in Inari a Lappish version which obviously reflects the Finnish text.

Apart from tales about kings and princesses and the like, the Polypheme motif, and so forth, there are several tales which are told in much the same way among the Lapps as among other peoples; for instance the story about the fox who coaxed the bear to put his tail into the ice hole, and the fable of the raven, the fox, and the piece of cheese. Several stories reflect the universal belief that people can be transformed into beasts, involuntarily or by their own free will. These stories make a more genuine impression than most of the beast fables. Werewolf legends are rare, and as far as I know the Lapp lycanthropes are of a rather innocuous character. Shamanism and the bear ceremonies may have contributed to keep such transformation ideas alive among the Lapps.

In the chapter on "The History of the Lapps" I have spoken of the legends about the Chudes (*Čuðek*), which may have a historic background, even if the details are fictitious and the localization is self-contradictory and otherwise dubious.

In Inari and the adjacent regions the Chude legends are often connected with a quasi-historical hero by the name of Lawrukaš (Finnish *Laurukainen*). Also in other parts of Lappland (for instance in Pite Lappmark) remarkable men and women live in popular tradition: *noaides*, protagonists of the Christian faith, and others.

The most specific kind of Lapp fiction is the *Stallo* legends. *Stallo* is always a dangerous enemy of the Lapps, but he appears in different shapes, and it is not easy to describe him in a few words. It is possible that he has a historical background, being from the beginning a Scandinavian (or Finnish or Karelian) viking, as Lars Levi Laestadius and J. A. Friis have suggested. But as he appears in the legends of the different parts of Lappland, Stallo is composed of quite a few ingredients, which I will try to isolate.

1. Stallo calls the Lapp, often a *noaide*, out to duel, in accordance with the most strict conditions of ancient chivalry. It is only a wrestling-match, but Stallo is so big and vigorous that few Lapps have a chance to beat him. He who wins the match is entitled to kill the other. If the Lapp wins, he has to give Stallo a decent interment; on the other hand, he gets the treasure which Stallo possesses. Stallo wears fine black clothes or an "iron frock."

Here we may have to deal with a viking or, as Rector Qvigstad has suggested, an ancient tax-collecting Scandinavian.

2. When the Lapp has won the wrestling-match, Stallo asks him to kill him with Stallo's own knife. If the Lapp follows this suggestion, the knife goes the wrong way, and he kills himself instead of killing Stallo. If a man is angry at somebody, he can send a Stallo to fight him; according to the Lapps of eastern Finnmark, this is a frequent habit in Russian Lappland. Stallo has a dog which can raise him from the dead. A Stallo can be made of peat, etc.

This black magic, which is known chiefly from the Stallo legends of northernmost Lappland, seems to originate in shamanism.

3. The Stallo-people are man-eaters; at any rate they eat human flesh when they have nothing else to eat. In Lule Lappmark this feature is fairly dominant.

Everybody knows that cannibalism is a widespread motif in European folk tales. But the Lapp legends about man-eaters are far more realistic than those which we know from our own childhood. These legends, like their Eskimo counterparts, may be products of a macabre imagination. If we take into account how precarious the existence of arctic hunters can be (an unsuccessful hunting expedition may mean famine), we may ask whether cannibalism is not a folk-way which the ancient Lapps may have heard of as a dire fact.

4. Stallo is a malignant and cruel giant, who collects children in a sack or carries them away in a boat. The children manage to cut a hole in the sack while the giant is asleep or has gone on an errand; they put stones into the sack and sew up the hole. Or (if they are in a boat) they take their chance when the giant passes under an overhanging birch and climb into the tree. This motif is well known from European folk tales.

5. Stallo moves around on Christmas Eve; he has a *raido* (caravan) drawn by mice or lemmings, or the like. Then the place before the tent must be free from chips and other trash, lest Stallo's *raido* be stuck there. An ample supply of water must be ready in the tent, for if Stallo happens to be thirsty and finds nothing to drink, he may suck the blood out of one of the children. The children are not allowed to romp or use bad language on Christmas Eve, lest Stallo kill them.

6. About 1800 and a little later it was the custom in Lyngen (at the western confines of Finnmark) at Christmas time that three or more young men went from one house to another asking for "the King's tax." The strongest of them was wrapped up in rags and impersonated Stallo. He had a phallus of wood with which he prodded the girls, asking them to pay "tax"; those who did not pay, he prodded so that they cried. Once it happened that the girls found Stallo alone before the house; they got hold of him and stripped him naked.

According to Professor Lid, the last-mentioned motif is the oldest of them all, and then comes the last but one. This has a counterpart in Norwegian traditions, and in Setesdal in southern Norway this Christmas procession was *Ståles-ferdi*. The leader of the procession was a giant called *Ståle*. As Lid has pointed out, the Norwegian tradition about Ståle has a few other traits in common with the Lapp Stallo tradition. "The decisive proof of the original identity of Stallo and Ståle is the name." Modern Norwegian *ståle* means "a tall strong man." *Stáli* occurs as a surname in Old Norse.

I have dwelt upon the Stallo legends because at first sight, they seem to be so peculiar and genuine. If Professor Lid is right, Stallo is an instance among many others of the almost ubiquitous Scandinavian influence which has put its stamp on the life and the ideas of the Lapps.

The lyrical poetry of the Lapps has been known in many countries for 275 years. In his *Lapponia* Johannes Schefferus published two anonymous Lappish song texts in the original and in Latin translation. He had obtained them from a theological student of Lapp descent, Olof Sirma, who had heard them in his home area in Kemi Lappmark. These songs were very much appreciated wherever Schefferus's book was read, in the Latin original or in English, German, French, or Dutch translation. Rather recently a Swedish scholar, Bergström, an English scholar, Wright, and a Hungarian scholar, Atányi, have been following the tracks along which these poems have spread from the *Lapponia* of Schefferus. In the eighteenth century the two songs were imitated rather than translated by several writers in England and Germany. Johann Gottlieb Herder published them in his epoch-making collection of folk songs and anonymous ballads, *Stimmen der Völker*. In the following century Longfellow alluded to them in his poem "My Lost Youth."[1] One of these old Lapp songs runs like this:

> *Shine bright, O Sun, upon Lake Oarrejaure!*
> *If I should climb the tops of yonder spruces,*
> *knowing I could behold the Oarrejaure,*
> *in the heather dale of which she dwells,*
> *then I would clear away all these trees*
> *which grow here now,*
> *and I would prune these twigs,*
> *all these good verdant twigs.*
> *I would accompany the speeding clouds*
> *which are moving toward the Oarrejaure.*

[1] " . . . a verse of a Lapland song
Is haunting my memory still:
'A boy's will is the wind's will,
And the thoughts of youth are long, long thoughts.' "

I wish I could fly there with wings, the wings of the
   crow!
I have no wings, the garrot's wings, with which
I might fly thither,
nor have I the goose's feet,
Forsooth thou hast been waiting long,
thy most delightful day,
with thine eyes, thy fervent heart.
Even if thou far shouldst flee,
soon I should catch up with thee.
What could be more tenacious
than sinew cord and iron chain
which press us hard,
wrapping up our head and changing all our thoughts?
A young man's mind is the mind of the wind,
the thoughts of the young are long thoughts.
If I should listen to them all,
then I would step on a wrong path.
I ought to take one trend of thought,
then I shall know how to find the better way.

These songs came from the parish of Sodankylä in Northern Finland. They came back to Finland in the nineteenth century, when the Swedish-speaking poet Frans Mikael Franzén imitated them in a song which is still very popular with the Swedes. The conclusion seems to be that the Lapps were introduced in the universal history of literature earlier than the Swedes.

In his book on the life of the Lapps Johan Turi describes the sentiments of the nomads on passing the Swedish-Norwegian frontier in the spring:

"When the Lapps are wandering in the spring across the mountain ridge where it is cold and where much snow has fallen, there are not many places where the ground is bare of snow, but there is just enough to allow the reindeer to find their forage. And when they arrive in Norway and begin to see the forests that stretch to the sea coast, where there

186

is grass and leaves, then the Lapps find that everything is beautiful and delicious, and when they approach and begin to hear the cuckoo and all the birds that are charming to the minds of the Lapps, then they start singing:

Mothers—oh beautiful grassy valleys,
mothers of the fawns, voya, voya, nana, nana.
All hail, all hail, you mothers, nana, nana, voya, voya.
Now receive my little herd
and tend it as you used to do,
voya, voya, nana, nana.
Now you mothers, be my friends again,
voya, voya, nana, nana.
Oh, mothers, let my reindeer graze and prosper,
nana, nana, voya, voya.

And then:

Oh, these beautiful regions,
voya, voya, nana, nana—
they are so beauteous that they shine.

"And everything is so delightful that the boys have only the girls in their minds, and the girls think only of the boys, and that they ought to meet."

In the beginning of the nineteenth century the Finnish priest Jacob Fellman noted some specimens of Lapp popular poetry. Two of these poems are of a considerable length (about two hundred lines together). They are about the first inhabitants of Lappland and the ancient history of the Lapps. It is a pity that one of these two epic poems exists only in translation. It is impossible to tell how old this kind of poetry is among the Lapps. Karl Bernhard Wiklund has remarked that there are Finnish elements in one of the epic songs communicated by Fellman. I should think that one of the songs about the first inhabitants of Lappland was written by a rather sophisticated person who knew Finnish very well. This unknown poet puts these words into the mouth of the first immigrants:

187

Let us look for a name to this our land!
You found land! Sameland be your name!
You found land, you shall be Sameland!

Same means "Lapp" in the Lappish language. The passage which I have just quoted seems to contain an endeavour towards an etymological explanation of the name *Same-aednam,* "Lappland." But as far as I know, *Same* cannot be connected with any Lappish word that means "find" or anything like that. On the other hand, the Finnish noun *saama* "capture, take" would make good sense here.

These poems would be well worth investigating because they are the only historical or quasi-historical epic poems recorded among the Lapps.

Anonymous poetry is known from all the regions where Lapps are living. Most of these are lyrical song texts.

The Lapps have a musical art of their own, hardly influenced by the music of the neighboring peoples up to these days. The first record of a Lapp melody was made 150 years ago by the Italian traveler Acerbi, who otherwise had a rather poor opinion of the Lapps. Nowadays European musicians find the music of the Lapps interesting even from an aesthetic point of view. The Swedish composer Vilhelm Peterson-Berger has written a symphonic rhapsody, called "Sameätnam," on the basis of Lapp melodies.

Whatever may be the aesthetic value of Lapp music, the way it is cultivated shows that the Lapps have a keen sense of music. They have no instruments, except a kind of shepherd's pipe made of the stalk of the Angelica plant and not much used. The only genre that plays a conspicuous role is solo song. The melody usually consists of a quite short theme that is repeated *ad libitum.* The rhythm seems to be at least as essential to the motif as the intervals. The absolute pitch is irrelevant, and as a matter of fact it often rises during the performance of a song while the intensity increases. The text usually bears the stamp of improvisation, and it may be replaced by meaningless sound sequences or vocalizations, as *voya, voya, nana, nana.* Everybody makes

188

new texts to old melodies, but it is not the fashion to sing old texts to new tunes.

For "melody" the Lapps use the indigenous term *vuolle*. In the Mordvin language the corresponding word means "word"; the corresponding Finnish word means "oath." In most cases the *vuolle* is used to characterize or denote the being or the thing which is the chief object of the song. Such objects or subject matters are: individual human beings and certain categories of human beings (as learned men, for instance), parishes, mountains, rivers, lakes, the ocean, the steamship, all kinds of animals, from the bear to the flea, but especially the reindeer and the different kinds of reindeer. In those districts where the indigenous art of singing has not been checked or jeopardized by the influence of modern music or by religious prejudice, every man of mark and distinction has his characteristic melody or *vuolle,* known by everybody. To some extent it may be legitimate to compare the Lapp *vuolles* to the *Leitmotifs,* used by Berlioz and Wagner.

The specimens on page 190 have been put in music score (from phonograph records in Uppsala Landsmåls- och Folkminnesarkiv) by Dr. A. O. Väisänen. They are all from Arjeplog.

Extensive collections of Lapp songs have been published by the Finnish composer Armas Launis (in 1908) and by the Swedish amateur musician Karl Tirén (in 1942). These publications are not satisfactory in so far as the song texts are concerned. Most of the melodies are accompanied by quite short texts or merely by vocalizations, and in Tirén's records the synchronization of text and melody is arbitrary. Questions of metrics cannot be attempted on the basis of these records. The metrical form of such song texts is linked to the melody, and it lives only in the musical performance. If the ties that connect the words with the melody are violently cut, as is the case when one asks the singer to dictate or write down the text, then the poem is transformed *eo ipso* into prose: the singer thinks in prose, and he makes additions and eliminations, distorting the verse more or less completely. The records of Ostyak and Vogul poetry are instructive so far. As late as about fifteen years ago the

189

1. "The Dog and the Man." Sung by Anders Fjellman.

2. "The Leitmotif of Old Skaile." Sung by Per Kibnu.

3. "The Leitmotiv of Lessik." Sung by Anna Fjellman.

4. "The Leitmotif of John Eriksson Steggo."
Sung by Anna Fjellman.

5. "The Fox." Sung by Sara Perrson.

well-established opinion of the specialists was that the Ostyaks and the Voguls had no regular rhythm in their poems.
Wolfgang Steinitz has shown that this opinion is un-
founded. When he took down the texts as they were sung,
the poems turned out to be strictly rhythmic. Usually they
consist of non-strophic trochaic dimeters, just as the old
epic and lyric popular poetry of the Finns and the Estonians.

This state of things made it imperative to provide for a
new collection of Lappish songs. In collaboration with the
Dialect and Folklore Archives of Uppsala I organized eight
phonograph expeditions to the different parts of Swedish
Lappland in the years 1942-1947, collecting among other
things about twelve hundred songs. Dr. Väisänen, the Finnish specialist in subarctic Eurasian music, is now transcrib-
ing these melodies on music scores. The writing down of
the texts from the records will take a considerable time, because many of the texts are rather long, but I hope we shall
be able to publish the whole material in a few years.

One of our Lapp informants, or rather performants,
deserves a special mention. He was a 72-year-old reindeer
owner, who had made a four-days' journey from his dwelling place close to the Norwegian frontier to the church
village where we met him. Before the microphone he related the story of his life; he told us about his childhood
and his youth, his native region, his parents, relatives, and
friends, about reindeer and beasts of prey, and hunting exploits, and experiences. He spoke for more than an hour;
when a disc was full he made a pause, and when the tech-
nician had turned the disc or put on a new one, he continued his story exactly where he had left it. His account
was an artistic achievement in itself, but it was only the
frame or border of his hoard of songs. All the way he illustrated his story with songs, and the total number of songs
was eighty-six. This achievement is interesting from the
point of view of literary form.

The first poet who is known to have written anything in
Lappish was a Finnish farmer, Anders Keksi. He wrote in
Finnish a jocose epic poem on a violent inundating spring

191

flood in the Tornio river in 1677. In the beginning of the poem we are told that the flood on its way through the parish of Pajala swept away a storehouse which contained the tithe grain of the vicar Olof Sirma (the same man who furnished Schefferus with his two specimens of Lappish poetry). In the burlesque imagination of the farmer-poet the grains transform the water of the Tornio river into malt brewage. The malt is washed ashore on the banks of the lake of Karunki, where people start brewing beer from it. One of the farmers of Karunki praises the beer in a speech, calling out to a renowned colleague from the parish of Olof Sirma:

> *Jukest taal tšaatsekortnest,*
> *juste vuolak šattai puurist!*

This is Lappish, meaning, "Now drink of the water-grains, of which an excellent beer was made!"

In the middle of the nineteenth century the rector Anders Fjellner related a few epic songs in Lappish: *Päiven parne'* or "the Offspring of the Sun," *Piššan Paššan pardne* or "The Son of Pišša and Pašša," *Päiven neita* or "The Sun-girl," and *Kassa muödda* or "The Thick Fur Coat." Otto Donner published them with German translation in his book *Lieder der Lappen* (1876). "The Sun-girl" and "The Thick Fur Coat" are poetical variants of Lappish legends which have been recorded in prose in different parts of Lappland. "The Offspring of the Sun" (or "the Sun-boy's Wooing in the Land of Giants") and "The Son of Pišša and Pašša" are of a considerable length and of a peculiar content, partly without any equivalent in Lappish folklore. They are written in the same meter as the Finnish Kalevala songs, with alliteration and parallelism. The linguistic usage is a rugged conglomerate of northern and southern Lappish, sometimes incorrect and unintelligible, whereas the rather artless poem of "The Sun-girl" is written in the very southernmost Lappish dialect as it is still spoken in Härjedalen. The poem of the Sun-boy shows an unmistakable poetical talent.

Fjellner was a nomad Lapp by birth; he was born in Härjedalen in 1795. After having finished his studies, he came to the Tornio Lappmark as an assistant priest. In 1842 he was appointed rector to Sorsele in the northern part of southern Lappland; he stayed there till he died in 1876. Through his whole life he seems to have been something of a Lapp nationalist, but at the same time he was a fervent Swedish patriot. He has published a poem written in honor of King Charles XIV, whom he admired very much. This poem is written in the same curious mixed dialect as the poem of the Sun-boy.

It appears that the poem of the Sun-boy and the poem of Pišša's and Pašša's son must have been written by Fjellner himself. This has been proved in detail by Wiklund.

Fjellner once told the naturalist von Düben, author of an extensive handbook on Lappland and the Lapps, that there has existed among the Lapps a gigantic epopee about the Sun-girl, comprising about one hundred songs; von Düben has given a brief account of the contents and a few short specimens in Swedish translation. In 1901 a Swedish writer who has been very much interested in the Lapps published a paper on "The Mythic Poetry of the Lapps," in which he communicates "in Swedish translation" a poem on "The Death of the Sun-girl." Sixteen lines of the poem are cited in the Lappish original. There is no doubt but that this poem has come from the literary remains of Fjellner.

The poem of the Sun-girl, as it was published by Donner in 1876, was written when Fjellner was twenty-six years old. This explains why the poem is written in the dialect of Härjedalen: the author had not mastered any other Lappish dialect at that time. But there is the rhythm and the frequent alliteration which makes it probable that Fjellner had already become acquainted with Finnish popular poetry and tried to imitate it. It is true that Lönnrot's *Kalevala* appeared in 1835 (fourteen years after Fjellner had written the poem of the Sun-girl). But when he was studying at Uppsala, Fjellner discussed questions of popular poetry with the Finnish scholar Carl Axel Gottlund, who was one

193

of the first collectors of Finnish poetry and even published a little volume of Finnish popular poems.

Fjellner made Donner, Düben, and other scholars believe that his poems were specimens of old popular poetry. Only thirty years after his death it was shown that he must have written them himself. So far he may be regarded as a Lapp counterpart of the Czech patriot Váceslav Hanka, who created with injudicious zeal a collection of alleged Old Czech epics and succeeded in duping the slavists for decades. But I do not think it is fair to call Fjellner a falsifier. It seems probable that he was through his whole life to some extent a child of Nature, with a rather immature judgment in scientific matters, in spite of his academic studies, which lasted only for a couple of years. When he allowed himself to mislead the scholars, he was not perhaps driven only by a misdirected zeal for the glory of the despised Lapp nation, but also by a kind of personal modesty. The fictions of poets should not be judged narrow-mindedly by the moral code of science. And there is no doubt that Anders Fjellner was a poet. He ventured to grapple with linguistic difficulties which sometimes became overwhelming, but even if his poems are hard to read, one often feels a vigorous vein of poetical inspiration breaking through the obstacles of his rugged style.

In this century ten Lapp authors have made their appearance, writing autobiographies, short stories or poems. One of them is a doctor of philosophy, and one was a member of the Norwegian parliament, but some of them had rather little or even no school education. The most remarkable of them all is the hunter Johan Turi.

Johan Turi was born in the Norwegian parish of Kautokeino in 1854 and died in the Swedish parish of Jukkasjärvi in 1936. He wrote two books, and one of these was translated into four languages. In his old age he lived in a small house which a Maecenas had given to him, and the Swedish parliament granted him six hundred crowns a year because of his literary merits.

In 1910, Turi published a book called *An Account of the Lapps*, in Lappish with Danish translation. The book was edited and translated by a Danish ethnologist, Mrs. Emilie Demant-Hatt. This book primarily had a practical purpose. In the preface, Turi says:

"I have thought that the best thing would be if there were a book in which everything were noted about the life and circumstances of the Lapps, so that it would not be necessary to ask: 'What are the circumstances of the Lapps like?,' and so that those people would not have any opportunity to distort everything, who wish to misrepresent the Lapps and twist everything to be the fault of the Lapps, when there are controversies between farmers and Lapps in Norway and Sweden. And in this book all the events and explanations must be written down, so that everybody understands it."

Turi's *Account* is no exhaustive handbook, and he was not always able to give a limpid account of complicated procedures and problems. But he had intuition and imagination, a keen sense of humor, and a kind heart.

In his second book he describes a drive with reindeer:

"When we were driving along the Karasjok river, the snow was deep and even, but the reindeer were lazy, because they had been wading in the deep snow all the day; they did not care to run fast.

"The journey went so slowly, and the landscape seemed to accompany us, when we were moving so slowly.

"Then I remembered an old trick. I brought the reindeer abreast of each other and slapped them with the rein, and then they started running, so that there was a constant creaking of the hoofs.

"And we drove at a terrible speed indeed. It was as if the forelands in the river had been shouting 'hello, hello!' and then 'good-bye, good-bye!' It was as if the forelands had seen that they would soon be left behind, when they had shouted those words."

Maybe this simile is not new, but Turi had not learned it from his reading, which was rather poor, and the shaping of the simile bears a personal mark.

I should like to say a few words of the so-called Homeric similes, as we find them for instance in the *Dead Souls* of

195

Nicolai Gogol and in the novel *Seven Brothers* by the famous Finnish author Alexis Kivi. Specialists in the history of literature say that Gogol and Kivi were influenced by the Homeric songs, and that is not unlikely. If you find such a prolix simile in a letter written by a Russian peasant soldier, recently taken from the plough, you cannot swear that he has not read *Dead Souls* and learned the trick from Gogol. But I think Johan Turi was exempt from influences of this kind. He too has that Homeric trait. One of the chapters of his *Account* has the rubric "On Girls and Courtship." In this chapter Turi has inserted a kind of short story about a young man called Nilas (Nick). He has many good qualities, and among other things he belongs to an opulent family, and even if he is not rich, he may be expected to become a rich man. And now comes a simile (or even two) which reasonably may be characterized as Homeric:

"A family is like a river. When it is a river that is long, as a family also is of long duration. One river has grassy source-streams from the very beginning. And in the same mountain there is also another river, and it begins as high up, but it has no grass, neither at the source-streams nor along the main river. And such are also the human families. And if the kind of trees in a given region is rich in branches and has fine straight branches, then further trees of the same sort come up in the same region. But if there are ugly trees in a district, then ugly trees come up; some trees become extinct, but instead of them other trees come up, the same sort of ugly trees. And such are the human families too. Therefore the Lapps used to consider of what family each man is. And therefore they also held Nilas in esteem, because he belonged to a well-to-do family."

Turi displayed a mordant irony when he wrote of reindeer thieves and other enemies of the Lapps, but his basic disposition of mind was kind and benevolent. One of his philippics finishes with this soft chord:

"But he who writes this nevertheless wishes that mercy might shine even before their eyes as well as before other terrestrial beings which the same God has created. At last we should be in the bosom of God like the child in its mother's arms, where its best refuge is."

Turi was fifty-six years old when he published his *Account*. At the age of seventy-seven he published another book, chiefly about travels and hunting exploits. In this book he described two trips which he made to Norwegian Finnmark and to Petsamo as the companion and interpreter of the English wine merchant and globe-trotter Frank Butler. Butler also wrote a book about these trips, with a few short contributions from Turi. Karl Bernhard Wiklund said in a review that Turi's report is in every respect by far superior to that of Butler, and I think he is right. But the short sketches of hunting expeditions in the mountains are still better in my opinion. They give a good insight into the unromantic life of those people to whom hunting is not a pastime, but a rather grim livelihood. Here is a passage:

"At dawn we found a fisher's hut, which was completely covered by snow, and as it was very cold, we had to dig in order to hide under the snow. The hut was so deep down in the snow that only the smoke hole was visible, and when we had dug a way into the snow, it led straight down as into a basement. When we had cleared the entrance we entered, and there the ground was bare, but it was dark, and we started searching for wood. There was small birch-wood there, but when we had found it, it was difficult to make it burn. But there was almost danger to life when the fire was burning, because the room was filled with smoke, so that one almost suffocated. But there were empty fish kegs there, which they had taken the bottoms out of. Then we made a chimney pipe from those kegs, and then we got a little draught, but nevertheless there was so much smoke that one had to lie with one's face turned down, and still one could not keep one's eyes open. Nevertheless we could eat a little, but the food had no taste, when there was such a smoke. When it got warmer, it began to drip at some places, and then it became wet and smoky, and when we went out there was a terrible cold and snowstorm, so that one could not possibly endure sleeping outdoors. Then I

197

started making holes at the lower edge of the hut, so that the air might come in. I made holes on both sides, and then the smoke began to go out to some extent, so that we could eat properly."

Turi had also some talent for drawing, and the *Account* is illustrated by himself. Another Swedish Lapp, Nils Nilsson Skum, has become famous as an artist. In 1937 his drawings were shown at the great international exhibition in Paris. In 1938 he published a volume containing about a hundred drawings, partly in colors, accompanied by an extensive text in which he described the annual cycle of reindeer breeding. Recently he has written an illustrated autobiography, which probably will appear soon. There have been many talented artists among the Lapps, but hitherto only one of them has been able to get a professional training. His name was John Savio (1902–1938). He was born in Finnmark, and he studied in Oslo and Paris. Influenced by Edvard Munch, he developed into a master of drawing and wood engraving. In the artistic treatment of Lapp motifs he is unparalleled.

In this context I ought to say a few words about the handiwork of the Lapps.

The Lapps of old have fabricated almost all their household goods and implements. Of wood they have made boats (formerly sewn together with root fibers), sleighs, skis and staffs, tent poles, boxes, trays, scoops, knife shafts, and cheese molds. Of reindeer horn they have made spoons, knife sheaths, knife shafts, needle cases, belt buckles, lasso loops, staff knobs (only for men's staffs), weaver's reeds, distaffs, netting pins, molds, decorative plates to be fixed on wooden scoops and staffs, and several other things. Of woolen yarn the women have plaited shoelaces and sashes, by means of a weaver's reed or without any implement. The fabrication of clothes and shoes also belongs to the duties of the women.

Root fibers (of birch and spruce) were used for twisting net ropes and net edgings and for plaiting baskets, cheese molds, and salt receptacles. The Lapp women have been extremely skilful in this trade. The cheese molds are some-times decorated with open-work zigzag patterns.

Tin embroidery has been accounted for in the chapter on Clothing. It is applied on caps, collars, belts, dickies, harness straps, pouches, and so forth.

The Lapps have mastered the art of casting decorative buttons of tin in horn molds of their own fabrication. All things made of metal they have bought or obtained by barter from their settled neighbors. As far as silver articles are concerned, they have stuck stubbornly to old patterns; even nowadays the Scandinavian goldsmiths make for the Lapps silver spoons of medieval fashion, with flat, blunt bowl and short handle, decorated with appending rings and leaves. (The Lapps have imitated this style in their horn spoons, except for the leaves.)

Little is known of the origin of the decorative patterns used by the Lapps. Some of these patterns one finds in the Scandinavian objects from the viking epoch, and earlier, as far back as the Stone Age. Most of them are purely geomet-ric. A few of the motifs are something intermediary between a geometric figure group and a conventionalized flower (of the chrysanthemum or lotus type). Pictures of animals, especially reindeer, occur chiefly in the northern regions, and this style is hardly of long standing.

The pattern elements are chiefly of two kinds, namely, lines and wedges. The wedges are engraved with the point of a knife and have the shape of an equilateral triangle, an acute-angled isosceles triangle, a square (always in oblique position), an arrow-head, or a "boomerang." The most common lines are: straight line, wavy line, ellipse, circle (with a point in the center), lozenge (rhomb), double loop (approximately a horizontal 8).

The most frequent combinations of elements are: cross (made of wedges), "bird's footprint," chequered triangle, toothed lines (single or in pairs), zigzag lines (preferably framed in two parallel straight lines), engraved or embossed, and an embossed twisted cord (screw). The zigzag line is the most widespread of all the patterns.

199

In the Lule Lappmark and farther south the interlace style is highly developed.

Openwork decoration (lozenge, triangle, heart) is characteristic of knife sheaths from Tornio Lappmark and the adjacent regions.

In decorating wood and horn, all the engraved lines and surfaces are stained with smoke-black.

In the last three decades Lapp handiwork has had a renaissance in Swedish Lappland and (to some extent) in Finnmark. The Swedish nomad schools have done a remarkable work in this field.

In the beginning of the 'thirties, the nomad Anta Pirak from Jockmock in Swedish Lappland dictated his autobiography to Dr. Harald Grundström, who published it first in Swedish translation and then in the Lappish original. Grundström has also published a complete Lappish-Swedish-German glossary to Pirak's book. This book, called *The Life of a Nomad Lapp*, is now being translated into English, so it will be the most easily accessible specimen of Lapp literary activities. It deserves to be widely known and thoroughly studied, since it is much more than an autobiography. It is a detailed account of all the aspects of Lappish life and mentality, a kind of miniature Lapp encyclopedia. Pirak is not a poet like Turi. He presents everything in a straightforward unsophisticated manner, and his style is plain. He is discursive rather than intuitive, but he has a remarkable talent for describing matters and events, and unraveling complicated questions. Of all the books that treat of the Lapps, this is the most instructive.

A few years ago another nomad Lapp, Abraham Johansson, eighty years old and rich in experience, started dictating his autobiography to his son, who is a distinguished investigator in the field of Lapp ethnology. The old man did not live to finish his autobiography, but the part of it that was taken down is a valuable contribution to the literature of the Lapps. I hope we shall be able to publish it soon.

In 1912 the Finnmark Lapp A. Larsen published a short novel called *Baeivve-Alggo* ("Dawn"). It is the story of a Lapp boy who manages to get a high-school education (there have not been many such cases in Norway) and then becomes a bank cashier in a town in northern Norway. There he is frustrated in a most serious love affair because of the race prejudice which is so common among the Norwegians in their attitude towards the Lapps. He renounces his post and retires to the small fishing hamlet where he was born. There he has the sad experience that his career has isolated him from his original milieu without giving him a firm foothold in the world of his schoolmates and colleagues. In this state of isolation the consciousness of his Lapp nationality grows stronger in him. He thinks it is a shame that he can read and write Norwegian, but not his own mother tongue, and he makes a point of rectifying this fault. Having done this, he decides to try to awaken the national consciousness of his kinsmen. He speaks to them in the following way:

"Hold together, *Same* brothers and sisters! As long as we are disunited, we are weak. When we hold together, we are strong. Let us cultivate and develop our kinship feeling! Let us defend the spiritual inheritance of our ancestors! We shall never disgrace the *Same* name! We have the same claim to the good things of life as other people. They will say that we are incapable people. Very well. Is it not so in the tales that the despised youngest son is the one who wins the princess and half the kingdom when he uses his gifts and his powers to the full?"

In substance this agrees with the message of the fairy people as we know it from the relation of Isaac Olsen; but in its verbal manifestation it is deeply influenced by the romantic-idealistic popular movements which flourished in the Scandinavian countries in the second half of the nineteenth century and a little later. In Lappish prose A. Larsen has beaten a new track; he is the first white-collar prose writer among his fellow-countrymen. He attempts the art of story-writing, but he has no strong grip of his subject, and he is a poor psychologist. Let us hope that he has initiated a new tradition, and that he will have able successors, so that his novel will mark a *baeive-algo,* the beginning of a new era.

201

In 1915, an Utsjoki Lapp, Pedar Jalvi (Helander), who had been studying in the normal school of Jyväskylä in central Finland, published a pretty booklet containing five short poems and seven sketches, one of them a translation from Finnish. The booklet has the same title as the first poem, *Muottačalmit* ("Snow-flakes"). The sketches are in the same style as the "chips" of the famous Finnish author Juhani Aho, who was then the unchallenged master of Finnish prose, and Pedar Palvi was no bad pupil. One of the sketches is a very good fragment of a description of the manners of the nomad Lapps, with a racy dialogue. The poems show a remarkable skill in handling the trochaic Kalevala meter, with its alliteration. Here are a few lines:

> *Vaarid viegam, duoddar duolmam,*
> *alla gaisa ala goarngum,*
> *Vuvdid vacam, gedgid gaečam . . .*

("I run in the mountains, I wander in the fjeld, I climb right to the summit; I walk in the forest, I look at the stones, . . .")

In 1940 another Utsjoki Lapp, Aslak Guttorm, published a booklet called *Koccam spalli* ("Rising blast"). It contains eleven poems and six sketches. Most of the sketches are skilful realistic snapshots of the toilsome (and sometimes dangerous) life of poor people in the border districts of Finland and Norway. Here I think we find the peak of consciously formed Lappish prose. The poems give evidence of a brisk and merry temperament and a keen eye for natural scenery. The poetic form is unaffected and artistic; Guttorm is especially interesting because his poems rhyme, even though he often, like the Hungarian poets, leaves the consonants out of account (e.g. *joðaša—jorada*), or neglects the vowels, like his Old Norse colleagues (e.g. *adda—guodda*).

A fortnightly newspaper, called *Nuorttanaste* (The Polar Star), written and printed by Lapps, has been appearing in northernmost Norway for fifty years.

In Finland, *Sami Čuvgitusseärvi* (The Lapp Educational Society) publishes a quarterly called *Sabmelaš* (The Lapp), with Lapp contributors. The same society has edited, among other things, Aslak Guttorms *Koccam spalli* and a Lappish hymnal. In Sweden the interests of the Lapps are taken care of by the quarterly *Samefolkets Egen Tidning* (The *Same* People's Own Newspaper), now thirty years old. It appears in Swedish, but it has also a Lappish section conducted by Dr. Ruong. The early volumes of this periodical contain many valuable articles on Lapp ethnology, chiefly written by its founder, the late county government official Torkel Tomasson. The society *Sameätnam*, founded by Swedes and Lapps in hearty collaboration, has recently started a publication series in Swedish and Lappish.

I should like to end this chapter with the Lapp National Anthem, written by the late Isak Saba, Member of the Norwegian Parliament, and published in 1906. It is written chiefly in the Kalevala meter (four trochees), but to each group of eight lines a catalectic line (with seven syllables instead of eight) has been added to form a strophe consisting of nine lines. The poem is very firm in its composition, and full of poetic visions. It has been translated into Finnish and Swedish. The first strophe is so beautiful that it is worth while to learn Lappish in order to enjoy it.

Gukken davven Dawgai vuolde
sabma suolgai Same-aednam:
Duoddar laebba duoddar duokken,
jawre saebba jawre lakka,
čokkak čilgiin, čorok čaeroin
allanaddik alme vuostai;
šavvik jogak, šuvvik vuowdek,
cakkik caeggo stalle-njargak
maraidaeggje maeraidi.

Far away in the North, under Charles's Wain,
is Lappland faintly to be seen in the distance.
Mountains lie stretched behind mountains;

203

lakes full to overflowing lie near each other;
summits with ridges, hills with stony slopes rise toward
  the sky.
Rivers rush, forests sigh,
steep steel-colored promontories jut into roaring seas.

Measured by the standard of world literature, the achievements of Lapp authors cannot claim a very high esteem. But they do not need any condescending benevolence on our part. They have a value of their own, and we cannot help admiring them if we take into account that they have been produced in the midst of a population of only thirty-three thousand souls, spread over an immense territory, divided between four countries, in the northernmost outskirts of the inhabited world.

CHAPTER XVIII

ANCIENT AND MODERN OPINIONS
OF THE LAPPS

CORNELIUS TACITUS in his ethnographic treatise *Germani*, written A.D. 98, gives a brief description of a primitive tribe called *Fenni*, living in the northeastern confines of *Germania*. There is no doubt but that *Fenni* is the same word as *Finns*; but this does not imply that the *Fenni* of Tacitus were the ancestors of the non-Scandinavian inhabitants of Finland. The picture which Tacitus gives of the *Fenni* does not fit in with what may be assumed of the civilization of the Finns even in the first century of our era. And there is another difficulty; in the Middle Ages the Swedes used the name Finns only (or chiefly) for the tribe which inhabited the southwestern corner of Finland. This usage was still alive in the middle of the sixteenth century, and even nowadays that part of Finland is called "Finland proper." Most archeologists think that the Finns came to Finland at the beginning of our era. The Finnish population of southwestern Finland came from Estonia. In their own language they called themselves *Suomi, Suomalainen*, plural *Suomalaiset*. The name *Finn, Finns* undoubtedly was given to them by the Swedes. At that time the forefathers of the *Suomalaiset* probably spoke the same language as the forefathers of the Tavastians, Karelians, Votes, Estonians, Livonians, and Vepses, and it is uncertain whether at that time they formed a distinct tribe and had a name of their own.

It is much more probable that Tacitus speaks of the Lapps. From time immemorial, the Norwegians have called the Lapps *Finner*, whereas in Sweden this word has denoted and still denotes the Finns. According to Hultman and other scholars, this word is of the same root as the verb *find* and originally meant a "finder," i.e. a person who is on the search and takes what he finds, or in other words, a migrating or roving hunter and fisherman. If this is so, the Scandinavians must have given this name to their migratory neighbors in the east and the north at a time when they themselves had begun to till the soil and live a more or less sedentary life. The Greek naturalist and geographer Ptolemaios (about A.D. 150) mentions, if the passage in question is not a later interpolation, *Finnoi* as the northernmost known inhabitants of *Skandia*. Here, in all probability, the Lapps are meant, and not a tribe living in the southwestern corner of Finland.

The *Fenni*, says Tacitus, are quite uncivilized and terribly poor; they have no hand weapons (or no implements?), no horses, no houses; they eat herbs, are dressed in furs, and sleep on the earth. They have no other weapons than arrows with points of bone. Obviously Tacitus does not mean that the Lapps were vegetarians, for he expressly states that they are hunters. The detail about herbs *may* be authentic, as the Lapps of our days collect and eat at least four different plants (*Rumex acetosa*, *Oxyria digyna*, *Mulgedium alpinum*, and *Angelica archangelica*).

Tacitus speaks of the Lapps in a style which we would characterize as romantic: "Children have no other refuge from wild beasts and storms than wattled hurdles. Thither the young repair, this is the abode of the old. But they consider this a happier existence than to groan in the fields, to work at the building of houses, to stake their possessions and those of other people on risky ventures. Safe from men, safe from the Gods, they have attained the most difficult thing: there is not even anything left for them to desire."

Professor Linkomies (Flinck) has pointed out that Tacitus's description of the *Fenni* chiefly consists of clichés which previous authors had used in their descriptions of other savage tribes. Obviously this does not imply that it is mere fiction. There is only one detail which does not seem to have any earlier parallels in Greek or Roman literature, namely, that the women take part in the hunting together

206

with the men. As Linkomies rightly observes, the Byzantine historian Procopios says exactly the same of the *Skrithifinoi* in his work on the Gothic Wars. According to Eduard Norden and other authorities, it is not probable that Procopios had read Tacitus's *Germania*. If he had, then it can be inferred that in the opinion of Procopios the *Fenni* of Tacitus were identical with the *Skrithifinoi*, i.e. the Lapps. If he had not, it seems that his relation confirms the account given by Tacitus, as far as the hunting habits of the Lapps are concerned.

The relation of Procopios, written in the middle of the sixth century, is worth reading for its own sake. In the second book of his work on the Gothic wars he wrote of the inhabitants of Thule. The first information on this distant country was given by the Greek explorer Pytheas of Marseilles, who lived at the time of Alexander the Great. He obviously visited northern Norway and was told by the natives that the land was called *Thule*. This seems to reflect a prehistoric shape of a Scandinavian word which is still preserved in place-names and meant an inlet with a narrow opening; thus, Thule means "the fjords" and is the oldest name of Norway. To Procopios Thule meant the Scandinavian peninsula, which, in his opinion, was an island. In his description of Thule he mentioned the *Skrithifinoi* as the only really savage people in this country. There is not the slightest doubt but that he meant the Lapps, and he expressed more than clichés. He wrote:

"Among the barbarians who live in Thule there is only one people, namely the so-called Skrithifinoi, who have a rather animal mode of living. They do not wear clothes or shoes, nor do they drink wine or get anything eatable out of the soil. For neither do they till the soil themselves, nor do their women do any such work for them, but the men always devote themselves to hunting together with the women. There is a great supply of wild beasts and other animals in the forests, which are very vast, and in the high mountains. And they eat the meat of the animals which they always hunt, and wear the skins, because they have neither linen nor sewing implements (?): they join the skins

207

together by means of the sinews of the animals, and thus they manage to cover the whole body. And they do not nurse their babies in the same way as other people do. For the children of the Skrithifinoi are not nourished with woman's milk nor do they get hold of their mother's breast, but they are fed with the marrow of the animals which are captured there. As soon as a woman has born her child, she sweeps the baby in a skin and hangs it at once in a tree, puts marrow in its mouth and goes with her husband to pursue the habitual hunting. For they perform this work in common like everything else they do."

This is not a true picture of the life of the Lapps, but for a second-hand report it is remarkably good. The skin in which the woman sweeps her baby may be interpreted as a wooden cradle covered with skin. The marrow is easily identified as reindeer marrow. In so far as the "habitual hunting" means the tending of the half-wild reindeer, Procopios is quite correct in stating that men and women do it together. The other traits may or may not be freehand drawing.

Skrithifinoi reflects a primitive Scandinavian word *skriðifinnōz*, which exactly corresponds to Old English *Scridefinnas,* used by King Alfred the Great as a synonym of *Finnas,* "Lapps." This compound literally means "ski-running Lapps." In Old Norse the verb *skriða* "to glide, to slide," is a technical term for running on skis. In *The Poetic Edda* we are told that Völund and his brothers, the sons of a Lapp king, *skriðu ok veiddu dýr,* i.e. used to run on skis and hunt. Ski-running was an activity, at which the Lapps excelled. In *Grágás,* the old lawbook of the Icelanders, there is an archaic formula about the outlawing of a man who breaks a truce:

". . . he shall be driven from God and all God's christendom as far as men drive wolves, Christian men go to church, heathen men sacrifice in fanes, mothers bear sons, a son cries to his mother, fires burn, *the Lapp runs on skis (Finnr skriðr),* the fir grows, the hawk flies during a long day, having a fair wind under both its wings."

208

Jordanes, the Goth, who was a contemporary of Procopios, published a poor summary of Cassiodorus's *History of the Goths* (which unfortunately has been lost). Among the peoples living in *Scandza* (the Scandinavian peninsula) he mentions the *Screrefennae* (or *Rerefeni*, or *Sirdfeni*), who according to him chiefly eat meat and eggs. It may be that he had heard of nesting boxes (or rather cavities cut into growing trees) for wild ducks, such as Forest Lapps have used in recent times to get eggs. Immediately after the Screrefennae he mentions the Swedes (*Svehans*).

Paulus Diaconus in his *History of the Langobards* (written about the middle of the eighth century or a little later) gives an account of the *Scritofini*. He says that their name is derived from a word which in the language of the barbarians means "to run"; for they are able to overtake wild animals by running on pieces of curved wood. In their country there is snow even in summer. They look like beasts, and they eat the raw flesh of wild animals, and they make themselves clothes out of the hairy skins of the same animals. In their country there is an animal that resembles the red deer. Paulus says that he himself has seen a garment such as the Scritofini use, made of the hairy skin of that animal; it reached to the knees and reminded him of a tunic.

To the court of King Alfred the Great there came a rich Norwegian landowner, whose name was Óttarr; the English called him Ohthere. He told the King that he lived farther north than any other Norwegian. Once he had made a voyage still farther north, and then east, and then south, and finally westward; in other words, he had rounded the Kola peninsula, which probably nobody had done before him. Ohthere was more than a pioneer and an explorer; he should also be mentioned in the annals of comparative linguistics. He said that the language of the *Beormas*, living in the Kola peninsula, resembles the language of the *Finnas*, i.e. Lappish. Now we know from the report of another Norwegian explorer, Thorir Hundr (the beginning of the eleventh century), that the *Bjarmar* of the Kola peninsula had a big wooden idol, which they called

209

Jómali (accusative *Jómala*). This word is identical with Finnish *Jumala*, "God," and suffices in itself to demonstrate that the *Beormas* were Finns or Karelians.

This is the substance of what Ohthere told King Alfred about the Lapps (*Finnas*):

"He said that he lived in the land to the northward, on the West Sea. He said, however, that the land is very long north from thence; but it is all waste, except that in a few places Lapps dwell here and there, hunting in the winter, and in the summer fishing in the sea. He said that he wished to find out, at one time, how far the land extended northward, or whether any one lived to the north of the wilderness. He then went northward along the land for three days. He was then as far north as the whalehunters go at the farthest. Then he went on northward as far as he could sail within another three days. Then the land there inclined eastward, or the sea into the land, he did not know which; he only knew that he there waited for a west wind and a little north, and then sailed eastward along the land as far as he could sail in four days. Then he had to wait there for a due north wind, because the land there inclined southward, or the sea into the land, he knew not which. He then sailed thence along the land southward as far as he could sail in five days. Then there lay a river up into the land. They then turned up into the river, because they dared not sail on past the river for fear of hostility, because all the land was inhabited on the other side of the river. He had not before met with any inhabited land since he left his own home. But all the way he had waste land on his starboard, except for fishers, fowlers, and hunters, and they were all Lapps. The Biarms had cultivated their country very well. But the country of the Ter Lapps was all waste, except where hunters, fishers, or fowlers lived.

"It seemed to him that the Lapps and the Biarms spoke nearly one language.

"He was very rich in the kind of property of which their riches consist, that is to say, in deer. He had six hundred unbought domesticated deer. These animals are called *hránas*. Six of them were decoy reindeer; they are very expensive among the Lapps, for with them they capture the wild reindeer. He was one of the greatest men in that country; and yet he had only twenty heads of cattle, and twenty sheep, and twenty pigs; the little that he ploughed, he ploughed with horses. But most of their income derives from the taxes which the Lapps pay to them. The taxes consist in skins and bird feathers and whale bones (teeth) and ship-ropes made of the hide of whales and seals. Everybody pays according to his condition. The most opulent shall pay fifteen marten skins and five reindeer and one bear skin and ten ambers (forty bushels) of feathers and a coat of bear skin or otter skin and two ship-ropes; each of them shall be sixty ells long, and one of them shall be made of whale's hide and the other one of seal's hide."

The decoy reindeer are known from later epochs. Samuel Rheen (seventeenth century) says that in the autumn, when the reindeer rut, the Lapps go into the woods where they know that the wild reindeer are, and bind their does there, and when the wild reindeer will come to the doe, he is shot.

Saxo Grammaticus in his admirable *Gesta Danorum*, written in the beginning of the thirteenth century, introduced Finnmark as an independent kingdom, involved in a war with a Swedish buccaneer. Having vanquished the *Finni*, the Swede resolved that they henceforth every three years should pay in tax a sleigh filled with wild skins for every ten persons.

As far as personal names and other details are concerned, we cannot give any credit to Saxo's relation, and the tradition about ancient kings of Finnmark he had no doubt taken from Norwegian folklore. But what he says of the *Finni*, that is, the Lapps, is interesting: "The *Finni* are the people who live farthest to the North. . . . No other people are more proficient in shooting. . . . They are busy with incantations; in hunting they are skilful. They have no fixed abodes, but their houses are movable and they settle down wherever they have got hold of some quarry. They run across the snowy mountains on curved pieces of wood."

There is no doubt but that this description refers to the Lapps. But on the other hand, Saxo gives the earliest evi-

211

dence of the name *Lapp* (or *Lappland*). He mentions "both Lapplands" (*utraque Lappia*) together with *Helsingia* and *Finnia* (which in this context obviously means Finland) and *Estia* (Estonia).

How should it be explained that Saxo used the word *Finn* in two meanings ("Lapp" and "Finn"), and that he has two different designations for Lappland? The answer is that he was influenced both by Norwegian and by Swedish nomenclature. Saxo's usage still prevails in that on many modern maps *Lappland* means (the northern parts of) the territories in Sweden and Finland where Lapps live, whereas the specific land of the Lapps in Norway is called *Finnmark*. Here we have an unbroken tradition from the time of Saxo or earlier up to these days. It should only be added that the term *Lappland* has sometimes been quite especially connected with Finland. The Swedish historian Ericus Olai (the second half of the fifteenth century) mentions *Lappia* (together with Tavastland, Karelia, and Nyland) as a province of Finland. The brothers Johannes and Olaus Magnus in the sixteenth century distinguish between *Biarmia, Scrikfinnia,* and *Lappia* (or *Lapponia*). From the maps published by Olaus Magnus it will appear that *Scrikfinnia* was to him approximately what is now called Finnmark, whereas *Biarmia* was the Kola peninsula, and *Lapponia* the Swedish-Finnish Lappmarks (Kemi, Tornio, Lule, and Pite Lappmark).

Damianus a Goës, who was a friend of Johannes and Olaus, explicitly states that Eastern Lappia was separated from Western Lappia by the Botnian Gulf, which ends at Tornio. According to him, Lappia extends in the east to the White Sea; its extension in the north is unknown.

The first mention of the Lapps (*Lappa*) in a document issued in Sweden dates from 1328.

All attempts to give an evident etymology of the word *Lapp,* that is to say, to find out what this word may have denoted before it was used as a proper name, have failed. Probably this term was coined by the Finnish fur traders in the Middle Ages (Finnish *Lappi,* "Lappland," earlier also "a Lapp," *lappalainen,* "Lapp") and then adopted by the

Swedes, perhaps not earlier, or not much earlier, than the twelfth century.

Johannes Magnus (Jonas Månsson) was the last catholic archbishop in Uppsala. He and his brother, the canon Olaus Magnus, remained faithful to the Roman Church when the Reformation was introduced in Sweden by King Gustav I in 1527. Both brothers went into exile and never returned to Sweden. Johannes died in 1544, and then Olaus Magnus was appointed archbishop of Uppsala *in partibus infidelium,* and in this capacity he took part in the famous Tridentine Council.

These two brothers have probably contributed more than anybody else to make the Lapps known to the world. In their great historical and ethnographical works they gave ample information on the Lapps. The first fruits of their activities in this field appeared in a work called *Scondia,* published by the Bajuvarian scholar Jacob Ziegler in 1532. In 1544 the Portuguese Damianus a Goës published a letter to the Pope on the deplorable spiritual state of the Lapp people, and a brief description of the Lapps (both in Latin). His knowledge he had got chiefly from Johannes Magnus. The exiled archbishop himself wrote a fantastic *History of the Peoples of the North,* published after his death by his brother.

In 1539 Olaus Magnus published a big map of Fennoscandia, with explanations in Italian. This map, the so-called Carta Marina, is a remarkable scientific achievement. It is illustrated with many ethnographic drawings, distributed across the map, in order to give an idea of the population or the chief means of livelihood characteristic of each region. There we see pictures of Lapps, reindeer, Bircarls in a fantastic vehicle drawn by reindeer of enormous size, and so on. We see a wolverine squeezing himself between two trees to get rid of the cumbersome consequences of its excessive gluttony. Here and there we find pieces of historico-political information; for instance an inscription located on the Arctic coast somewhere in the western confines of the Kola peninsula: "Here is the limit of Sweden." On this map Fennoscandia, with the Kingdom of Sweden in its center, clearly appeared as the true wonderland that it was, made still more wonderful by distance and obscurity. In his great ethnographic *History of the Peoples of the North,* published in 1555, Olaus made this hyperborean world accessible to his European contemporaries. Of all the themes which Olaus Magnus treated, none was more apt to stir the imagination of his readers than Lappland.

Olaus seems to have taken some part of his information on the Lapps from Ziegler, but Ziegler probably had got most of his knowledge from Olaus or his brother Johannes. In any case, Olaus was the first to give a detailed account of the life and the material ethnography of the Lapps. Olaus said that the Lapps worshipped the sun and the moon; the sun was worshipped as the divinity which illuminated and warmed the earth and made the grass grow to feed the reindeer.

Speaking of the witchcraft of the Lapps, Olaus said that if somebody came to ask a Lapp what might have happened to an absent person, the Lapp went together with a companion and his wife into another room and there he put a brass frog or serpent upon an anvil and started beating the anvil muttering incantations till he swooned and lay as if he were dead. The companion had to watch him carefully during this trance. When he had returned to consciousness he could give information about the absent person and show a ring, a knife, or something else which he had taken from him. The Lapp sorcerers used to make magic arrows of lead, which they shot from an ever so great distance; those who were hit by such a shot received a wound in the leg or the arm and died within three days.

Olaus seems to distinguish between reindeer-breeding Lapps and fishing and hunting Lapps. He knew that the eastern Lapps in summer migrate from one dwelling-place to another in the forests, whereas they spend the winter "on the banks of the waters"(?). He knew about the wild reindeer and the domesticated reindeer and their winter food. He said that one Lapp may own ten, fifteen, thirty, seventy, or four to five hundred reindeer. He gave detailed, if not quite reliable, information on the tending of the reindeer, on milking, cheese-making, and the preparation and use of the skin, horns, bones, and sinews of the reindeer. He has described and depicted the boat-shaped sleigh and the reindeer-harness.

Olaus Magnus had a fairly good idea of the skis of the Lapps. He was quite right in stating that one of the two skis was longer than the other. He was also correct in saying that the skis are clad below with the hairy skin of a reindeer fawn in order to make it easier to go uphill.

According to Olaus the women hunted together with the men, but the men distributed the kill and decided what parts should be broiled. It is uncertain whether Olaus was right in asserting that the Lapps used to broil the meat. He may have been right in saying that they used to drink the fresh blood of the killed animal; as a matter of fact it is not unheard of nowadays that a Lapp having killed a reindeer, immediately drinks the blood from the wound, and such a habit is not unknown to Finnish or Swedish hunters either.[1]

Kaspar Peucer is known in the history of the Reformation as the leader of the so-called Crypto-calvinists, who tried to introduce the symbolic interpretations of the Eucharist in the electorate of Saxony. For this bold endeavor Peucer had to atone by twelve years' imprisonment. If the word humanist means a man who writes good Latin and can read Greek books, then Peucer was one. But he was more than that; he was also a specialist in mathematics and medicine. He got his education at the University of Wittenberg, the greenhouse of the evangelistic reformation. He was the son-in-law of Philip Melanchthon. In 1553 he published a standard work on the art of divination (*Commentarius de praecipuis divinationum generibus*) which proved to be a good seller, as learned handbooks go. In this work there is a paragraph on the magic practices of the Lapps. It contains such detailed information that one cannot help thinking that Peucer must have got his knowledge from a Swedish student at Wittenberg. This paragraph is well worth quoting at length.

[1] Karl Ahlenius has given a systematic account of Olaus Magnus's contributions to the ethnography of the Lapps.

215

Peucer says that the *Pilappii* (where did he get the prefix *pi-?*) live in the farthest part of the Scandinavian peninsula, near the Arctic Sea. They do not till the soil and they have no domestic animals except the reindeer, which they use as a draught-animal. They live by hunting and fishing. Hitherto they have had pieces of wood and stones for gods. They do not use quite as many incantations as they did earlier, because the king of Sweden has prohibited them severely from doing so, and he tries to have them instructed about our religion, although this is difficult because they have no fixed dwellings, and the regions where they live are marshy and one cannot travel there except in winter when everything is frozen. Priests from Finland, Norrbotten, Ångermanland, Medelpad, Hälsingland, and the adjacent regions used to visit them, and those whom they can find they teach to pray, and having given them a mediocre instruction, they baptize them. It is said that those who are baptized at an advanced age usually die within seven or eight days after their baptism.

"When they are going to hunt or fish or start doing something else, they use some conjuration and then try to move from their place the gods which they consult. If they are easy to move, then they approve of the endeavor and promise success. If they resist, they do not admit any success. If they cannot be moved at all, they feel obviously offended. In such case they think that the gods should be placated by a sacrifice, which is made in the following way. They have a brass drum on which they have depicted different kinds of quadrupeds, birds, and fishes. They have also a brass frog at the end of an iron stick, which they fix vertically in the middle of the drum. Then, having uttered adjurations, they beat the drum, and when it sounds, the frog leaps down on one of the depicted animals. The animal, to the picture of which the frog goes, must be sacrificed to the gods. They hang the head in a tree which they regard as holy. The rest they cook and eat, and they all pour over themselves the juice in which the victim has been boiled.

"If a stranger wishes to know something about his own people, they are able to make him know within twenty-four hours what has happened to them even if they are three hundred miles away. The sorcerer, having called and addressed his gods with traditional ceremonies, suddenly collapses and turns unconscious, as if he really were dead and the soul had quitted his body. There must always be some people present to watch over the outstretched lifeless body, else the demons may carry him away. After twenty-four hours the body with a deep sigh returns to life. Then he answers questions, and in order to convince the person who asks him, he tells him something which makes him sure that the sorcerer has visited his house or the house of his relatives.

"They have a vast multitude of the most powerful spectres, which visit them and keep company with them and speak to them, and it is impossible to keep them off or drive them away. They are especially frightened and harassed by the ghosts of their dead relatives, and to avoid this, they bury their relatives under the hearth."

One or two details of this account are doubtful, as the description of the magic drum and its accessories, which is not found in the first edition of the work; but on the whole it is no doubt authentic. The belief that a holy stone might be lighter or heavier according to its disposition towards the sacrificers occurs also in the relation of Samuel Rheen a hundred years later. He says that if the stone gods are portentously heavy when the Lapps lift them in order to put fresh twigs under them, this means that the god is adverse to them, and then they have to promise him a special sacrifice. Edgar Reuterskiöld has shown that an analogous belief has existed in southern Sweden. It may be added that the Yukaghir in northeastern Siberia, who use a shaman's skeleton for an oracle, think that it is a bad omen if the skeleton cannot be lifted from the ground.

In the middle of the sixteenth century the English found their way to the Kola peninsula and saw Lapps with their own eyes. The first Lappish word-list, comprising about one hundred words, was written down by the Englishman Stephen Borough in 1557. He met some Lapps at Svjatoi Nos, not far from the outflow of the river Ekonga:

". . . there came aboard us certaine Lappians in a boate, to the number of sixteene persons, and amongst them there were two wenches, and some of them could speake the Russe tongue. I asked them where their abiding was, and they tolde me that there was a companie or heard of them, to the number of 100 men, besides women and children, but a little from us in the river Iekonga. They tolde me that they had bene to seeke meate among the rockes, saying, If wee get no meate, wee eate none. I sawe them eate rocke wedes as hungerly, as a cowe doeth grass when she is hungrie. I sawe them also eate foules egges rawe, and the yong birdes also that were in the egges."

Richard Johnson, who traveled together with Borough, says that in Lappia there live two peoples, namely, Scrickfinnes and Lappians, but they resemble each other in every respect. Of the former he states expressly that they live in tents of deer-skins; they are clothed in deer-skins, they eat raw flesh but no bread, and drink only water. According to Johnson's informants, these two peoples seem to have differed chiefly in matter of religion: The Scrickfinnes "neither know God, nor yet good order," whereas the Lappians, or at least those who have been subdued by the Russian Emperor, "will say that they beleeve in the Russes God."

Anthony Jenkinson visited Russian Lappland at the same time as Borough. I do not know in how far his account was founded on autopsy, but it is worth quoting because it is so lively and because he says, just as Tacitus and Procopios, that the Lapp women take part in hunting together with the men. Anthony Jenkinson wrote:

"The land of Lappia is an high land, having snow lying on it commonly all the yeere. The people of the country are halfe Gentiles: they live in the summer neare the sea side, and use to take fish, of which they make bread, and in the winter they remove up into the countrey into the woods, where they use hunting, and kill Deere, Beares, Woolves, and other beasts, with whose flesh they be nourished, and with their skinnes apparelled in such strange fashion, that there is nothing seene of them bare but their eies. They have none other habitation, but onely in tents, removing

218

from place to place, according to the season of the yeere. They know no arte nor facultie, but onely shooting, which they exercise dayly, as well men as women, and kill such beasts as serve them for their foode."

Giles Fletcher visited the Kola peninsula in the year that the Spanish Armada was destroyed. Most of what he said about the Lapps he learned from Russian sources. He praises the Lapps as excellent huntsmen. In summer, he said, they come in great companies to the sea coast "to fish for Codde, Salmon, and But-fish. When their fishing is done their manner is to drawe their carbasses or boates on shore, and there to leave them with the keele turned upwardes, till the next spring tide. Their travaile to and fro is upon sleddes drawen by the Olen² Deere: which they use to turne a grasing all the Sommer time in an Island called Kildyn . . . and towards the Winter time, when the snow beginneth to fall, they fetch them home for the use of their sledde."

"For practise of witchcraft and sorcerie they passe all nations of the worlde," says Fletcher. But he does not believe in their alleged faculty of regulating the wind on the sea by tying and untying magic knots; this is "a very fable, devised by themselves, to terrifie sailers for comming neere their coast."

In 1613 the Norwegian clergyman Peder Claussøn (Friis) wrote a detailed *Description of Norway*, published 1632. He devoted a chapter to the Lapps, especially the Sea Lapps of Finnmark, praising them as efficient ship-builders, fishermen, and hunters. Although they are lean, he said, they are much stronger than other people: a Norwegian is not able to pull a bow half as much as a Lapp can. The Lapps keep a lot of domesticated reindeer, from which they get milk, butter, and cheese. In autumn they sell their reindeer to butchers. They also keep goats, but no sheep. When a Lapp shoots a wild reindeer he keeps his bow and arrow between the antlers of a domesticated reindeer, and so he shoots one animal after another. The Lapps are keen about hunting seals "because a Lapp likes to have a quart of train-oil to drink at every meal."

² The Russian word for "reindeer."

Peder Claussøn said that the Lapps must be regarded as pagans because of their terrible sorcery and idolatry; they worship idols made of wood. Peder related the same story as Olaus Magnus and others about how the Lapp sorcerers manage to know what happens at distant places. His relation is remarkable because of its conscientious exactness; it reminds one of a scientific report of a hypnotic experiment:

"... one has witnessed in Johan Delling's German boardinghouse at Bergen that a Lapp who had come to Bergen together with a man called Jacob Smaasvend, was asked to tell them what the above-mentioned Johan Delling's principals in Germany were doing. He made himself ready, and sat reeling as if he had been drunk, and suddenly he jumped to his feet and ran around a few times, and then he fell to the floor and there he remained lying as if he had been dead, and when he awakened later on, he told them what Johan Delling's principals were doing at the same time, and that was noted at once in the diary of the boardinghouse, and subsequently it turned out that he had told the truth."

A variant of this story circulated in Sweden as late as the first decade of this century. In this variant the Lapp during his trance travels from Lappland to Uppsala (or some other remote place) to visit the fiancée or wife of a man of distinction who is present at the séance (the missionary Petrus Laestadius, or even Linnaeus, who was not engaged when he went to Lappland), and when he wakes up out of his trance he hands over the engagement ring (or wedding-ring) of the young lady, who later on states that exactly on that day and hour a Lapp had appeared while she was baking bread; when she left the kitchen for a moment, the Lapp disappeared with her ring. I am not quite sure that there are not still people who believe such stories. Anyhow, most of what Peder Claussøn said about the practices of Lapp sorcerers is interesting as evidence of the compact superstition which prevailed even among learned men in Scandinavia (and in other countries too) as late as three hundred years ago. We must not forget that Peder Claussøn was born in a century during which about twenty thousand women were burned alive as "witches."

220

Queen Christina of Sweden was eager to engage prominent foreign scholars. She invited Descartes to teach her philosophy; unfortunately, the famous philosopher was not accustomed to rising at five o'clock in the morning, and he died after his first winter in Stockholm. Another of the queen's protegés lived to plough a long furrow in the soil of Swedish civilization, namely, the Alsatian philologist Johannes Schefferus. He gained a world-wide reputation by his book *Lapponia*, which appeared (in Latin) in 1673 and was soon translated into English, German, French, and Dutch. *Lapponia* was the very first monograph on the Lapps to be printed in any language, and it is still regarded as the standard work in this field. This is most remarkable because Schefferus never saw Lappland, and I do not know if he was ever north of Uppsala. Linnaeus has justly remarked that *Lapponia* is an astonishingly good work if this circumstance is taken into account. Schefferus says in the preface to his book that he never neglected any opportunity to talk to Lapps, but there is not much evidence of this in the book.

Schefferus wrote *Lapponia* at the request of the Swedish authorities, and all the material available was put at his disposal. Clergymen who knew Lappland thoroughly were commanded to furnish him with detailed systematic descriptions, and it is not the least of Schefferus's merits that he quoted his informants on every page of his dissertation. The descriptions written by Samuel Rheen, Olaus Petri Niurenius, and Johannes Tornaeus have been published in Swedish by K. B. Wiklund (Niurenius wrote in Latin, Rheen and Tornaeus in Swedish).

Rheen's *Relation about the Life, Customs, and Superstitions of the Lapps* is a masterpiece of concise ethnographical description; it is the chief source of Schefferus's *Lapponia*. Rheen had a favorable opinion of the physical attainments of the Lapps. He wrote:

"The Lapps are almost all of low stature, not very strong, but very swift and supple, so that the Lapp can run on his skis down the high mountains, which seems to be above all understanding. [Yes, to a farmer's son from Piteå in the

221

middle of the seventeenth century. The same was reported about the Norwegian king, Olaf Tryggvason, who lived in the tenth century.] Some of them are white of complexion, and although they always dwell in smoky tents, they nevertheless keep clean, washing their hands and face pretty well every day. [Fifty years later, Linneaus said that he could not help wondering at the snow-white bodies of these black-faced people.] The Lapps are by nature a healthy people, generally not afflicted with bodily infirmities, as people of other nations are.

"In their commerce the Lapps are very false and fraudulent, so that he who does not understand their tricks can hardly escape being cheated by them. They try in particular to cheat those who just begin to trade with them, and having done so, they deride those whom they have thus deceived."

To this judgment Schefferus adds the reasonable remark that the Lapps probably learned the noble art of trading from their settled neighbors. Lapp paganism is treated at some length in Rheen's treatise, and to this chapter he added four splendid drawings.

Johannes Tornaeus did a remarkable pioneer work in his *Manuale Lapponicum,* which I have mentioned in the chapter on the literature of the Lapps. He knew thoroughly the conditions of the Lapps in Tornio Lappmark. From his valuable *Account of the Lappmarks and their State* I should like to quote the following characterization of the Lapps:

"In stature the Lapps are mostly small people. Some of them are of a medium height, but there are not many tall persons to be found among them. They usually have black and coarse hair . . . , and I have never seen but one Lapp with blond hair. Under the eyes and in the face they are broad, with empty cheeks and long chin, so that their women can easily be distinguished from other women, without being misshapen. . . . Their body is quite white, and the women are rather well shaped, so that their comeliness would be quite passable if they could afford to keep out of the smoke. These people are also quite lithe and nimble, and although they are small of stature they have nevertheless a considerable power and agility, and also patience on journeys and perseverance in working. . . . They have a good understanding and a strong memory; they are prudent and astute in all their proceedings and fraudulent in business transactions, but very inclined and willing to entertain and advance strangers and travelers. They readily take care of poor people and keep them for a whole year, or a half year or a quarter, more or less, according to their resources and circumstances, and then they take them with their own reindeer to somebody else, as it is impossible to walk because of the deep snow. The children are always well disciplined, and the parents are respected and honored properly, nay, when they are aged their children never leave them untended, but maintain and nurse them most carefully to their dying day. The wives are found to be obedient towards their husbands, and the husbands are affectionate towards them. . . . . With their neighbors they live confidentially and candidly. They abhor stealth, and they are so conscientious that if someone happens to see that a wild reindeer or another animal has got caught in his neighbor's or somebody else's snare, he tells him that immediately. . . . About Lapp women it is known that most of the old ones cannot stand any sudden movement, change, or consternation, but if anybody provokes them, vexes them with a bad or unseemly word, points to them, imitates them, or turns her swiftly around, or if a spark from the fire hits her, then she goes wild, rushes against him who has caused it, tears his hair, beats people with pieces of burning wood, or whatever else she gets hold of, and even if a very distinguished man should be present, in her excitement she does not shrink from showing her private and secret parts. In a word she behaves quite like a madman, which she then really is."

Tornaeus gives the following account of the role which the reindeer plays in the economy of the Lapps:

"It is impossible fully to describe what a useful and noble animal the reindeer is. For from the reindeer the Lapp has his food and his clothes, his conveyance and his sustenance, and many household articles. While it lives, it gives the Lapp both milk and cheese, and moreover it is not only quite handy, but also pretty swift on all journeys. And yet the Lapp is not bound to incur any expenses for it: it needs neither any stable in winter, nor forage; wherever it comes in the night it sleeps under the open sky, and it finds its food for itself. When it is slaughtered there is nothing to be found in it which is not useful. First, the meat is not only eatable, but it is as fat, good, and savory as any meat can be. In the bones there is an excellent marrow, of which the Lapps make such a feast as we make of oysters or some early fruit. From the skin they get fur coats, from the leg-skin and the head-skin leggings, shoes and gloves, and harnesses, and what else may be needed for straps and the like. The sinews are always used instead of thread, and also to seam together the boards of their boats and boat-shaped sleighs. With the hides they do their best trading and pay all their taxes. Out of the bones and the horns, spoons and all kinds of household goods can be made. In short, to the Lapp the reindeer is more valuable and useful than any other animal is to any people on the earth."

In 1732, Carl Linnaeus went to Lappland, with the backing of a Royal Scientific Society. He was twenty-five years old, full of pluck and enterprise. His keen eye grasped everything that met him. His diary has been published, though it never was intended for publication, and it contains a few remarks and descriptions that would have been shocking to Victorian minds. It is written in casual Swedish, with an admixture of slipshod Latin jargon.

Linnaeus was obviously thrown off his balance by the first sight of the snowy alps of Lappland, even if he did not admit it explicitly. He wrote: "When we were on the mountain Skalka seven miles from Tjâmotis, there appeared in the northwest a gap between the mountains, through which there glared mountains at a distance of seventy or eighty miles, all white, as if they had not been more than seven miles away, rising with their peaks up into the sky, as when white clouds rise above the horizon . . . , in a word, I saw the fjelds."

Linnaeus is chiefly known to posterity for his binary nomenclature for both animals and plants. He classified all the living beings, except the microbes, which he found too variegated and puzzling. He greatly admired the Lapp women in Jockmock, when he saw them handle their half-domesticated reindeer herds. He wrote: "I wondered how the milkers could know them. For as soon as they were milked, they were let loose. They told me that all the reindeer have their specific names, which they know quite distinctly. This seemed to me most strange, because the shape (of the animals) is the same, the color is similar, and varies from one month to another. The size differs according to the age, and to know such a muddle, like ants in an ant-hill, seemed to me to be a most puzzling thing."

Per Fjellström published the first Lappish grammar, the first Lappish dictionary, and the first Lappish translation of the New Testament. He has also written a detailed account of the bear hunting ceremonies of the Lapps.

In 1746 the Swedish clergyman, Per Högström, who was the first rector of the parish of Gällivare, published his *Description of the Lappmarks of the Crown of Sweden,* which was twice translated into German; it was the first systematic handbook on the Lapps founded on autopsy.

In 1752 the Norwegian clergyman, Knud Leem, was appointed headmaster and docent of Lappish in the newly founded Seminarium Lapponicum at Trondheim. This humble-minded man did a gigantic work in teaching and preaching as well as in linguistic investigations. He wrote a good Lappish grammar (the first description of Finnmark Lappish) and a voluminous Lappish dictionary, an epoch-making work. He also published an ample *Description of the Lapps of Finnmark* in Danish and Latin. This is a standard work in its kind. It is illustrated with a hundred engravings, which are not all quite as realistic as the text.

Leem devoted a few chapters of his excellent treatise to the superstitions and the ancient pagan religion of the

225

Lapps, but he also added to his work a treatise by Erich Johannes Jessen on the same subject. Jessen, a Supreme Court Judge, was no specialist in this field, and as a matter of fact, his work is only a revised version of a part of a manuscript written by the Norwegian clergyman and missionary Hans Skanke. This treatise has justly been regarded as a chief source of our knowledge of Lapp paganism.

After Leem's death the missionary work among the Lapps of Finnmark was neglected. The authorities thought that they could do without the Lappish language. But most of the Lapps did not understand Norwegian, and the consequences of the new policy of christianization turned out to be destructive. Reform was called for, and it was brought about by the clergyman Niels Vibe Stockfleth, who came to Finnmark in 1825. He thought that the only means of improving the religious condition of the Lapps was to teach them in their own language, and he made up his mind to start by learning Lappish himself. In order to achieve this aim he took a badly paid position in a region where he could live in daily contact with the Lapps. He devoted several years to the study of the Lappish language and he wrote a Lappish grammar and a big dictionary (Norwegian and Lappish). In collaboration with the famous Danish linguist Rasmus Rask he worked out a new orthography for Lappish and printed books written in that orthography for the use of the Lapps. In 1836 he renounced his ecclesiastic career and moved to the capital, where he was busy until his death working for the benefit of the Lapps. He published a diary describing his life as a missionary in Finnmark and his other activities. This work contains rich information on the life and the conditions of the Norwegian Lapps.

Petrus Laestadius was a younger brother of the famous preacher and religious reformer Lars Levi Laestadius. The two brothers were different in many respects. In religion Lars Levi strongly stressed the Law, whereas Petrus exclusively preached the Gospel. Lars Levi was a fanatic, Petrus had a peaceful mind and a keen sense of humor. It seems as if two souls had dwelt in the bosom of Lars Levi Laestadius,

226

the vehement subjective sectarian and the calm objective naturalist. He was interested in the material as well as in the spiritual wellbeing of his countrymen. At the age of twenty-two he published a treatise on the *Possibility of Cultivation in Lappland,* with a classic characterization of the different climatic zones. His work on the ancient mythology of the Lapps, written for the publications of the French scientific expedition to Northern Lappland, of which he had been a member, was not published during his lifetime.

Petrus Laestadius functioned for a few years as a "missionary," that is a traveling priest or preacher in Lule Lappmark. In 1831 he published a diary of his first year as a missionary in Lappland. This book, with its continuation which appeared two years later, is much more than a diary. It is one of the best books ever written on Lappland and the Lapps, and many later travelers and other writers have drawn from it. It was no success when it appeared, and Laestadius wrote later that he was forever disconsolate about this literary shipwreck. But his work is a masterpiece, and it occupies a place of its own in Swedish literature. The straightforward simplicity of its style has an irresistible charm. From the very first page the reader is led on and made familiar with the topographical, economic, educational, and ecclesiastic conditions of Lappland. Lively descriptions alternate with theoretic expositions of mint value and other difficult themes. In an unsystematic way the author treats almost all questions which have anything to do with Lappland and its settled and nomadic inhabitants. Laestadius was born in Lappland and spent most of his life there. He was partly if not chiefly of Lapp extraction, and in matter of language he was a "Mountain Lapp of the Sirkas tribe of Lule Lappmark." He is the first author to give a detailed picture of the intellectual and emotional life of the Lapps. He is not sentimental, and he does not take an optimistic view on the future of the Lapps. He says that some Lapps are "employed in the parishes of Norrland as flayers, hangman's jackals, and the like," and he adds the following prognosis: "A nation of flayers has arisen which is likely to

227

be everlasting like Jews and Gypsies, and it will certainly remain after the rest of the Lapp nation has disappeared." Fortunately Laestadius was mistaken.

Petrus Laestadius had a very favorable opinion of the Forest Lapps and a rather poor opinion of the Mountain Lapps. There is a touch of romanticism in his judgment of the Forest Lapps of Pite Lappmark:

"They are on a higher level of civilization than the other, so that they are undoubtedly the best among the Lapps. And their manner of life is so happy that I do not know if any other way of living is superior to theirs, if one takes into account those who must eat bread in the sweat of their brows and eat of the ground in sorrow, as it is said. . . . The poets praise the shepherd's life, hunting is a pleasure even for kings, and certainly many a man knows no occupation more pleasant than fishing. All three together compose the whole life of the Forest Lapp. Moreover he is free from the usual dog's-life of the Mountain Lapp, who is exposed to every kind of bad weather in the bare snow-mountains and has to tend his reindeer incessantly day and night."

Jacob Fellman was rector in Utsjoki, the northernmost parish of Finland, from 1819 to 1832. He learned the Lappish language thoroughly, preached in Lappish, and translated religious texts into this language. He was accomplished in both science and letters, and with unfailing energy he spent all his spare time in botanical, zoological, meteorological, ethnological, and philological observations and investigations, till he had to quit his outpost with broken health. Among other things he noted down a few Lapp epic songs which are more archaic than anything else we know of that kind. Many years after his death Jacob Fellman's diaries and notes were edited in full by his son, Isak Fellman. To the four volumes of this posthumous work Isak Fellman added another four volumes of documents and essays on Finnish Lappland and the Lapps, from Swedish and Finnish archives. It is a pity that we do not have such a collection concerning Swedish Lappland from Lule Lappmark southward.

228

Jens Andreas Friis was appointed professor of the Lappish language at the University of Cristiania (Oslo) 1866. He was a worthy follower of Leem and Stockfleth, not only as a teacher but also as a lexicographer and grammarian. His *Lexicon Lapponicum* (with Norwegian and Latin glosses) remained unchallenged for a half century; now it is superseded. His description of a journey to Finnmark, Russian Lappland, and Karelia is still worth reading. He also wrote a romantic Lapp novel, *Lajla* which has been translated into several languages and even filmed.

Exactly two hundred years after the appearance of Schefferus's *Lapponia,* the Swedish naturalist Gustaf von Düben published a richly illustrated handbook on *Lappland and the Lapps* (especially the Swedish Lapps). In the beginning the author had planned only an ethnological introduction to a description of a collection of Lapp skulls, but he became so interested in this subject that he made a trip to Lappland and entered deeply into all aspects of this study. Von Düben knew more about the Lapps than Schefferus, but most of his knowledge was second hand. In his attitude towards informants and previous authors he is mostly critical, often hypercritical (as of Petrus Laestadius, and Stockfleth), sometimes uncritical (as of Anders Fjellner, who is discussed in Chapter XVII). Von Düben also published a French summary of his handbook.

In the summer of 1885 a student by the name of Karl Bernhard Wiklund came to Uppsala to begin his academic career. He was only seventeen, but he had already been studying Finnish independently. Now he had made up his mind to study phonetics and Lappish. As he could not get any training in these branches of linguistics in Uppsala, so he went to Lule Lappmark and there spent most of his time during that academic year. He continued to investigate the Lappish language for five decades and extended his sphere of interest to the comparative study of the Uralic family of languages and the ethnology of the peoples of the Northern hemisphere. He became expert in almost everything that had anything to do with the Lapps. His works are so numerous and so many of them are of an outstanding importance that it is impossible to give in a few words an idea of what he achieved in the domain which he designated with a rather slipshod term, "Lappology." In his attitude towards the Lapps, Wiklund was realistic and unromantic. He understood and appreciated them and never dreamed of dealing with them in a condescending manner. He heartily disliked the habit some people have of regarding the Lapps as museum curiosities or objects of cheap philanthropy. He used to assert that the Lapps are citizens of their country with the same rights and the same duties as everybody else, and that they are able to take care of themselves and get along if they are given a fair chance.

This chapter would be incomplete if I should not mention a few research workers who are still living.

Just Knud Qvigstad was born in Lyngen in Finnmark in 1853. He was headmaster of the normal school at Tromsö for decades, but this did not keep him from tremendous activity as a field-worker and author in the domains of linguistics and folklore. He is quoted as having said that two years of his life have been of no avail, namely the two years he spent in Oslo as President of the Board of Education. All his activities have been focussed on the Lapps, their language, folklore, history, traditions, customs, and livelihood. Few folklorists have collected as much material as Qvigstad and very few have published so much of their material. Especially important is his mighty collection of Lapp folktales and legends (with Norwegian translation) in four big volumes, completed by his systematic catalogue of motif variants.

Some forty years ago a young Danish ethnologist, Emilie Demant (later married to the anthropologist Gudmund Hatt) made a unique experiment: she made up her mind to live with a nomadic Lapp family for a whole year as a member of the household. She prepared herself by studying Lappish in Copenhagen under the direction of the famous linguist Vilhelm Thomsen. Then during her migratory existence in Lappland she learned the language thoroughly. Her Lapp year was a success; the Lapps took "Emilie" to

230

their bosom, and she learned to know and appreciate and like them very much. The first literary fruit of her roving experience was her excellent book, *With the Lapps in the High Mountains*. And we are indebted to Emilie Demant-Hatt for another achievement: under her influence the Lapp Johan Turi wrote his remarkable book, *Muittalus samid birra*. But for her efforts it would probably never have been written.

Norway has a paramount record in the cultivation and the systematic description of the Lappish language. A two-century-old tradition has culminated in Konrad Nielsen's great *Lapp Dictionary* (with glosses in Norwegian and English). If both completeness and phonetic accuracy are taken into account it is safe to say that Nielsen's dictionary is equalled by few dictionaries in the world, and second to none. Nielsen has also written the classic grammar of the Lappish language. It is a pity that it is accessible only to those who understand Norwegian.

It is still more to be regretted that most of the works of Toivo Itkonen have been published only in Finnish. Dr. Itkonen belongs to a family of "lappologues," he is a specialist in the entire field of Lapp studies, and his production is very extensive. He has recently published a great synthetic systematic work on the Finnish Lapps.

BIBLIOGRAPHY

ABBREVIATIONS:

Ac. Sc. Fenn., *Annales—Suomalaisen tiedeaka-
temian toimituksia. Annales Academiæ
Scientiarum Fennicæ.*
*Archives des traditions—Archives des tradi-
tions populaires Suédoises. Nyare bidrag
till kännedom om de svenska landsmålen
ock svenskt folklif.* (Later title:) *Svenska
landsmål och svenskt folkliv.*
Diss.—Doctor's dissertation.
Hki—Helsinki (Helsingfors).
SFOu, *Journal — Suomalais-ugrilaisen seuran
aikakauskirja. Journal de la Société finno-
ougrienne.*
SFOu, *Mémoires—Suomalais-ugrilaisen seuran
toimituksia. Mémoires de la Société finno-
ougrienne.*
Sthm—Stockholm.
Ups—Uppsala (Upsala).

BIBLIOGRAPHY*

Abercromby, John. "The earliest list of Russian Lapp words." (SFOu, *Journal*, XIII. No. 2.) Hki, 1895.

Acerbi, Joseph. *Travels through Sweden, Finland, and Lapland to the North Cape, in the years 1798 and 1799.* I–II. London, 1802. (Vol. II, pp. 137–211, is a treatise on the Lapps, based on Leem's Description.)

Äimä, Frans. "Russ. kebovat'—lp. *gievvot.*" (Ac. Sc. Fenn., *Annales.* Ser. B. Tom. XXVII, pp. 409–432.) Hki, 1932.

Ahlenius, Karl. *Olaus Magnus och hans framställning af Nordens geografi.* Diss., Ups, 1895.

Arbman, Ernst. "Kallbad och rännskjuts. En norrländsk folktradition och dess verklighetsunderlag." (*Festskrift till Iwan Wikström*, pp. 11–66.) Lund, 1947.

Atányi, István. "Kahden vanhimman tunnetun lappalaisen runon vaikutus maailmankirjallisuuteen." (*Virittäjä*, 1941, pp. 110–122.) Hki, 1941. (With a Summary in French.)

Bergström, Richard. "Spring, min snälla ren!" (*Archives des traditions*, V. 4, pp. 1–20.) Sthm, 1885.

Bromé, Janrik. *Nasafjäll. Ett norrländskt silververks historia.* Sthm, 1923.

Brooke, Sir Arthur de Capell. *Travels through Sweden, Norway, and Finmark, to the North Cape, in the summer of 1820.* London, 1823.

——. *A Winter in Lapland and Sweden, with various observations relating to Finmark and its inhabitants; made during a residence at Hammerfest, near the North Cape.* London, 1827.

Bruhn, Karl. *Uppfostran hos de nordiska nomaderna.* Hki and Sthm, 1935.

Bryn, Halfdan. *Troms fylkes antropologi.* (*Videnskapsselskapet i Kristiania. Skrifter.* I. Matematisk-naturvidenskabelig klasse, 1921, No. 20.) Kristiania, 1922. (With a Summary in German.)

Butler, Frank Hedges. *Through Lapland with skis and reindeer*,

*Note. Apart from publications in the English language, this bibliography comprises only such sources as I have drawn on for this book.

235

with some account of ancient Lapland and the Murman coast. London, 1917.

Charnoluskĭ, V. V. *Materialy po bytu lopareĭ.* Leningrad, 1930.

——. "Zametki o past'be i organizatsii stada u lopareĭ." ("Notes on pasturage and organization of the herd among the Lapps." *Kol'skiĭ sbornik.* Akademiia nauk Soiuza Sovetskikh Sotsialisticheskikh Respublik. *Materialy Komissii ėkspeditsionnykh issledovaniĭ.* Vpy. 23. Seriia severnaia, pp. 23–69.) Leningrad, 1930.

Clarke, Edward Daniel. *Travels in various countries of Europe, Asia and Africa.* Part 3: *Scandinavia.* (Vol. 9–10.) London, 1824.

Collinder, Björn. "The Affinities of Lapp." (*Uppsala Universitets Årsskrift,* 1945:12. *Språkvetenskapliga Sällskapets i Uppsala Förhandlingar,* 1943–1945, pp. 129–143.) Ups, 1945.

——. "Den lapska litteraturen." (*Saga och sed,* 1944, pp. 1–17.) Ups, 1945.

——. *Lapparna, deras kultur och arbetsliv.* (*Verdandis småskrifter,* 352.) Sthm, 1932.

Consett, Matthew. *A tour through Sweden, Swedish-Lapland, Finland and Denmark.* London (Stockton), 1789.

Czekanowski, Jan. "Zur Anthropologie der Ugrofinnen." (SFOu, *Mémoires,* LXVII, pp. 65–71.) Hki, 1933.

Daunius, Erik. "Om de hedniska lapparnas gudabilder." (*Västerbotten,* 1926, pp. 17–85.) Umeå, 1926.

Demant-Hatt, Emilie, *Med lapperne i höjfjeldet.* Sthm, 1913.

——. "Offerforestillinger og erindringer om troldtrommen hos nulevende lapper." (*Festskrift til Rektor J. Qvigstad,* pp. 47–58.) Oslo, 1928.

Dergachev, N. *Russkaia Laplandiia.* ("Russian Lappland.") Archangel, 1877.

Donner, Otto. *Lieder der Lappen.* Hki, 1876.

Drake, Sigrid. *Västerbottenslapparna under förra hälften av 1800-talet.* Diss., Ups, 1918.

Düben, Gustaf von. "La Laponie et les Lapons." (*Congrès international des sciences géographiques tenu à Paris du 1er au 11 Août 1875. Compte rendu des séances.* T. I, pp. 323–341.) Paris, 1878.

——. *Om Lappland och Lapparne, företrädesvis de svenske.* Sthm, 1873. (With a map.)

Ekvall, Sven. "On the history and conditions of life of the West Bothnian nomad Lapps, their food and health conditions." (*Acta Medica Scandinavica*, Vol. CV:4, pp. 329–359.) Sthm, 1940.

Engelhardt, Alexander Platonovich. *A Russian Province of the North*. Translated from the Russian by Henry Cooke. Westminster, 1899.

Fellman, Isak. *Handlingar och uppsatser angående finska Lappmarken och lapparne, samlade och utgifna af Isak Fellman. I anslutning till Jacob Fellmans "Anteckningar under min vistelse i Lappmarken."* 4 v. Hki, 1910–1915.

Fellman, Jacob. *Anteckningar under min vistelse i Lappmarken.* 4 v. Hki, 1906.

Fett, Harry. "Finnmarksviddens kunst—John Savio." (*Kunst og kultur*, Vol. 26, pp. 221–246.) Oslo, 1940.

Fjellström, Pehr. *Kort Berättelse Om Lapparnas Björna-fänge, Samt Deras der wid brukade widskeppelser.* Sthm, 1755.

Friis, Jens Andreas. *En Sommer i Finmarken, Russisk Lapland og Nordkarelen. Skildringer af Land og Folk.* Christiania, 1871. (The same, 2nd ed., Christiania, 1880.)

——. *Lappisk Mythologi, Eventyr og Folkesagn.* Christiania, 1871.

——. "Russisch-Lappland." (*Mittheilungen aus Justus Perthes' geographischer Anstalt über wichtige neue Erforschungen auf dem Gesammtgebiete der Geographie* von Dr. A. Petermann, Vol. 16, pp. 358–364.) Gotha, 1870. (With a map.)

(Friis), Peder Claussøn. *Norriges Oc Omliggende Øers sandfærdige Bescriffuelse.* Copenhagen, 1632.

Fritzner, Johan. "Lappernes Hedenskab og Trolddomskunst sammenholdt med andre Folks, især Normændenes, Tro og Overtro." (*Historisk Tidsskrift.* Udgivet af Den Norske Historiske Forening. Vol. IV, pp. 135–217.) Christiania, 1877.

Geĭman, Vasiliĭ Georgievich, ed. *Materialy po istorii Karelii XII–XVI v.v.* Petrozavodsk, 1941.

Genetz, Arvid. *Wörterbuch der Kola-lappischen Dialekte nebst Sprachproben.* (Also with Finnish title:) *Kuollan lapin murteiden sanakirja ynnä kielennäytteitä. (Bidrag till kännedom af Finlands natur och folk.* Utgifna af Finska Vetenskaps-Societeten. Vol. 50.) Hki, 1891.

Goes, Damião de. "Deploratio Lappianae gentis. Lappiae descriptio." (*Damiani a Goes eqvitis Lvsitani Opvscvla aliqvot historica . . .*) Louvain, 1544.

Gourlie, Norah. *A Winter with Finnish Lapps.* London and Glasgow, 1939.

Grundström, Harald. *Barnaundervisningen i en lappmarksför-samling.* Ups, 1942.

Guttorm, Aslak. *Koccam spalli.* (*Sami Čuvgitusseärvi toaima-tusak,* Vol. 6.) Hki, 1940.

Hadwen, Seymour, and Palmer, Lawrence J. *Reindeer in Alaska.* (United States Department of Agriculture. *Bulletin* No. 1089.) Washington, 1922.

Hämäläinen, Antti. *Koltta-Lappia sanoin ja kuvin.* Porvoo (Borgå), Hki, 1938.

Hakluyt, Richard. *The Principal Navigations Voiages Traffiques and Discoveries of the English Nation.* 2nd ed. 3 v. London, 1598–1600. (Reprinted, in 12 v., Glasgow, 1903–1905.)

Hallström, Gustaf. "Gravplatser och offerplatser i ryska lappmarken." (*Rig,* Vol. V, pp. 162–192.) Sthm, 1922.

——. "Kolalapparnas hotade existens." (*Ymer,* Vol. 31, pp. 239–316.) Sthm, 1911.

——. "Lapska offerplatser." (*Arkeologiska studier tillägnade H.K.H. kronprins Gustaf Adolf,* utgivna av Svenska Fornminnesföreningen, pp. 111–131.) Sthm, 1932.

Harva, Uno. *Lappalaisten uskonto.* (*Suomen suvun uskonnot.* II.) Porvoo (Borgå), 1915.

——. "Skoltelapparnas 'följeslagare'." (*Festskrift til Rektor J. Qvigstad,* pp. 65–67.) Oslo, 1928.

——. "Vänster hand och motsols." (*Rig,* Vol. 8, pp. 23–36.) Sthm, 1925.

Hatt, Gudmund. *Arktiske Skinddragter i Eurasien og Amerika.* Diss., Copenhagen, 1914.

——. "Notes on Reindeer Nomadism." (*Memoirs of the American Anthropological Association.* Vol. VI, No. 2, pp. 75–133.) Lancaster, Pa., 1919.

Helland, Amund. *Topografisk-statistisk beskrivelse over Finmarkens amt. 2. Befolkning og historie.* (*Norges land og folk, topografisk-statistisk beskrevet,* XX:2.) Kristiania, 1906.

——. *Topografisk-statistisk beskrivelse over Tromsø amt.* (*Norges land og folk, topografisk-statistisk beskrevet,* XIX.) Kristiania, 1899.

Högström, Pehr. *Beskrifning öfwer de til Sweriges Krona lydande Lapmarker.* Sthm (1747).

Holmbäck, Åke. *Om Lappskattelandsinstitutet och dess historiska utveckling.* (Statens offentliga utredningar. Socialdep:t, 1922:10.) Sthm, 1922.

BIBLIOGRAPHY

Holmberg, Uno. See: Harva, Uno.

Homén, Theodor. *East Carelia and Kola Lapmark.* Described by Finnish scientists and philologists. (*Fennia*, 42, No. 3.) Hki, 1921.

Huldt, H. Hampusson. *Mönsterbok för lapsk hemslöjd i Västerbottens län.* Hälsingborg, 1920.

Itkonen, Erkki. "Olaus Sirman kotiseudusta ja kielestä." (*Virittäjä*, 1940, pp. 334–349.) Hki, 1940. (With a Summary in German.)

Itkonen, Toivo Immanuel. *Heidnische Religion und späterer Aberglaube bei den finnischen Lappen.* (SFOu, *Mémoires*, LXXXVII.) Hki, 1946.

——. *Koltan- ja kuolanlappalaisia satuja.* I–II. Kolttalaisia ja kildiniläisiä satuja, koonnut T. I. Itkonen. III. Jokongalaisia satuja, koonnut D. E. D. Europæus. (SFOu, *Mémoires*, LX.) Hki, 1931.

——. "Lapparnas förekomst i Finland." (*Ymer*, Vol. 67, pp. 43–57.) Sthm, 1947.

——. *Suomen lappalaiset vuoteen 1945.* I–II. Porvoo (Borgå), Hki, 1948.

Jaakkola, Jalmari. *Pirkkalaisliikkeen synty.* (*Annales Universitatis Fennicæ Aboensis.* Ser. B. Tom. II, No. 1.) Turku, 1924.

Jacobi, Arnold. *Das Rentier. Eine zoologische Monographie der Gattung Rangifer.* Leipzig, 1931.

Jalvi, Pedar. *Muottačalmit.* Jyväskylä, 1915.

James, Neill. *Petticoat Vagabond among the Nomads.* New York, 1939.

Jessen-S(chardebøll), Erich Johan. *Afhandling om de Norske Finners og Lappers Hedenske Religion.* . . . *De Finnorum Lapponumque Norwegicorum Religione Pagana.* . . . (Leem, Knud: *Beskrivelse over Finmarkens Lapper* . . . Appendix.) Copenhagen, 1767.

Johansson, Carl. "Om kultplatser och heliga områden i Torne och Lule lappmarker." (*Archives des traditions*, 1941, pp. 44–82.) Sthm, 1944.

Johansson, Levi. *Bebyggelse och folkliv i det gamla Frostviken.* (*Skrifter utgivna genom Landsmåls-och Folkminnesarkivet i Uppsala.* Ser. B. 3.) Ups, 1947.

Kajava, Yrjö. *Beiträge zur Kenntnis der Rasseneigenschaften der Lappen Finnlands, hauptsächlich nach den Untersuchungen von Dr. Arvo Elfving.* (Ac. Sc. Fenn., *Annales.* Ser. A. Tom. XXV, No. 1.) Hki, 1925.

Keane, A. H. "The Lapps: their Origin, Ethnical Affinities, Physical and Mental Characteristics, Usages, Present Status, and Future Prospects." (*The Journal of the Anthropological Institute of Great Britain and Ireland*, Vol. XV, pp. 213–235.) London, 1886.

Kharuzin, Nikolai N. "K voprosu o dvukh tipakh loparei." ("Contribution toward the question of two types of Lapps." *Izviestiia Imperatorskago Obshchestva Liubitelei Estestvoznaniia, Antropologii i Ètnografii*. Tom LXVIII. *Trudy Antropologicheskago Otdiela*, XII, pp. 131–140.) Moscow, 1890.

——. *Russkie lopari*. ("The Russian Lapps." *Izviestiia Imperatorskago Obshchestva Liubitelei Estestvoznaniia, Antropologii i Ètnografii*. Tom LXVI. *Trudy Ètnograficheskago Otdiela*, X.) Moscow, 1890.

Krohn, Kaarle. "Lappische beiträge zur germanischen mythologie." *(Finnisch-ugrische forschungen*, Vol. VI, pp. 155–180.) Hki, 1906.

Læstadius, Petrus. *Journal för första året af hans tjenstgöring såsom missionaire i Lappmarken*. Sthm, 1831.

——. *Fortsättning af Journalen öfver missions-resor i Lappmarken*. Sthm, 1833.

Lagercrantz, Eliel. "Synopsis des Lappischen." (*Oslo Etnografiske Museums Skrifter*, Vol. 2:4, pp. 227–350.) Oslo, 1941.

Larsen, A. *Bæivve-Alggo. Muittalus*. Kristiania, 1912.

Laufer, Berthold. "The reindeer and its domestication." *(Memoirs of the American Anthropological Association*. Vol. IV, No. 2, pp. 91–147.) Lancaster, Pa., 1917.

Launis, Armas. *Lappische Juoigos-Melodien, gesammelt und herausgegeben*. (SFOu, *Mémoires*, XXVI.) Hki, 1908.

Leem, Knud. *Beskrivelse over Finmarkens Lapper, deres Tungemaal, Levemaade og forrige Afgudsdyrkelse, oplyst ved mange Kaaberstykker med J. E. Gunneri Anmærkninger og E. J. Jessen-S Afhandling om de Norske Finners og Lappers Hedenske Religion. De Lapponibus Finnmarchiæ . . . commentatio*. Copenhagen, 1767.

Lid, Nils. *Jolesveinar og grøderikdomsgudar*. (*Skrifter utgitt av Det Norske Videnskaps-Akademi i Oslo*. II. Hist.-Filos. Kl., 1932, No. 5.) Oslo, 1933.

——. "Stainak og rodno. Tvo urnordiske lånord i samisk." (*Norsk tidsskrift for sprogvidenskap*, Vol. V, pp. 87–104.) Oslo, 1932.

L(inde)r, (J. A.). "Om Swenska Lappmarken och dess In-
wånare." (*Läsning för folket,* Vol. 15, pp. 146–165, 200–
250, 341–351, Vol. 16, pp. 147–169, 265–283, 345–361, Vol.
17, pp. 120–146, 271–287, 351–361, Vol. 18, pp. 249–269,
Vol. 19, pp. 63–76, Vol. 20, pp. 154–178.) Sthm, 1849–1854.
Linkomies (Flinck), Edwin. "Suomalaisten ensimmäinen mai-
ninta historiassa." (*Aika,* Vol. 15, pp. 238–254.) Hki, 1921.
——. "Vad visste romarna om de nordiska folken?" (*Kejsar
Augustus och arvet från Rom,* översatt från finskan av
Henrik Zilliacus, pp. 190–219.) Hki and Sthm, 1948.
Linné, Carl von. *Iter Lapponicum.* Andra upplagan med bi-
lagor och noter. Ombesörjd af Th. M. Fries. (*Skrifter af
Carl von Linné,* utgifna af Kungl. Svenska Vetenskapsaka-
demien. Vol. V.) Ups, 1913.
Lönnberg, Einar. *Om renarne och deras lefnadsvanor.* (Appen-
dix to *Förhandlingarna inför skiljedomstolen af 1909 i
renbetesfrågan.* Afdelning I, Svensk inlaga No. 3.) Ups,
1909.
Lundius, Nicolaus. *Descriptio Lapponiæ.* Ed. K. B. Wiklund.
(*Archives des traditions,* XVII. 5.) Ups, 1905.
Lundman, Bertil. "On the Origin of the Lapps. Physico-anthro-
pological Observations." (*Ethnos,* 1946, pp. 71–88.) Sthm,
1946.
Magnus, Johannes. *Gothorum Sveonumque historia.* Rome,
1554.
Magnus, Olaus. *Historia de gentibus septentrionalibus.* Rome,
1555.
Manker, Ernst. *Die lappische Zaubertrommel. Eine ethno-
logische Monographie. I. Die Trommel als Denkmal ma-
terieller Kultur.* (Nordiska museet: *Acta Lapponica.* I.)
Sthm, 1938.
Mikkola, J. J. *Kolttakylän arkisto.* (*Lapin sivistysseuran Jul-
kaisuja,* Vol. 8.) Porvoo (Borgå), Hki, 1941.
Näätänen, Esko K. *Über die Anthropologie der Lappen in
Suomi.* (Ac. Sc. Fenn., *Annales.* Ser. A. Tom. XLVII, No.
2.) Hki, 1936.
Nickul, Karl. *The Skolt Lapp community Suenjelsijd during
the year 1938.* (Nordiska museet: *Acta Lapponica.* V.)
Sthm, 1948.
Nielsen, Konrad. "Et tredelt bidrag. 3. Litt om nordiske lånord
i den lappiske ren- og rendriftsterminologi." (*Festskrift til
Rektor J. Qvigstad,* pp. 179–183.) Oslo, 1928.
——. *Lærebok i lappisk utarbeidet på grunnlag av dialektene i*

241

BIBLIOGRAPHY

Polmak, Karasjok og Kautokeino. Utgitt på offentlig foranstaltning. 3 v.: I. Grammatikk. II. Tekster. III. Glossar. Oslo, 1926–1929.

——. "Spörsmaalet om den lappiske torvgammes oprindelse." (SFOu, *Journal,* XXIII. No. 7.) Hki, 1906.

Nordberg, Erik. "Om lapparnas brudköp. Ruta-seden hos arjeplogslapparna." (*Archives des traditions,* 1948, pp. 1–33.) Sthm, 1948.

Norden, Eduard. *Die germanische Urgeschichte in Tacitus Germania.* Leipzig and Berlin, 1920.

Nordlandet. Utgit av Oplysningsfondet av 1914 ved Carl Schøyen. Kristiania, 1920.

Olrik, Axel. "Nordisk og lappisk gudsdyrkelse." (*Danske Studier,* 1905, pp. 39–57.) Copenhagen, 1905.

——. "Tordenguden og hans dreng i lappernes myteverden." (*Danske Studier,* 1906, pp. 65–69.) Copenhagen, 1906.

Paulaharju, Samuli. *Lapin muisteluksia.* Hki, 1922.

——. *Taka-Lappia.* Hki, 1927.

Pettersson, O. P. "Fornlapparnas sätt att begrafva sina döda." (*Fataburen,* 1912, pp. 92–97.) Sthm, 1912.

Peucer, Kaspar (Casparus Peucerus). *Commentarius de praecipuis divinationum generibus.* Wittenberg, 1553. (Several later issues.)

Pirak, Anta. *En nomad och hans liv.* Upptecknat och översatt av H. Grundström. Med förord av K. B. Wiklund. (*Skrifter utgivna av K. Humanistiska Vetenskaps-Samfundet i Uppsala.* Vol. 28, No. 3.) Ups, 1933.

——. *Jåhttee saamee viessoom.* Upptecknat och försett med inledning av H. Grundström samt fonetiskt upptecknat språkprov av B. Collinder. (*Skrifter utgivna av K. Humanistiska Vetenskaps-Samfundet i Uppsala.* Vol. 31, No. 2.) Ups, 1937.

Qvigstad, Just Knud. *Kildeskrifter til den lappiske Mythologi.* (*Det Kongelige Norske Videnskabers Selskabs Skrifter,* 1903:1.) Trondhjem, 1903.

——. *Kildeskrifter til den lappiske Mythologi.* II. Om Lappernes Vildfarelser og Overtro af Isaac Olsen. (*Det Kongelige Norske Videnskabers Selskabs Skrifter,* 1910:4.) Trondhjem, 1910.

——. *Lappische Heilkunde.* Mit Beiträgen von K. B. Wiklund. (*Instituttet for sammenlignende kulturforskning.* Serie B: Skrifter, XX.) Oslo, 1932.

BIBLIOGRAPHY

——. "Lappische Opfersteine und heilige Berge in Norwegen." (Zur Sprach– und Volkskunde der norwegischen Lappen, pp. 317–356.)

——. "Lappischer Aberglaube." (Zur Sprach- und Volkskunde der norwegischen Lappen, pp. 41–135.)

——. "Lappische Sprichwörter und Rätsel." (Zur Sprach- und Volkskunde der norwegischen Lappen, pp. 137–251.)

——. Lappiske eventyr og sagn. 4 v. (Instituttet for sammenlignende kulturforskning. Serie B: Skrifter, III, X, XII, XV.) Oslo, 1927–1929.

——. Nordische Lehnwörter im Lappischen. (Forhandlinger i Videnskabs-Selskabet i Christiania, 1893, No. 1.) Christiania, 1893.

——. Zur Sprach- und Volkskunde der norwegischen Lappen. (Oslo Etnografiske Museums Skrifter. Vol. I.) Oslo, 1920–1934.

(Qvigstad, Just Knud.) Festskrift til Rektor J. Qvigstad. (Tromsø Museums Skrifter. Vol. II.) Oslo, 1928.

The Race Biology of the Swedish Lapps. I. General Survey. Prehistory. Demography. With the collaboration of . . . K. B. Wiklund edited by H. Lundborg and S. Wahlund. Ups, 1932. II. Anthropometrical Survey by Gunnar Dahlberg and Sten Wahlund. Ups, 1941. (The Swedish State Institute for Race Biology.)

Ränk, Gustav. "Kysymys Lapin madderakan ja hänen tyttäriensä alkuperästä." ("The problem of the origin of the Lapp Madderakka and her daughters." Kalevalaseuran Vuosikirja, Vol. 29, pp. 180–247.) Porvoo (Borgå), Hki, 1949.

Ravila, Paavo. "Die stellung des lappischen innerhalb der finnisch-ugrischen sprachfamilie." (Finnisch-ugrische forschungen, Vol. XXIII, pp. 20–65.) Hki, 1935.

——. Reste lappischen Volksglaubens. (SFOu, Mémoires, LXVIII.) Hki, 1934.

Rennerfeldt, A. F. "Anteckningar öfver Frostviken i Jemtland, med särskildt afseende å de derinom vistande lappar." (1849.) (Ströms Hembygdsförenings årspublikation, 9, pp. 17–27.) Strömsund, 1941.

Reuterskiöld, Edgar. De nordiska lapparnas religion. Sthm, 1912.

——. Källskrifter till lapparnas mytologi. Sthm, 1910.

Rheen, Samuel. En kortt Relation om Lapparnes Lefwarne och

Sedher, wijd-Skiepellsser, sampt i många Stycken Grofwe wildfarellsser. Ed. K. B. Wiklund. (*Archives des traditions,* XVII. 1.) Ups. 1897.

Rode, Fredrik. *Optegnelser fra Finmarken, samlede i Aarene 1826–1834.* Skien, 1842.

Rosberg, J. E. *Lapplynne.* Ups, 1923.

Rosen, Eric von. "En nyupptäckt lapsk offerplats vid Vidja-kuoika." (*Ymer,* Vol. 31, pp. 177–179.) Sthm, 1911.

Ruong, Israel. *Fjällapparna i Jukkasjärvi socken.* (*Geographica.* Skrifter från Uppsala Universitets Geografiska Institution, 3.) Ups, 1937.

——. "Om rennomadens rätt till jorden och gårdsbrukarens." (*Norrlandica.* Skriftserie utgiven av Norrlands nation i Uppsala, II, pp. 71–83.) Ups, 1942.

——. "Studier i lapsk kultur i Pite lappmark och angränsande områden." (*Archives des traditions,* 1943–1944, pp. 123–194 + 1 map.) Sthm, 1945.

Scheffer (Schefferus), Johannes. *Lapponia, id est regionis Lapponum et gentis nova et verissima descriptio.* Frankfurt, 1673.

——. *The History of Lapland.* Oxford, 1674. (Second enlarged ed.: *The History of Lapland.* Translated from the last Edition in Latin. London, 1704. Third abridged ed. London, 1751.)

Setälä, Emil Nestor. "Lappische lieder aus dem XVII:ten jahrhundert." (SFOu, *Journal,* VIII, pp. 105–123.) Hki, 1890.

Sirelius, Uuno Taavi. "Über die Art und Zeit der Zähmung des Renntiers." (SFOu, *Journal,* XXXIII. No. 2.) Hki, 1916–1920.

Skum, Nils Nilsson. *Same sita—Lappbyn.* Bilder och lapsk text av Nils Nilsson Skum. Svensk översättning av Israel Ruong. (Nordiska museet: *Acta Lapponica.* II.) Sthm, 1938.

Smith, P. L. *Kautokeino og Kautokeino-lappene.* En historisk og ergologisk regionalstudie. (*Instituttet for sammenlignende kulturforskning.* Serie B: *Skrifter,* XXXIV.) Oslo, 1938. (With a Summary in German.)

Solem, Erik. *Lappiske rettsstudier.* (*Instituttet for sammenlignende kulturforskning.* Serie B: *Skrifter,* XXIV.) Oslo, 1933. (With a Summary in German.)

Stockfleth, Niels Vibe. *Dagbog over mine Missionsreiser i Finmarken.* Christiania, 1860.

Strömbäck, Dag. *Sejd. Textstudier i nordisk religionshistoria.* Diss., Ups. Sthm, 1935.

Tanner, Väinö. *Antropogeografiska studier inom Petsamo-området. I. Skoltlapparna. (Fennia,* 49:4.) Hki, 1929. (With a Summary in French.)

Temple, George T. "Notes on Russian Lappland." *(Proceedings of the Royal Geographical Society and Monthly Record of Geography.* New Monthly Series. Vol. II, No. 10, pp. 593–602.) London, 1880.

Tirén, Karl. *Die lappische Volksmusik.* (Nordiska museet: *Acta Lapponica.* III.) Sthm, 1942.

Tomasson, Torkel. "Bidrag till kännedomen om de s. k. stalotomterna." *(Samefolkets egen tidning.* 1929, pp. 33–35, 1930, pp. 6–8, 15–16.) Ups, 1929–1930.

——. "Historisk översikt av folkundervisningen bland sameh." *(Samefolkets egen tidning.* 1921, pp. 14–16.) Ups, 1921.

——. "Renskötseln, dess utveckling och betingelser." *(Svenska lapparnas landsmöte i Östersund,* pp. 69–99.) Ups and Sthm, 1918.

Tornæus, Johannes. *Berättelse om Lapmarckerna och Deras Tillstånd.* Ed. K. B. Wiklund. *(Archives des traditions,* XVII. 3.) Ups, 1900.

Tuderus, Gabriel. *En kort underrättelse Om the Österbothniske Lappar som under Kiemi Gebiet lyda.* Ed. K. B. Wiklund. *(Archives des traditions,* XVII. 6.) Ups, 1905.

Turi, Johan. *Från fjället.* (Swedish translation by Anna Bielke, and the Lappish original.) Lund, 1931.

——. *Muittalus samid birra. En bog om Lappernes liv.* Udgivet med dansk oversættelse af Emilie Demant. Andet gennemsete oplag. Sthm, 1910. (With an atlas, comprising 14 pictures.)

——. *Turi's Book of Lapland.* Edited and translated into Danish by Emilie Demant Hatt. Translated from the Danish by E. Gee Nash. New York and London (1931).

——. *Lappish texts written by Johan Turi and Per Turi.* With the cooperation of K. B. Wiklund, ed. by Emilie Demant-Hatt. *(Det Kgl. Danske Videnskabernes Selskabs Skrifter,* 7. Række, historisk og filosofisk Afd. IV. 2.) Copenhagen, 1918–1919.

Unwerth, Wolf von. *Untersuchungen über Totenkult und Ödinnverehrung bei Nordgermanen und Lappen, mit Excursen zur altnordischen Literaturgeschichte.* (Germanistische Abhandlungen, hrsg. von F. Vogt, 37.) Breslau, 1911.

Vår nordliga hembygd. En hembygdsbok för Malå, Arvidsjaur

och Arjeplog. Utg. till skolornas tjänst av Nils Ramselius. Örnsköldsvik and Lund, 1920.

Wiklund, Karl Bernhard. "De första lapska böckerna." (*Nordisk tidskrift för bok- och biblioteksväsen,* IX, pp. 13–28.) Ups, 1922.

——. "De svenska lapparnas skolundervisning i äldsta tid." (*ABC-bok på lapska 1619.* Fac-simile edition.) Sthm, 1922.

——. *De svenska nomadlapparnas flyttningar till Norge i äldre och nyare tid.* Ups, 1908.

——. "Die Erforschung der germanischen Lehnwörter im Finnischen und Lappischen." (*Indogermanisches Jahrbuch,* Vol. V, pp. 1–21.) Strassburg, 1918.

——. "Die Herkunft der Lappen." (*Folkliv,* 1937, pp. 109–123.) Sthm, 1937.

——. "Die nordischen lehnwörter in den russisch-lappischen dialekten." (SFOu, *Journal,* X, pp. 146–206.) Hki, 1892.

——. "En nyfunnen skildring av lapparnas björnfest." (*Le monde oriental,* Vol. VI, pp. 27–46.) Ups, 1912.

——. *Entwurf einer urlappischen lautlehre.* I. Einleitung, Quantitätsgesetze, Accent, Geschichte der hauptbetonten vokale. Diss., Ups. (Printed as No. X.1 of SFOu, *Mémoires.*) Hki, 1896.

——. "Finno-Ugrier. B. Sprache und Anthropologie." (*Reallexikon der Vorgeschichte,* unter Mitwirkung zahlreicher Fachgelehrter hrsg. von Max Ebert. Vol. III, pp. 364–382.) Berlin, 1925.

——. "Huru länge har det funnits lappar i Jämtland och Härjedalen?" (*Jämtländska Studier,* Festskrift till Eric Festin,* pp. 931–412.) Ups, 1928.

——. "Lapparnas forna utbredning i Finland och Ryssland, belyst av ortnamnen." (*Le monde oriental,* Vol. V, pp. 101–136, 175–196.) Ups, 1912.

——. *Lapparnes sång och poesi.* Ups, 1906.

——. "Lappar och renar i Alaska." (*Ymer,* Vol. 26, pp. 181–185.) Sthm, 1906.

——. "The Lapps in Sweden." (*The Geographical Review,* Vol. XIII, pp. 223–242.) New York, 1923.

——. *Nomadskolans läsebok. Tredje boken.* Ups, 1929.

——. *Om lapparna i Sverige.* 2nd ed. (*Verdandis småskrifter,* 82.) Sthm, 1910.

——. "Om lapparnas mössor." (*Svenska kulturbilder,* Vol. VI [Part XII], pp. 281–310.) Sthm, 1932.

——. "Om renskötselns uppkomst." (*Ymer,* Vol. 38, pp. 249–273.) Sthm, 1918.

——. "Saivo. Till frågan om de nordiska beståndsdelarna i lapparnas religion." (*Le monde oriental*, Vol. X, pp. 45–74.) Ups, 1916. German translation: "Saivo. Zur Frage von den nordischen Bestandteilen in der Religion der Lappen." (*Beiträge zur Religionswissenschaft*, hrsg. von der Religionswissenschaftlichen Gesellschaft in Stockholm. Vol. 2:2, pp. 155–201.) Leipzig, 1918.

——. "Untersuchungen über die älteste Geschichte der Lappen und die Entstehung der Renntierzucht." (*Folkliv*, 1938, pp. 12–47, 362–404.) Sthm, 1938.

——. "Zur kenntnis der ältesten germanischen lehnwörter im finnischen und lappischen." (*Le monde oriental*, Vol. V, pp. 217–252.) Ups, 1912.

Wright, Herbert. "Lapp Songs in English Literature." (*The Modern Language Review*, Vol. XIII, pp. 412–419.) Cambridge, 1918.

Ziegler, Jacob. "Schondia." (*Qvæ intvs continentvr. Syria, ud Ptolomaici* [!] *operis rationem* . . . , pp. LXXXIV–CIX.) Strassburg, 1532.

Zolotarev, D. A. *Kol'skie lopari.* ("The Kola Lapps." *Akademiia nauk Soiuza Sovetskikh Sotsialisticheskikh Respublik. Materialy Komissii ėkspeditsionnykh issledovaniı̆.* Vyp. 9. Seriia severnaia.) Leningrad, 1928. (With a Summary in French.)

INDEX

INDEX

251

INDEX

252